This book is due on the last date stamped below.
Failure to return books on the date due may result
in assessment of overdue fees.

| | |
|---|---|
| NOV 1 6 2005 | MAR 2 9 2011 |
| APR 1 7 2006 | MAY 0 3 2011 |
| APR 1 7 REC'D | MAY 1 6 REC'D |
| DEC 0 4 2006 | NOV 1 3 2012 |
| DEC 1 2 REC'D | NOV 1 5 REC'D |
| NOV 0 1 2007 | |
| OCT 1 8 REC'D | |
| FINES | .50 per day |

# Homeland Security

Other books in the Current Controversies series:

The Abortion Controversy
Afghanistan
Alcoholism
America's Battle Against
    Terrorism
Assisted Suicide
Biodiversity
Capital Punishment
Censorship
Child Abuse
Civil Liberties
Civil Rights
Computers and Society
Conserving the Environment
Crime
Developing Nations
The Disabled
Drug Abuse
Drug Legalization
Drug Trafficking
Espionage and Intelligence
    Gathering
Ethics
Family Violence
Free Speech
Garbage and Waste
Gay Rights
Genetic Engineering
Guns and Violence
Hate Crimes
Homosexuality
Illegal Drugs
Illegal Immigration

The Information Age
Interventionism
Iraq
Marriage and Divorce
Medical Ethics
Mental Health
The Middle East
Minorities
Nationalism and Ethnic
    Conflict
Native American Rights
Police Brutality
Politicians and Ethics
Pollution
Poverty and the Homeless
Prisons
Racism
The Rights of Animals
Sexual Harassment
Sexually Transmitted Diseases
Smoking
Suicide
Teen Addiction
Teen Pregnancy and Parenting
Teens and Alcohol
The Terrorist Attack on
    America
Urban Terrorism
Violence Against Women
Violence in the Media
Women in the Military
Youth Violence

# Homeland Security

**Andrea C. Nakaya,** *Book Editor*

**Bruce Glassman,** *Vice President*
**Bonnie Szumski,** *Publisher*
**Helen Cothran,** *Managing Editor*

CURRENT CONTROVERSIES

**GREENHAVEN PRESS**
*An imprint of Thomson Gale, a part of The Thomson Corporation*

THOMSON
™
GALE

Detroit • New York • San Francisco • San Diego • New Haven, Conn.
Waterville, Maine • London • Munich

THOMSON
GALE

© 2005 Thomson Gale, a part of The Thomson Corporation.

Thomson and Star Logo are trademarks and Gale and Greenhaven Press are registered trademarks used herein under license.

*For more information, contact*
Greenhaven Press
27500 Drake Rd.
Farmington Hills, MI 48331-3535
Or you can visit our Internet site at http://www.gale.com

| LIBRARY OF CONGRESS CATALOGING-IN-PUBLICATION DATA |
| --- |
| Homeland security / Andrea C. Nakaya, book editor.<br>    p. cm. — (Current controversies)<br>Includes bibliographical references and index.<br>ISBN 0-7377-2777-2 (lib. bdg. : alk. paper) —<br>ISBN 0-7377-2778-0 (pbk. : alk. paper)<br>    1. U.S. Dept. of Homeland Security. 2. Terrorism—United States—Prevention.<br>3. Internal security—United States. 4. National security—United States. 5. Civil<br>rights—United States. I. Nakaya, Andrea C., 1976– . II. Series.<br>HV6432.4.H65  2005<br>363.32'0973—dc22                                                              2004052292 |

Printed in the United States of America

# Contents

Foreword                                                                   10

Introduction                                                               12

## Chapter 1: Is the American Homeland Secure?

Homeland Security: An Overview *by Martin Kady II*                          16
While there have been a number of successes in improving homeland
security, experts warn of critical security gaps in many areas, including
America's borders, ports, and airports.

### Yes: The American Homeland Is Secure

The Threat of Terrorism Has Been Exaggerated *by John L. Scherer*          26
Terrorism experts exaggerate the likelihood of another large terrorist
attack occurring. Chemical, biological, and nuclear attacks are difficult to
launch successfully, thus there is not likely to be another large terrorist
attack against the United States.

America Is Prepared for a Bioterrorist Attack *Part I by George W. Bush;*
*Part II by the Centers for Disease Control and Prevention*                30
The United States has stockpiled enough smallpox vaccine to inoculate
the entire population if necessary. In addition, the U.S. public emergency
response system is prepared to respond quickly and effectively to a
bioterrorist attack.

Improved Monitoring of Immigrants Is Protecting the United States
*by Asa Hutchinson*                                                        34
With the 2003 implementation of the U.S. Visitor and Immigrant Status
Indicator Technology (US-VISIT) program, the Department of Homeland
Security can efficiently monitor U.S. borders.

### No: The American Homeland Is Not Secure

Terrorism Is a Serious Threat to Homeland Security
*by Larry A. Mefford*                                                      37
The United States continues to be threatened by a wide range of international terrorist groups, with al Qaeda posing the greatest threat.

America Is Not Prepared for a Bioterrorist Attack
*by James Jay Carafano*                                                    43
The federal government is currently unprepared for a bioterrorist attack.
Federal agencies should be reorganized to provide an effective strategy
for meeting this threat.

Current Immigration Policies Are Failing to Protect the United States
*by Michelle Malkin, interviewed by Stephen Goode*     50
A lack of enforcement of U.S. immigration laws is compromising homeland security. In order to protect America against foreign-born terrorists,
immigrants should be more closely monitored, and penalties against illegal aliens should be strictly enforced.

Security Lapses at Nuclear Plants Threaten America
*by Alexander Cockburn*     55
The United States has large quantities of nuclear waste and radioactive
materials that are not well guarded and thus vulnerable to terrorist attack.
These potential targets are a deadly threat to homeland security.

Reliance on Technology May Make America Less Secure from
Terrorism *by Charles C. Mann*     58
Centralized databases and increasingly complex technology such as face-
recognition software have been designed to protect America; however,
these new technologies may actually make America less safe because of
the likelihood that they will fail.

# Chapter 2: Is the Department of Homeland Security Effective?

The Department of Homeland Security: An Overview
*by the U.S. Department of Homeland Security*     70
The U.S. Department of Homeland Security, created in 2003, unifies the
large number of federal organizations charged with preserving homeland
security. Guided by the principles of service, protection, and accountability, its goal is to make America safe.

## Yes: The Department of Homeland Security Is Effective

The Department of Homeland Security Is the Best Way to Protect
America *by Todd Tiahrt*     78
The Department of Homeland Security brings over one hundred security
organizations together in one cabinet department. The new department
will facilitate effective communication between security agencies, thus
helping to protect America.

The Department of Homeland Security Is Making America Safer
*by George W. Bush*     81
The Department of Homeland Security has made significant progress in
making the American homeland safe. The nation's borders are more
secure, air travel is safer, and first responders to national emergencies are
now getting the training they need.

The Homeland Security Advisory System Is Effective *by Tom Ridge*     86
The Homeland Security Advisory System is an effective way to evaluate
terrorist threats and communicate them to the public. It helps government
and citizens understand the level of threat and take the necessary actions
to stay safe.

## No: The Department of Homeland Security Is Ineffective

The Department of Homeland Security Is Not the Best Way to Protect
America *by Ivan Eland*     90
> The government already has the necessary agencies to coordinate secu-
> rity; creating a new department that combines these agencies merely adds
> another layer of bureaucracy to the federal government and may actually
> make the United States less effective in fighting terrorism.

The Department of Homeland Security Is Unlikely to Prevent Another
Terrorist Attack on America *by Andrew Stephen*     96
> Despite the creation of the Department of Homeland Security, the U.S.
> homeland is not completely secure. It is likely that there will be another
> terrorist attack on America no matter what steps the new department takes
> to prevent it.

The Homeland Security Advisory System Does Not Work
*by Charles V. Peña*     99
> The Homeland Security Advisory System is not an effective way to pro-
> tect America. It has no practical utility for ordinary citizens, and it may
> actually help terrorists plan attacks by letting them know when U.S. secu-
> rity is relaxed.

# Chapter 3: What Measures Should Be Taken to Enhance Homeland Security?

Chapter Preface     102

Airline Pilots Should Be Armed *by John R. Lott Jr.*     104
> America's air-travel system is vulnerable to another terrorist hijacking.
> Arming pilots would pose minimal risks to the safety of passengers and is
> the best way to prevent another terrorist attack involving airliners.

Airline Pilots Should Not Be Armed *by George F. Will*     109
> Arming airline pilots is not a good way to protect against potential airline
> hijackings and could actually make flying more dangerous. Pilots should
> be focused on flying the aircraft, not on protecting it.

National ID Cards Would Make Americans Safer *by David Bursky*     111
> The creation of a national ID card could help prevent terrorist attacks by
> allowing officials to verify the identities of American citizens and in the
> process identify individuals illegally in the country.

National ID Cards Would Not Make Americans Safer
*by Timothy Lynch and Charlotte Twight*     113
> The implementation of a national ID card will not make Americans safer
> because terrorists will easily defeat the system by recruiting people who
> have valid ID cards. In addition, ID cards will mark the beginning of a
> loss of important civil liberties.

A Home Guard Should Be Created to Increase Homeland Security
*by Robert Cottrol*     117
> In order to effectively protect the homeland in the case of an emergency,
> the United States needs to create a home guard. It should do this by reviv-
> ing the Reserve Officers Training Corps (ROTC).

A New Intelligence System Must Be Created for Effective Homeland
  Security *by James B. Steinberg, Mary Graham, and Andrew Eggers*    121
   The U.S. intelligence system is outdated and ineffective against new
   threats facing America. A new intelligence system should be built that
   emphasizes information-sharing while maintaining privacy and protecting
   important secrets.

## Chapter 4: Do Efforts to Enhance Homeland Security Threaten Civil Liberties?

Chapter Preface                                                      129

### Yes: Efforts to Enhance Homeland Security Threaten Civil Liberties

The USA PATRIOT Act Has Decimated Many Civil Liberties
  *by Barbara Dority*                                                 130
   Since the passage of the USA PATRIOT Act, both immigrants and American citizens have lost many basic civil liberties. Immigrants suspected of
   terrorist acts are being detained without due cause, and Americans' privacy is being violated.

New Surveillance Technologies Threaten Civil Liberties
  *by Clyde Wayne Crews Jr.*                                          137
   The increasing use of privacy-invading technologies, such as biometric
   face cameras and wire-tap enhancements, to enhance homeland security
   is a threat to civil liberties.

Efforts to Increase Homeland Security Have Resulted in the
  Mistreatment of Immigrants *by Mark Engler*                         140
   Immigrants' civil liberties have been increasingly violated since the
   September 11, 2001, terrorist attacks. Many immigrants suspected of
   links to terrorism have been detained without due process.

Using the U.S. Military to Aid Domestic Security Efforts Would
  Lead to Violations of Civil Liberties *by Gene Healy*               144
   The historical record of military involvement in domestic affairs shows
   that an active military presence in the homeland is dangerous. Using the
   military for domestic police work will violate Americans' civil liberties.

### No: Efforts to Enhance Homeland Security Do Not Threaten Civil Liberties

The USA PATRIOT Act Provides the Security That Protects Americans'
  Liberty *by John Ashcroft*                                          156
   The USA PATRIOT Act helps the government more effectively prevent
   terrorism and preserve homeland security. That security is essential to
   preserving Americans' freedom.

New Surveillance Technologies Can Be Used Without Endangering
  Civil Liberties *by Tony Tether*                                    162
   The U.S. government is developing technology that can run narrow
   surveillance searches of suspicious activities, which eliminates the need
   to examine mass amounts of data on American citizens.

Immigrants Have Been Treated Fairly in Efforts to Increase Homeland
Security *by Michael Chertoff*                                      169
   In order to protect homeland security, the United States has been forced
   to detain numerous immigrants suspected of having knowledge of terrorists or terrorist activity. These detentions are legal, and the immigrants'
   rights have not been violated.

Chronology                                                          176
Organizations to Contact                                            178
Bibliography                                                        183
Index                                                              187

# Foreword

By definition, controversies are "discussions of questions in which opposing opinions clash" (Webster's Twentieth Century Dictionary Unabridged). Few would deny that controversies are a pervasive part of the human condition and exist on virtually every level of human enterprise. Controversies transpire between individuals and among groups, within nations and between nations. Controversies supply the grist necessary for progress by providing challenges and challengers to the status quo. They also create atmospheres where strife and warfare can flourish. A world without controversies would be a peaceful world; but it also would be, by and large, static and prosaic.

## The Series' Purpose

The purpose of the Current Controversies series is to explore many of the social, political, and economic controversies dominating the national and international scenes today. Titles selected for inclusion in the series are highly focused and specific. For example, from the larger category of criminal justice, Current Controversies deals with specific topics such as police brutality, gun control, white collar crime, and others. The debates in Current Controversies also are presented in a useful, timeless fashion. Articles and book excerpts included in each title are selected if they contribute valuable, long-range ideas to the overall debate. And wherever possible, current information is enhanced with historical documents and other relevant materials. Thus, while individual titles are current in focus, every effort is made to ensure that they will not become quickly outdated. Books in the Current Controversies series will remain important resources for librarians, teachers, and students for many years.

In addition to keeping the titles focused and specific, great care is taken in the editorial format of each book in the series. Book introductions and chapter prefaces are offered to provide background material for readers. Chapters are organized around several key questions that are answered with diverse opinions representing all points on the political spectrum. Materials in each chapter include opinions in which authors clearly disagree as well as alternative opinions in which authors may agree on a broader issue but disagree on the possible solutions. In this way, the content of each volume in Current Controversies mirrors the mosaic of opinions encountered in society. Readers will quickly realize that there are many viable answers to these complex issues. By questioning each au-

10

thor's conclusions, students and casual readers can begin to develop the critical thinking skills so important to evaluating opinionated material.

Current Controversies is also ideal for controlled research. Each anthology in the series is composed of primary sources taken from a wide gamut of informational categories including periodicals, newspapers, books, United States and foreign government documents, and the publications of private and public organizations. Readers will find factual support for reports, debates, and research papers covering all areas of important issues. In addition, an annotated table of contents, an index, a book and periodical bibliography, and a list of organizations to contact are included in each book to expedite further research.

Perhaps more than ever before in history, people are confronted with diverse and contradictory information. During the Persian Gulf War, for example, the public was not only treated to minute-to-minute coverage of the war, it was also inundated with critiques of the coverage and countless analyses of the factors motivating U.S. involvement. Being able to sort through the plethora of opinions accompanying today's major issues, and to draw one's own conclusions, can be a complicated and frustrating struggle. It is the editors' hope that Current Controversies will help readers with this struggle.

Greenhaven Press anthologies primarily consist of previously published material taken from a variety of sources, including periodicals, books, scholarly journals, newspapers, government documents, and position papers from private and public organizations. These original sources are often edited for length and to ensure their accessibility for a young adult audience. The anthology editors also change the original titles of these works in order to clearly present the main thesis of each viewpoint and to explicitly indicate the opinion presented in the viewpoint. These alterations are made in consideration of both the reading and comprehension levels of a young adult audience. Every effort is made to ensure that Greenhaven Press accurately reflects the original intent of the authors included in this anthology.

# Introduction

In 2002 Jamal Udeen, a suspected terrorist, was arrested in Afghanistan by American soldiers during the war there to oust the ruling Taliban, which was harboring terrorists. The thirty-seven-year-old British Muslim, who denies any links to terrorism, was taken to a U.S. detention camp in Guantánamo Bay, Cuba, and held for more than two years without being charged or tried. Following his release in March 2004, Udeen spoke about his experience, claiming that U.S. guards at the camp tortured him. In an interview with the British *Daily Mirror*, he described the conditions at Guantánamo Bay, including the cells where inmates were kept. According to Udeen, the cells were no more than wire cages with concrete floors and no protection from the elements. Udeen maintains that water to the cells was often cut off before prayers so Muslim prisoners could not wash themselves as their religion instructs them to. Prisoners were shackled and attached to metal rings on the floor during interrogations, he says, and he claims that he was beaten by men in riot gear after refusing to have a mystery injection. According to Udeen, "They actually said: 'You have no rights here.' After a while, we stopped asking for human rights—we wanted animal rights."

Following the September 11, 2001, terrorist attacks, the United States began taking more aggressive actions to protect its homeland. Among these efforts have been the indefinite imprisonment of suspected terrorists and the use of military trials to assess their guilt. Many experts believe that these steps are necessary to ensure homeland security because they allow the government to prevent suspected terrorists from committing future terrorist acts, and enable U.S. officials to obtain information about other terrorists and future attacks. However, America's treatment of these suspected terrorists has been a source of heated controversy.

In a November 2001 order, President George W. Bush authorized the indefinite detention of any noncitizen accused of terrorism, and since then, thousands of suspected terrorists have been detained indefinitely without being formally charged or tried. U.S. officials have defended these actions as necessary for the protection of America against future terrorist attacks. According to Vice President Richard Cheney, "These [terrorists] are bad people. . . . They may well have information about future terrorist attacks against the United States. We need that information. We need to be able to interrogate them and extract from them whatever information they have." Cheney adds, "People will object to it, but we are absolutely determined to get the balance right between human rights, which are important, and society's right to live free from terror." Secretary of Defense Donald Rumsfeld echoes Cheney's argument that detention of suspected terrorists is vital to the preservation of homeland security. "America is a nation at war," Rumsfeld argues. "It is a war we did not ask for, but it is a war we must fight. It is a war we must win and we will. . . . Detaining 'enemy combatants' is a part of that war." According to Rumsfeld, "The reason for their detention is that they're dangerous," and keeping them detained is "just plain common sense."

However, critics of indefinite detentions believe that the new laws have resulted in many people being falsely imprisoned, leaving them no way to appeal their position. Attorney and professor David Cole believes that a large number of immigrants have been unfairly detained. He asserts in the journal *Human Rights* that "hundreds of immigrants not charged with any crime, much less involvement in the September 11 attack, are being detained in secret, even where judges rule that there is no basis for detention, and without going before a judge at all." Anthony D. Romero, executive director of the American Civil Liberties Union, argues that the new laws pertaining to detention are dangerous because they allow the U.S. government to detain people in secret, without allowing the American public to judge the legitimacy of their actions. In *Human Rights* he states, "The proceedings surrounding . . . detention have been shrouded in secrecy, thereby impeding the public's ability to scrutinize the actions of the [former] Immigration and Naturalization Service (INS) and other law enforcement officials."

In addition to approving the indefinite detention of suspected terrorists, in November 2001 President George W. Bush also signed an order allowing non-U.S. citizens to be tried in military courts for activities that the president determines to be terrorism-related. Military courts differ from civil courts in a number of ways; the trial can be closed, the normal rules of evidence used in civil courts do not apply, there is no civilian judicial review of the decision, and no right to appeal. According to the U.S. government, military courts are necessary for the effective conduct of military operations and the protection of sensitive information about future terrorist plans. Rumsfeld explains the necessity of the courts: "[Suspected terrorists are] not common criminals," he claims. "They're enemy combatants and terrorists who are being detained for acts of war against our country, and that is why different rules have to apply."

However, the authorization of military trials for suspected terrorists has caused opposition from human rights advocates, who believe that these courts may not provide a fair trial. According to activist Maryam Elahi, "The president's order establishing military trials . . . is not only in violation of international human rights law, but it also flies in the face of U.S. domestic law." Elahi describes how, in her experience, military courts often do not provide defendants with a fair trial:

As a lawyer working for [human rights organization] Amnesty International, I observed numerous trials in the 1990s before military courts in Egypt and Turkey. It would be impossible to argue that any of the defendants in these courts were given the basic due process rights that are legally guaranteed. . . . Defendants were often assumed guilty prior to the presentation of the evidence, judges were biased, defendants' access to defense lawyers was limited at best, and the opportunity for appeal was nonexistent or futile. Many were subjected to the death penalty following unfair trials.

Indefinite detention and military trials for suspected terrorists have caused debate over how to maintain the balance between civil liberties and homeland security. U.S. Attorney General John Ashcroft defends the measures that the United States has taken. He states: "Our efforts have been crafted carefully to avoid infringing on constitutional rights, while saving American lives." Ashcroft argues that debates over civil liberties weaken the U.S. war on terror. In a speech to the Senate Judiciary Committee he maintained, "To those who scare peace-loving people with phantoms of lost liberty, my message is this: Your tactics only aid terrorists for they erode our national unity and diminish our resolve."

Many civil liberties groups have challenged measures passed by the U.S. government, however, alleging that these laws remove important restrictions on governmental authority, and are a dangerous encroachment on civil liberties. They argue that the United States can, and must, protect civil liberties at the same time that it preserves homeland security. Romero emphasizes the importance of protecting the freedom America has traditionally symbolized. He states, "Admittedly, the terrorists who attacked the United States on September 11, 2001, took insidious advantage of American liberties and tolerance. . . . That does not mean, however, that those freedoms are at fault." He emphasizes the importance of preserving freedom while fighting terrorism, stating, "If we are intimidated to the point of restricting our freedoms, the terrorists will have won." In *Human Rights* David Cole writes about the danger of giving up civil liberties in the pursuit of security: "By conducting law enforcement in secret," he says, "and jettisoning procedures designed to protect the innocent and afford legitimacy to the outcome of trials, we will encourage people to fear the worst about our government. . . . Freedom and security need not necessarily be traded off against one another; maintaining our freedoms is itself critical to maintaining our security."

How to treat suspected terrorists is only one of the many controversies related to maintaining homeland security. The authors in *Current Controversies: Homeland Security* offer various perspectives on the security of the United States. They debate how safe the United States is, whether the Department of Homeland Security is effective, what measures should be taken to ensure homeland security, and whether these measures threaten civil liberties.

# Chapter 1

# Is the American Homeland Secure?

# Homeland Security: An Overview

## by Martin Kady II

**About the author:** *Martin Kady II covers homeland security and technology for* CQ Weekly *and* CQ Today. *He has won twelve writing awards from the Virginia, North Carolina, and Maryland press associations.*

Two years after one of the darkest days in U.S. history [the September 11, 2001, terrorist attacks], the fundamental question remains: Are we safer? Many experts and government officials believe that, yes, the United States is safer. But the nature of terrorism is to surprise the victims and exploit a security weakness, and even the most optimistic experts say that despite the efforts of the new Department of Homeland Security [DHS], America's defenses remain vulnerable.

"I think we're safer, but we're not safe enough," says Rep. Jim Turner, D-Texas, the ranking Democrat on the House Select Committee on Homeland Security. "We're still in the infant stages of developing a national strategy on homeland security. But our terrorist enemies are not waiting. We have a long way to go."

Meanwhile, since Sept. 11 about $20 billion has been funneled to local police and fire "first responders," for equipment and training in responding to a terrorist attack. The training includes mock-disaster exercises nationwide involving local responders, coordinated by the DHS.

Top homeland-security officials say federal, state and local agencies are ready to respond to another attack, but several security studies, including one from the New York–based Council on Foreign Relations, rate the nation's first responders as "dangerously unprepared." Other recent studies say the nation's schools and health-care providers feel vulnerable and unprepared to respond to another terrorist attack.

Another lingering homeland-defense question: Are the CIA, FBI and other U.S. intelligence agencies now working together effectively and able to "connect the dots" in order to avoid the massive communication failures that enabled the

9/11 terrorist attacks to succeed? The agencies acknowledge that the answer is still no. Two years after the Sept. 11 attacks, their dozen or so different terrorist "watch lists" have not been electronically connected, despite a mandate in last year's [2002] Homeland Security Act to consolidate the databases.

Information-sharing has become a new priority of the Terrorist Threat Integration Center, but critics worry that the new Bush administration initiative will not be effective because it was placed under the authority of the Central Intelligence Agency (CIA). Opponents of the move say terrorism data-analysis should be independent of the intelligence community's old guard, entrenched at the CIA.

## The Success of Homeland Security

Although firm answers to many of these fundamental security questions are elusive, the Bush administration consistently touts its homeland-security successes in the two years following the terrorist attacks.

"We are . . . far safer than we were," DHS Secretary Tom Ridge said on Sept. 2 [2003], citing improvements in airport security, border controls and coordination with state and local officials. "So on an incremental basis, but a steady basis day by day, we get to a new level of readiness every day."

Defenders of the administration and the Department of Homeland Security cite several "wins" in the war on terrorism as evidence of the success of their homeland-defense policies. Domestically, they point to the detention in 2002 of an alleged terrorist ring from Lackawanna, N.Y., and the August [2003] arrest of the man accused of trying to buy shoulder-fired missile launchers. Overseas, high-ranking al Qaeda [terrorist group] operatives have been arrested, including a top lieutenant of terrorist leader Osama bin Laden, Khalid Shaikh Mohammed, in Pakistan in March [2003].

But, some national security experts and Democrats—especially those looking to score political points—say America is unprepared for another attack. They say the administration is not spending enough money on homeland security and that its terrorism intelligence-sharing procedures are suspect.

On Sept. 5 [2003], Democrats issued a scathing, eight-page critique of the administration's war on terrorism calling for consolidation of disparate terrorist watch lists; better information-sharing with local law enforcement; more border patrols

> *"Even the most optimistic experts say that despite the efforts of the new Department of Homeland Security, America's defenses remain vulnerable."*

and better tracking of foreign visitors; screening of all air cargo in passenger jets, more inspections of cargo containers headed for U.S. ports and mandatory vulnerability assessments of chemical plants.

Others are critical of President [George W.] Bush's latest request [in 2003] for

$87 billion for continuing operations in Iraq, contending that the administration sold the [2003] war in Iraq as part of the war on international terrorists, even though no clear, indisputable link has ever been made between [former Iraqi president] Saddam Hussein and al Qaeda or Osama bin Laden. In making the request, however, Bush said Iraq had become "the central front" in the war against terrorism. He said $66 billion of the funds would be for military and intelligence operations over the next year in Iraq and Afghanistan. Critics have said the Iraq war has been distracting Bush from pursuing bin Laden and other terrorists in Afghanistan.

> *"'On an incremental basis, but a steady basis day by day, we get to a new level of readiness every day.'"*

One of Bush's leading terrorism advisers, Rand Beers, made waves in March [2003] when he resigned from the White House, complaining later that "the administration wasn't matching its deeds to its words in the war on terrorism." Beers contended the war in Iraq is "making us less secure, not more secure." He later joined the 2004 presidential campaign of Democratic Sen. John F. Kerry of Massachusetts.

Kerry has wasted no time in making homeland security a political issue. "Here on the home front, every investigation, every commission, every piece of evidence we have tells us that this president has failed to make us as safe as we should be," Kerry said on Sept. 2 [2003] as he formally announced his candidacy.

## Defense Gaps

Critics and security experts cite several gaps in the nation's defenses. For instance, while airport security nationwide has been beefed up since the Sept. 11 hijackings, experts say other areas of air travel remain vulnerable. Air cargo on passenger jets is not screened. Jets are still vulnerable to ground-to-air missile launchers, and the airline industry is hesitant to endorse a proposal by Sen. Barbara Boxer, D-Calif., to equip all passenger airliners with missile-defense shields. In one of the most recent airport alerts, the Homeland Security Department warned that terrorists have been experimenting with turning electronic devices like cameras or cell phones into weapons or bombs. And on Sept. 4 [2003], the FBI warned that hijackers may be planning to hijack planes in neighboring nations, such as Canada.

In addition to the airlines, other potential terrorist targets also are seeking a balance between security and freedom of commerce and movement of people. Chemical plants, nuclear-power facilities, railroads, transit systems, utilities, computer networks, seaports and even sewage systems have increased security, yet congressional legislation to mandate security upgrades for certain industries, like chemical companies, has stalled. In other areas, including firefighter grants, advocates say less money has been appropriated for security than they had hoped for.

Meanwhile, the 180,000-employee DHS is still experiencing growing pains following the mega-merger of 22 federal agencies that created the new agency.

"We're making progress, but the jury is still out on how the department is doing," says Sen. Susan Collins, R-Maine, chairwoman of the Senate Governmental Affairs Committee, which overseas the DHS. "We still have a lot to do to coordinate the agencies" that were consolidated to create the department.

DHS Secretary Ridge has received generally positive reviews from members of Congress on both sides of the aisle. However, the department's color-coded terrorist-alert system has been both ridiculed by the public and criticized as inefficient by the Congressional Research Service (CRS).

Ridge has said the department is developing more specific ways to issue terrorist threat alerts, but he nonetheless has defended the color-coded system. Ridge also has his hands full with the new Transportation Security Administration (TSA), which took over airline screening after Sept. 11 [2001] but has been criticized by some key members of Congress, including Rep. Harold Rogers, R-Ky., chairman of the House Homeland Security Appropriations Subcommittee. Rogers criticized the TSA for being overstaffed and also for failing to complete background checks on all its employees, many of whom were found to have criminal records.

Meanwhile, a federal commission that is mandated to investigate the Sept. 11 attacks reportedly has run into numerous obstacles, including lack of sufficient funding and the Bush administration's alleged reluctance to turn over intelligence about the attack and let witnesses testify freely to commission members.

> *"While airport security nationwide has been beefed up since the Sept. 11 hijackings, experts say other areas of air travel remain vulnerable."*

The commission is run by former New Jersey Gov. Thomas Kean, a moderate Republican who has complained that witnesses have felt "intimidated" by administration officials who have insisted on sitting in on interviews. The commission's report is due next fall [2004], but Kean says if the commission does not get more money and move cooperation, it may not finish the investigation on time. The 10-member commission, formally known as the National Commission on Terrorist Attacks, will investigate events leading up to the attacks, including aviation security, immigration and U.S. diplomacy.

As citizens, lawmakers and security experts confront the continuing threat of terrorism, here are some of the key questions they are asking:

## Is America Safer Today?

In his State of the Union address last Jan. 28 [2003], President Bush said, "we are winning" the war on terrorism. Seven months later, at a press conference at his ranch in Crawford, Texas, on Aug. 13, he said, "We're doing everything we can to protect the homeland." Asked about the threat of missile launchers and a

. . . breach in security at John F. Kennedy International Airport in New York City, Bush responded, "America is a safe place for people to fly."

Frank Cilluffo, a consultant on national security and a former terrorism consultant for the Bush administration, says, "Unequivocally we are safer, but the question is how do you define safer? If you're asking, 'Are we ever going to be able to protect everything from every possible attack?' the answer is no. Defining success is difficult because the good guys have to bat a thousand, and the bad guys only have to be right once."

> *"'We're making progress, but the jury is still out on how the [Department of Homeland Security] is doing.'"*

Most agree that airports and airplanes are indeed safer. The government will spend more than $5 billion on the TSA in fiscal 2004, largely to cover costs for 45,000 new airport screeners, as well as baggage-screening equipment. However, many critics say the TSA is overstaffed and suffers from image problems due to longer security lines at airports.

"The TSA still has a big job to do in getting 100 percent of all bags screened electronically [by bomb detectors] by the end of the year [2003]," says Todd Hauptli, a lobbyist for the American Association of Airport Executives and the Airports Council International, two leading aviation associations. "Vigilance is up, security has increased, but there are still soft spots.". . .

Many security experts agree the country is safer than before Sept. 11, but they also note a laundry list of vulnerabilities, including the electricity grid and chemical plants. The DHS has been assessing the nation's "critical infrastructure"—such as telecommunications networks, dams and power plants—for vulnerabilities. The assessments, some of which will be completed within the year, are expected to lay the groundwork for tougher, new security regulations and legislation in the future.

Not surprisingly, the debate over security has reflected political agendas. In the Senate debate over chemical-plant security, for instance, the Democrats, led by Sen. Jon Corzine of New Jersey, support a plan with a heavier regulatory agenda. They want all chemical facilities to conduct security studies and submit them to the Environmental Protection Agency (EPA) for approval. Chemical plants would also be required to study using alternative—and potentially safer—chemicals—a move the industry believes is meddlesome and has little to do with security.

The Republicans' own bill takes a lighter regulatory approach, requiring chemical plants only to keep their security plans on file, rather than submitting them for approval to the federal government. Sponsored by Oklahoma Sen. James M. Inhofe, it also does not require companies to consider switching to alternative chemicals. Moreover, it would shift chemical-security oversight from the EPA to the DHS. Inhofe's bill is more likely to move forward because he is chairman of the Senate Environmental and Public Works Committee.

## Port Security

Port security is another headache for security officials. Only about 5 percent of the millions of shipping containers that enter U.S. seaports every year are physically inspected. The rest of the cargo containers go uninspected, although homeland-security officials have said that they inspect all suspicious cargo. Along with Customs agents, they try to keep tabs on all containers by using computers to monitor shipping manifests, looking for suspicious cargoes originating from ports with questionable security.

The 2002 Maritime Transportation Security Act was supposed to address the gap in port security, but the bill did not authorize any money to assess security at the country's major ports. The proposed fiscal 2004 homeland security appropriations bills could provide up to $150 million for port security, but the Coast Guard says it would need $1 billion to carry out recommendations of the Maritime Transportation Security Act, which mandates vulnerability assessments be conducted at all the nation's major ports.

"An area of vulnerability remains in our ports," says Sen. Collins, whose home state has hundreds of miles of coastline. "We need to step up programs to put Customs inspectors in foreign ports, and identify risky cargo."

Determining whether the country is safer, Collins and other experts say, will be a day-to-day, ongoing assessment as the war against terrorism continues without any end in sight.

## Are Rescue Personnel Prepared to Respond?

As the World Trade Center towers teetered on the brink of collapse on Sept. 11, the New York City Police Department realized it had to get all emergency personnel out of the towers. But it could not alert fire department personnel inside the towers because the two departments did not have adequate interoperable radios. The city lost 343 firefighters in the collapse, while the police department lost 23. Since Sept. 11, police and firefighters have demanded better training, better communication and better equipment, including interoperable radios.

> *"Many security experts agree the country is safer than before Sept. 11, but they also note a laundry list of vulnerabilities."*

The nationwide effort to improve preparations for another terrorist attack has been watched over by Michael Brown, DHS undersecretary for emergency preparedness and response. Brown has overseen major mock-terrorism exercises in Seattle and Washington, D.C. In the aftermath of a terrorist attack, Brown's federal emergency responders are prepared to sweep in and help run command centers, as they did during the mid-August [2003] blackout in New York, Detroit, Cleveland and other cities.

"We're learning you have to put in a command-and-control structure, because otherwise it'll be chaos," Brown says. "First responders know how to do their jobs, but they need to be able to reach back into the federal government for resources. If we take care of first responders, we take care of the homeland."

However, funding for state and local first responders has become a major political football. Democrats have regularly attacked the Republican Congress and the Bush administration, saying they are underfunding the people who will be on the front lines of a terrorist attack. Democrats have proposed adding anywhere from $1 billion to $14 billion to the fiscal 2004 appropriations bills in an attempt to funnel more homeland-security grants to cities and states.

> *"Determining whether the country is safer . . . will be a day-to-day, ongoing assessment as the war against terrorism continues without any end in sight."*

The Council on Foreign Relations bolstered the Democrats' argument in June [2003] when it said America's first responders were "dangerously unprepared" for another attack. "Based on our analysis, America will fall roughly $98.4 billion short of meeting critical emergency-responder needs over the next five years if current overall funding levels are maintained," the report said. "Covering this shortfall using federal funds alone would require quintupling federal funding."

The report carried considerable weight because it was co-authored by Richard A. Clarke, a former terrorism and national security adviser who served in four presidential administrations and was among the first senior administration officials to raise warnings about al Qaeda before the Sept. 11 attacks.

The report also noted that:

• On average, fire departments have only enough radios for half the firefighters on a shift and breathing apparatuses for only a third.

• Police departments do not have the protective gear to safely secure a site after an attack with weapons of mass destruction.

• Public-health labs in most states still lack basic equipment and expertise to adequately respond to a chemical or biological attack.

Two other studies, released in August [2003], also raised doubts about whether front-line responders are prepared for another attack. A study by the federal Centers for Disease Control and Prevention said police officers and firefighters "feel vastly unprepared" for another attack and do not have the equipment and training they need to handle biological, chemical or radiological weapons. Another study, released by the National Association of School Resource Officers, showed that 76 percent of the resource officers surveyed believe schools are not prepared for a terrorist attack.

Other critics argue that too much money is being spent on preparations in some areas while not enough is being spent in others. For example, because of the way the funds are distributed, Wyoming gets much more anti-terrorism money per capita than New York and New Jersey. Homeland-security funds have reached well beyond traditional terrorism targets, to places like Springdale, Ark., where the police department received a $760,000 homeland-security grant for its bomb squad. The Clearmont, Wyo., fire department, meanwhile, recently received $81,000 for firefighter safety and training. Small towns like Clearmont receive homeland-security grants because the current formula for grant money guarantees every state a minimum amount of money, which is then funneled down to counties and towns.

## Reorganizing for Preparedness

Rep. William M. "Mac" Thornberry, R-Texas, says the sweeping reorganization that created the DHS has forced federal agencies and employees involved in terrorism response to refocus their mission away from prevention to preparedness. "One of the biggest challenges in homeland security is making up for years of neglect," Thornberry says. "We are more prepared [for an attack]. But in some areas we may not be as prepared as we were [before 9/11] because we shuffled the deck, and it takes time to develop relationships again."

Jamie F. Metzl, who directed the Council on Foreign Relations task force on first-responder preparedness, says he and other researchers visited emergency personnel nationwide to see if they had the specific equipment and training needed to handle various terrorist events. It was not a pretty picture, Metzl says.

*"Critics argue that too much money is being spent on preparations in some areas while not enough is being spent in others."*

"We're not nearly as prepared as we need to be in multiple areas," he warns. "We came away with the conclusion that America's first responders are not prepared for another terrorist attack."

In San Francisco, for example, all the search-and-rescue teams, which specialize in digging through the rubble of buildings after explosions, earthquakes or other calamities, are scattered throughout the region outside of the city. Thus, the team that would respond to a disaster anywhere in the San Francisco Bay area is located in Berkeley—across the Golden Gate and Bay bridges from the city and the rest of the bay area. If there is a major disaster in San Francisco and the bridges are shut down, it could take hours for the Berkeley-based team to get to the disaster, Metzl says. Such gaps in preparedness were repeated in firehouses and police departments around the country, he says.

Undersecretary Brown, however, defends his department's preparations. All 28 of the nation's urban search-and-rescue teams are now certified to handle the aftermath of a weapon of mass destruction, he says. And disaster-response exercises are being done somewhere in the country on almost a daily basis. At the Federal Emergency Management Administration (FEMA) headquarters in southwest Washington, the command center that used to be open only during hurricanes or after other disasters is now a 24-hour operation.

"That is a quantitative leap in preparedness," Brown says. "I want it to be up 24/7, so any agency or locality can reach into DHS and start communicating [instantly]."

## Is Congress Spending Enough on Homeland Security?

While members of Congress, the Bush administration and state and local officials have all shifted their spending priorities to put homeland defense at the top, the big question—both in Washington and in state capitals—remains hotly debated: How much is enough? . . .

Democrats have made homeland-security spending one of their top national-security issues this year [2003]. They complain that the Bush administration is shortchanging homeland-defense spending, putting first responders in the position of being unprepared for another attack. Senate Democrats forced nearly a dozen votes on amendments to the Senate's homeland-security appropriations bill in an effort to increase funding for ports, border security and first responders. Republicans complained that the Democrats' tactics were part of a political strategy to get the GOP on the record as voting against homeland-security spending.

"Police and fire departments say they don't have enough money, chemical plants say they don't have enough money [for security]," Rep. Markey says. "Al Qaeda is still targeting the same objectives" as they were on Sept. 11.

Republicans say it's not how much you spend but how you spend it. As evidence that the Bush administration has its spending priorities straight, they point to major increases in critical areas, such as terrorism intelligence, which focus on preventing an attack and analyzing data that could lead to arrests of terrorists.

The National Governors' Association, however, warns that states' homeland-security obligations are continuing to grow and that governors want to make sure they have a guaranteed stream of funding from the federal government to cover state and local homeland-defense costs. At the outset of the Iraq war in March [2003], the governors point out, the DHS launched "Operation Liberty Shield," a homeland-security program that raised nationwide terrorist alerts to Code Orange, the second-highest threat level. During the alert, which lasted several weeks, states had to cover millions of dollars worth of overtime costs for local and state

> *"'One of the biggest challenges in homeland security is making up for years of neglect.'"*

law-enforcement officers. Most governors believe that when the federal government issues a nationwide alert that will cost local law enforcement extra overtime, Washington should help defray the extra costs.

"In the face of possible terrorist threats, we cannot overstate the importance of . . . the need for a stable, multiyear federal funding commitment," says Delaware's Democratic Gov. Ruth Ann Minner, the association's spokeswoman on homeland security.

In a speech to the governors, DHS Secretary Ridge defended the administration's outreach to states and localities but said extra dollars do not equate to better security. "It's just not a matter of putting billions of dollars in this system," Ridge said. "We need to make sure at all levels of government that we are building up a national capacity, which, in my mind, means we need to rely on the governors to coordinate statewide security plans, working in collaboration with their partners at the local government."

# The Threat of Terrorism Has Been Exaggerated

**by John L. Scherer**

**About the author:** *John L. Scherer, a Minneapolis, Minnesota–based freelance writer, edited the yearbook* Terrorism: An Annual Survey *in 1982–1983 and the quarterly* Terrorism *from 1986 to 2001.*

The threat of terrorism in the U.S. is not over, but [the] Sept. 11 [2001 terrorist attacks] may have been an anomaly. Intelligence agencies are unlikely to uncover an impending attack, no matter what they spend on human intelligence, because it is virtually impossible to infiltrate terrorist cells whose members are friends and relatives. At least five of the 19 Al Qaeda[1] hijackers came from Asir province in Saudi Arabia, and possibly eight were related.

The U.S. was not defended on 9/11. As soon as the aircraft were hijacked, helicopters armed with missiles should have risen to protect coastal cities. Two F-16s dispatched from Langley and Otis Air Force bases in Virginia and New Jersey, respectively, were too distant to reach New York and Washington, D.C., in time. On a cautionary note, the penetration of White House air space by a Cessna aircraft in June, 2002, and by several other flights since the World Trade Center and Pentagon attacks, indicates nothing much has been done.

Although there will be small-scale terrorist attacks in the U.S. in the next 10 years, major Al Qaeda operations are over. Of the more than 1,200 people arrested after 9/11, none has been charged in the conspiracy. This suggests the hijackers did not and do not have an extensive operational American network. Some intelligence officials have estimated that up to 5,000 "sleepers"—persons with connections to Al Qaeda—are living in this country, including hundreds of hard-core members, yet nothing significant has happened in more than a year. The arrests [of five suspected terrorists on September 13, 2002] in the Buffalo, N.Y., area back up the possibility of such sleeper cells.

1. the terrorist group believed to be responsible for the September 11, 2001, terrorist attacks on the World Trade Center in New York and the Pentagon in Washington, D.C.

*Chapter 1*

## The Al Qaeda Threat Is Exaggerated

Al Qaeda attacks are more likely to occur abroad, but the danger of this group is being exaggerated overseas as well. Members of Al Qaeda cells have been arrested in Spain, Italy, England, Germany, Malaysia, and elsewhere, but scarcely more than a score anywhere except Pakistan.

The threat of terrorism in the U.S. has greatly diminished, but Al Qaeda and Taliban[2] prisoners realize they can terrorize citizens merely by "confessing" to plans to blow up bridges in California, attack schools in Texas, bomb apartments in Florida, rob banks in the Northeast, set off a series of "dirty bombs" [nuclear bombs], and have scuba divers operate in coastal areas.

A recent book on Al Qaeda states that the organization plans 100 attacks at any one time. This is nonsense. There have been a handful of small-scale attacks with fatalities linked to Al Qaeda since Sept. 11, nothing near 100. These include a church bombing in Islamabad (five deaths); the explosion of a gasoline truck and bus outside a synagogue on Djerba Island, Tunisia (19 dead); a bus bombing outside the Sheraton Hotel in Karachi (14 killed); and a bombing at the U.S. consulate in Karachi (12 fatalities). Three of these incidents occurred in Pakistan. In addition, Al Qaeda links are suspected in late-2002 bombings in Bali and Kenya. The claim by Sept. 11 terrorist suspect Zacarias Moussaoui of an ongoing Al Qaeda plot in this country is a subterfuge to save himself.

Al Qaeda had planned attacks in London, Paris, Marseilles, Strasbourg, Singapore, and Rome, but most of the conspirators were arrested a short time after the Sept. 11 attacks. Meanwhile, no one had hijacked an aircraft in the U.S. using a "real" weapon in almost 15 years, although crashing planes into structures is not new. The Israelis shot down a Libyan jetliner they said was headed for a building in Tel Aviv in the 1980s. A Cessna 150 fell 50 yards short of the White House in September, 1994. French commandos prevented a jumbo jet, hijacked in Algeria by the Armed Islamic Group, from crashing into the Eiffel Tower the following December. In the mid 1990s, terrorist Ramzi Yousef plotted to have his friend Abdul Hakim Murad fly a light plane loaded with chemical weapons into CIA headquarters at Langley, Va., or to have him spray the area with poison gas. A Turkish hijacker attempted to crash an aircraft into the tomb of former Pres. Kemal Ataturk in Ankara in 1998. With enhanced security on at airports and passengers on commercial airliners who will react to any danger, this threat has diminished.

> *"Although there will be small-scale terrorist attacks in the U.S. in the next 10 years, major Al Qaeda operations are over."*

Terrorists have attacked on holidays, but authorities are now especially alert

---

2. The Taliban was a fundamentalist Islamic regime that ruled Afghanistan from 1996 to 2001.

on those occasions, and the number and violence of anniversary attacks have lessened. Al Qaeda has never staged an incident on a holiday.

## Difficulty of Launching a Terrorist Attack

Chemical, biological, and nuclear (CBN) attacks are possible, but difficult and unlikely. Only one has succeeded over the last two decades—the 1995 Sarin incident on the Tokyo subway.[3] Thousands were injured, but just six people died.

There have been no CBN attacks with mass fatalities anywhere. Terrorist "experts" simply have thought up everything terrible that can happen, and then assumed it will. Terrorists would encounter problems dispersing biological toxins. Most quickly dilute in any open space, and others need perfect weather conditions to cause mass casualties. Some biological agents, although not anthrax, are killed by exposure to ultraviolet light. The Washington, D.C., subway system has devices that can detect biological toxins. New York has the highest-density population of any American city, and for this reason might have the greatest probability of such an attack, but it also has the best-prepared public health system.

In one instance, Essid Sami Ben Khemais, a Moroccan who ran Al Qaeda's European logistics center in Milan, Italy, received a five-year prison sentence in February, 2002. His cell planned to poison Rome's water supply near the U.S. embassy

> *"Americans must remain vigilant, of course, but there is no need to raid the Treasury or turn the country upside down pursuing phantoms."*

on the Via Veneto. This group had 10 pounds of potassium ferro-cyanide, a chemical used to make wine and ink dye, but extracting a deadly amount of cyanide from this compound would have proved extremely difficult.

Americans are rightly concerned about a strike against a nuclear power facility, but terrorists would have to get through a series of gates and fences, bypass motion sensors, and outfight a heavily armed security force to enter a containment building. Once inside the structure, they would need to know the exact sequence to shut down a reactor. An aircraft diving at a nuclear station would have to hit a small target, nothing like the World Trade Center buildings, which rose 1,400 feet into the air. Containment vessels are 160 feet high by 130 feet wide, and storage casks are even smaller.

Politicians have proposed creating a bureau to protect food from terrorists, but no one in the U.S. has ever died from a terrorist food poisoning. In fact, the nation has experienced just one instance of tampering with agricultural produce, when members of a cult contaminated several salad bars at restaurants in Oregon. The biggest danger to the food supply would be from salmonella, E.

---

3. In 1995 the Japanese cult Aum Shinrikyo released sarin nerve gas in the Tokyo subway system.

coli 0157, clostridium botulinum, and cholera, but careless handling and im-proper preparation of food are far-greater menaces than terrorism.

There are 168,000 public water systems in the U.S. Some serve as many as 8,000,000 people, while others as few as 25. None has ever been poisoned, al-though there have been attempts.

## The Need to Remain Vigilant

The FBI may need reorganization, especially since its failures preceding Sept. 11 resulted from officials making bad decisions. It is well-known that in mid August, 2001, officials at a flight school in Eagan, Minn., told the FBI that a French citizen of Algerian descent, Moussaoui, had offered $30,000 cash for lessons on a flight-simulator to learn how to fly a Boeing 747. He had no inter-est in learning how to land the plane. Moussaoui was arrested three weeks be-fore the attacks. One week before the hijackings, French intelligence informed the FBI that he was an Islamic militant who had visited Afghanistan and had links to Al Qaeda. FBI agents could have entered Moussaoui's computer and obtained his phone records using the Federal statutes already in place, but which were ignored or forgotten by officials.

Reorganizations refuse to acknowledge that some individuals are smarter and more knowledgeable than others, and new personnel will eventually resolve these problems. The new Department of Homeland Security will disrupt normal channels of communication and create even more bureaucratic confusion. It will compete for resources with the National Security Council and it will be costly trying to coordinate 46 agencies and, judging from actual terrorist events in the U.S., wholly unnecessary. Americans must remain vigilant, of course, but there is no need to raid the Treasury or turn the country upside down pursuing phantoms.

# America Is Prepared for a Bioterrorist Attack

**Part I: George W. Bush**
**Part II: Centers for Disease Control and Prevention**

**About the authors:** *George W. Bush was elected the forty-third president of the United States in November 2000. Prior to that he was governor of Texas. The Centers for Disease Control and Prevention is the federal agency dedicated to protecting the health and safety of Americans.*

## Part I

Since our country was attacked [on September 11, 2001], Americans have been forced to prepare for a variety of threats we hope will never come. We have stepped up security at our ports and borders, we've expanded our ability to detect chemical and biological threats, we've increased support for first responders, . . . [and] made our public health care system better able to track and treat disease. By preparing at home and by pursuing enemies abroad, we're adding to the security of our nation. I thank the members of my team who are here who are adding to the security of our nation.

One potential danger to America is the use of the smallpox virus as a weapon of terror. Smallpox is a deadly but preventable disease. Most Americans who are 34 or older had a smallpox vaccination when they were children. By 1972, the risk of smallpox was so remote that routine vaccinations were discontinued in the United States. In 1980, the World Health Organization declared that smallpox had been completely [eradicated] and, since then, there has not been a single natural case of the disease anywhere in the world.

We know, however, that the smallpox virus still exists in laboratories, and we believe that regimes hostile to the United States may possess this dangerous virus. To protect our citizens in the aftermath of September the 11th, we are evaluating old threats in a new light. Our government has no information that a

Part I: George W. Bush, "President Delivers Remarks on Smallpox," www.dhs.gov, December 13, 2002.
Part II: Centers for Disease Control and Prevention, "Bioterrism Preparedness FAQs," www.cdc.gov, October 25, 2001.

smallpox attack is imminent. Yet it is prudent to prepare for the possibility that terrorists . . . who kill indiscriminately would use diseases as a weapon.

## Smallpox Vaccination

Our public health agencies began preparations more than a year ago. Today, through the hard work of our Department of Health and Human Services, ably led by Tommy Thompson, and state and local officials, America has stockpiled enough vaccine, and is now prepared to inoculate our entire population in the event of a smallpox attack. Americans and anyone who would think of harming Americans can be certain that this nation is ready to respond quickly and effectively to a smallpox emergency or an increase in the level of threat.

Today [December 2002] I am directing additional steps to protect the health of our nation. I'm ordering that the military and other personnel who serve America in high-risk parts of the world receive the smallpox vaccine; men and women who could be on the front lines of a biological attack must be protected.

This particular vaccine does involve a small risk of serious health considerations. As Commander-in-Chief, I do not believe I can ask others to accept this risk unless I am willing to do the same. Therefore, I will receive the vaccine along with our military.

These vaccinations are a precaution only and not a response to any information concerning imminent danger. Given the current level of threat and the inherent health risks of the vaccine, we have decided not to initiate a broader vaccination program for all Americans at this time. Neither my family nor my staff will be receiving the vaccine, because our health and national security experts do not believe vaccination is necessary for the general public.

At present, the responsible course is to make careful and thorough preparations in case a broader vaccination program should become necessary in the future. There may be some citizens, however, who insist on being vaccinated now. The public health agencies will work to accommodate them. But that is not our recommendation at this time.

We do recommend vaccinations for one other group of Americans that could be on the front lines of a biological attack. We will make the vaccine available on a voluntary basis to medical professionals and emergency personnel and response teams that would be the first on the scene in a

> *"Anyone who would think of harming Americans can be certain that this nation is ready to respond quickly and effectively to a smallpox emergency."*

smallpox emergency. These teams would immediately provide vaccine and treatment to Americans in a crisis and, to do this job effectively, members of these teams should be protected against the disease.

I understand that many first responders will have questions before deciding whether to be vaccinated. We will make sure they have the medical advice they need to make an informed decision. Smallpox is a serious disease and we know that our enemies are trying to inflict serious harm. Yet there's no evidence that smallpox imminently threatens this country.

We will continue taking every essential step to guard against the threats to our nation and I deeply appreciate the good efforts of state and local health officials who are facing difficult challenges with great skill. The actions we are taking together will help safeguard the health of our people in a measured and responsible way.

## Part II

We continue to hear stories of the public buying gas masks and hoarding medicine in anticipation of a possible bioterrorist or chemical attack. We do not recommend either. As Secretary [of Health and Human Services Tommy G.] Thompson said recently, people should not be scared into thinking they need a gas mask. In the event of a public health emergency, local and state health departments will inform the public about the actions individuals need to take.

*Does every city have an adequate emergency response system, especially one geared for a bioterrorist attack? How quickly can it be implemented?* The emergency response system varies from community to community on the basis of each community's investment in its public health infrastructure. Some components of these emergency systems can be implemented very quickly, while others may take longer.

*Are hospitals prepared to handle a sudden surge in demand for health care?* The preparedness level in hospitals depends on the biological agent used in an attack. Because a sudden surge in demand could overwhelm an individual hospital's resources, hospitals collaborate with other hospitals in their area in order to respond to a bioterrorist attack on a citywide or regional

> *"The United States public water supply system is one of the safest in the world."*

basis. Hospitals are required to maintain disaster response plans and to practice applying them as part of their accreditation process. Many components of such plans are useful in responding to bioterrorism. Specific plans for bioterrorism have been added to the latest accreditation requirements of the Joint Commission on Accreditation of Healthcare Organizations. In an emergency, local medical care capacity will be supplemented with federal resources.

*Are health department labs equipped/capable of doing testing?* CDC [Centers for Disease Control and Prevention], the Association of Public Health Laboratories, and other officials are working together to ensure that all state health departments are capable of obtaining results of tests on suspected infectious agents. . . .

Every state has a Laboratory Response Network (LRN) contact. The LRN links state and local public health laboratories with advanced-capacity laboratories, including clinical, military, veterinary, agricultural, water, and food-testing laboratories. . . .

## Water Safety

*With all this talk about possible biochemical agents, just how safe is our water? Should I be disinfecting my water just in case?* The United States public water supply system is one of the safest in the world. The general public should continue to drink and use water just as they would under normal conditions. Your local water treatment supplier and local governments are on the alert for any unusual activity and will notify you immediately in the event of any public health threat. At this point, we have no reason to believe that additional measures need to be taken.

The U.S. Environmental Protection Agency (EPA) is the lead federal agency that makes recommendations about water utility issues. The EPA is working closely with the CDC and the U.S. Departments of Defense and Energy to help water agencies assess their systems, determine actions that need to be taken to guard against possible attack, and develop emergency response plans.

# Improved Monitoring of Immigrants Is Protecting the United States

**by Asa Hutchinson**

**About the author:** *Asa Hutchinson is undersecretary for Border and Transportation Security at the Department of Homeland Security.*

*Editor's Note: In December 2003 the U.S. Citizenship and Immigration Services implemented the U.S. Visitor and Immigrant Status Indicator Technology (US-VISIT) program in an effort to enhance border security. US-VISIT uses scanning equipment to collect biometric identifiers such as fingerprints, in an inkless process, along with a digital photograph of the visitor. Together with the standard information gathered from a visitor about their identity and travel, the new program will verify the visitor's identity and compliance with visa and immigration policies. The following viewpoint was originally given as testimony on the US-VISIT program on March 4, 2004.*

US-VISIT represents the greatest advance in border technology in three decades. It is an historic achievement in which we, for the first time in history, can use a biometric ability to confirm the identity of those traveling to our country with visas.

The Department of Homeland Security deployed the first increment of US-VISIT on time, within budget, and has exceeded the mandate established by Congress. We also met the challenge that was given by Secretary [of Homeland Security Tom] Ridge to include biometrics ahead of schedule.

But what US-VISIT also delivers is the ability to have security without sacrificing the open flow of legitimate travel and trade through our borders. We are now on the road to having an overall system where we can catch the few who mean harm while remaining a welcoming nation to the millions of legitimate visitors here for education, business, and travel. With US-VISIT, we can do both.

Asa Hutchinson, testimony before the House Committee on Government Reform, Washington, DC, March 4, 2004.

US-VISIT entry procedures are currently [in March 2004] deployed at 115 airports and 14 seaports. As of today, almost 2 million foreign visitors have been processed under the new US-VISIT entry procedures with no measurable increase in wait times. And, even more importantly, we have prevented over 60 criminals from entering the country. Without the biometric capabilities US-VISIT delivers, we would not have caught these people.

We are currently meeting the deadline for exit as well. Our exit procedures are based upon passenger departure information shared with us by the carriers. We match this information with the visa information and this allows us to identify visa overstays.

We currently have, let me emphasize, the biographic data that will allow us to determine visa overstays. We want to be able to enhance this with the biometric feature. We are testing this with various pilots, one of them being at Baltimore Washington International Airport.

## How US-VISIT Works

Let me take a minute to explain how US-VISIT works. The biographic and biometric information are collected overseas at the visa issuing posts and then verified at the port of entry. I will explain the process from the perspective of the United States Customs and Border Protection Officer. The example I am using is a visitor who has had their fingers scanned and digital photo taken at an overseas post.

The visitor arrives at the inspection booth and provides their travel documents—passport and visa—to the officer. The officer swipes the machine-readable part of the visa; the system immediately selects the correct file from the State Department's database to display. This information is seen on the officer's monitor.

The officer asks the visitor to place first their left index finger and then their right index finger on the finger-scanner device that captures their fingerscans. The officer then takes a digital photograph of the visitor.

> *"We are now on the road to having an overall system where we can catch the few who mean harm while remaining a welcoming nation to . . . legitimate visitors."*

While the officer continues the entry questioning, the fingerscans are compared against a criminal and terrorist watchlist, and the biographic and biometric data are matched against the data captured by the State Department. This ensures that the person entering the country is the same person who received a visa.

In addition, the digital picture that was taken of the visitor at the visa issuing post is displayed to the Customs and Border Protection officer for visual comparison. Let's remember, that the biometric checking is only a tool that an officer uses to determine admissibility, not the entire process. The biometric check through the select watchlist takes a matter of seconds.

When the system has completed its check, the officer sees a response that says either "No Hit" or "Hit." If a "No Hit" is received, the officer completes the interview, updates the screen with the duration of the visitor's stay and, unless other questions arise, welcomes the visitor into the United States. The addition of biometrics, collected abroad and verified at the port of entry, is one of many tools U.S. Customs and Border Protection Officers use to make their decision to admit a visitor to the country.

## Successes Under US-VISIT

Since the US-VISIT entry procedures were implemented, we have caught a fugitive who escaped from prison 20 years ago. We have caught and extradited a felon wanted for manslaughter. We stopped a drug dealer who had entered our country more than 60 times in the past four years using different names and dates of birth.

And just this Monday [March 1, 2004], a woman attempted to enter through Puerto Rico, and though there was a lookout for her in the Interagency Border Inspection System, or IBIS, because she had a fairly common surname, her biographic information didn't give us a match. But the US-VISIT biometric check allowed officers to confirm that she was the same person wanted in New Jersey for possession of stolen property. The US-VISIT biometric match also tied her to an additional 17 aliases and 7 different dates of birth.

Her criminal history dates back to 1994 and includes multiple arrests in New York for larceny, an arrest in Maryland for theft, and arrests in New Jersey for possession of stolen property, theft and possession of burglary tools. She had been deported from the United States in 1998. After being caught by US-VISIT, extradition to New Jersey was refused and she was given an expedited removal from the United States.

It is important to note that these important security measures currently are not just capturing those that are attempting to enter our country under false identity and with previous convictions, many times under orders to be expelled from the country. But it also serves as a deterrent as the word goes out that we have this capability. . . .

The successful deployment of US-VISIT was done with the 2003 budget of $367 million. In 2004 we have $330 million that has been allocated and appropriated by Congress for this purpose. The biggest challenge is to accomplish US-VISIT implementation in the 50 busiest land ports by the deadline of December of 2004. . . .

We are committed to building a program that enhances the integrity of our immigration system by catching the few and expediting the many. And we recognize that the U.S. is leading the way in helping other countries around the world keep their borders secure and their doors open.

# Terrorism Is a Serious Threat to Homeland Security

by Larry A. Mefford

**About the author:** *Larry A. Mefford is the assistant director of the Counterterrorism Division of the Federal Bureau of Investigation.*

*Editor's Note: The following viewpoint was originally given as testimony before the U.S. Senate on June 27, 2003.*

Let me emphasize the commitment of the FBI to investigating and disrupting terrorist activity both in this country and against U.S. interests overseas. There is no more important mission within the FBI. We are dedicating tremendous resources to this effort and will continue to do so as long as the threat exists.

Since [the terrorist attacks of] September 11, 2001, the FBI has investigated more than 4,000 terrorist threats to the U.S. and the number of active FBI investigations into potential terrorist activity has quadrupled since 9/11. Working with our partners in local and state law enforcement and with the U.S. Intelligence community, we have also disrupted terrorist activities in over 35 instances inside the United States since September 11, 2001. These include both domestic and international terrorism matters and consist of a variety of preventive actions, including arrests, seizure of funds, and disruption of terrorist recruiting and training efforts. No threat or investigative lead goes unanswered today. At headquarters, in our field offices, and through our offices overseas, we run every lead to ground until we either find evidence of terrorist activity, which we pursue, or determine that the information is not substantiated. While we have disrupted terrorist plots since 9/11, we remain constantly vigilant as a result of the ongoing nature of the threat. The greatest danger to our safety and security comes not from what we know and can prevent, but from what we do not know.

Larry A. Mefford, testimony before the Senate Subcommittee on Terrorism, Technology, and Homeland Security, Washington, DC, June 27, 2003.

## The Threat from Al Qaeda

We know this: The Al Qaeda terrorist network remains the most serious threat to U.S. interests both here and overseas. That network includes groups committed to the "international jihad movement," and it has demonstrated the ability to survive setbacks. Since September 11, 2001, we believe that Al Qaeda has been involved in at least twelve terrorist attacks against the United States and our allies around the world. This fact requires that we continue to work closely with our partners to fight Al Qaeda in all its forms both here and overseas.

On March 1, 2003, counterterrorism forces in Pakistan captured Al Qaeda operational commander Khalid Shaikh Mohammed and financier Mustafa Ahmed al-Hawsawi. In early 2002, another high ranking Al Qaeda operational commander, Mohamed Atef, was killed in a U.S. bombing raid. Many more suspected Al Qaeda operatives have been arrested in the United States and abroad.

> *"The Al Qaeda terrorist network remains the most serious threat to U.S. interests both here and overseas."*

Despite these strikes against the leadership of Al Qaeda, it remains a potent, highly capable and extremely dangerous terrorist network—the number one terrorist threat to the U.S. today. The very recent attacks in Riyadh, Saudi Arabia and in Casablanca, Morocco—for which we believe to be either sponsored or inspired by Al Qaeda—clearly demonstrate that network's continued ability to kill and injure innocent, unsuspecting victims.

In Riyadh on May 12, 2003, the simultaneous strikes on three foreign compounds were carried out by 12 to 15 individuals, nine of whom were suicide bombers. The overall death toll rose to 34, including at least seven Americans and the nine attackers. Nearly 200 people were wounded. Forty of those were Americans.

In Casablanca on May 16, 2003, as many as 12 suicide bombers orchestrated the simultaneous bombing of 5 targets. A targeted Jewish center was closed and unoccupied when one of the bombs was detonated. The deadliest attack occurred inside a Spanish restaurant where 19 were killed. Outside one targeted hotel, a security guard and a bellboy scuffled with bombers intent on entering the hotel. They prevented them from entering but lost their lives, along with those of their terrorist attackers, when the bombs were detonated outside. The terrorists even targeted a Jewish cemetery.

We know that the Al Qaeda network maintains a presence in dozens of countries around the world, including the United States. Audiotaped messages released in early October 2002 from [Al Qaeda leader] Usama bin Laden and his senior deputy, Ayman al-Zawahiri, urged renewed attacks on U.S. and Western interests. Intelligence analysis indicates that subsequent attacks against Western targets may have been carried out in response to these audiotaped appeals that were broadcast on the al-Jazeera [Arabic television] network beginning on October 6, 2002.

Two subsequent audiotapes attributed to bin Laden, released on February 11 and February 14, 2003, linked a call for terrorist attacks against Western targets with the pending war in Iraq. In the latter of these audiotaped messages, bin Laden appeared to express his desire to die in an attack against the United States. The most recent audiotape attributed to bin Laden, released on April 9, 2003, urged jihadists to carry out suicide attacks against those countries supporting the [2003] war in Iraq. And while individual suicide attacks have the potential to cause significant destruction and loss of life, we remain concerned about Al Qaeda's ability to mount simultaneous and large-scale terrorist attacks.

While large-scale, coordinated attacks remain an Al Qaeda objective, disruptions to the network's command and logistics structures during the past 20 months increase the possibility that operatives will attempt to carry out smaller scale, random attacks, as evidenced by Richard Reid's failed attempt to detonate a shoe-bomb on board a trans-Atlantic flight in December 2001. Such attacks, particularly against softer or lightly secured targets, may be easier to execute and less likely to require centralized control. We remain vigilant to the ability and willingness of individual terrorists, acting on their own in the name of "jihad," to carry out random acts of terror wherever and whenever they can.

We also know that jihadists tend to focus on returning to "unfinished projects," such as the destruction of the World Trade Center and attacks on U.S. Navy vessels. Consequently, a continuing threat exists to high profile targets previously selected by Al Qaeda. These include high profile government buildings, and encompass the possibility of more terrorist attacks on major U.S. cities and infrastructures. While we know that Al Qaeda has focused on attacks that have economic impact, we believe that its goals still include the infliction of mass casualties.

> *"Disruptions to [Al Qaeda's] command and logistics structures . . . increase the possibility that operatives will . . . carry out smaller scale, random attacks."*

## Disruption of Terrorist Activities

As I mentioned earlier, we have made significant progress in disrupting terrorist activities and planning; and this includes Islamic extremists activities within the United States. For example:

• On October 3, 2002, five men and one woman were indicted in Portland, Oregon, for conspiracy to levy war against the United States, conspiracy to provide material support and resources to a terrorist organization, and conspiracy to contribute services to Al Qaeda and the Taliban [which, as the ruling regime in Afghanistan, harbored Al Qaeda]. Five of the individuals were arrested. The sixth remains at large.

• On September 13, 2002, five members of a suspected Al Qaeda cell were arrested in Lackawanna, New York. They were charged with "providing, attempting to provide, and conspiring to provide material support and resources to a designated foreign terrorist organization." In addition, a sixth member was rendered to the United States from Bahrain in mid-September 2002, pursuant to an arrest warrant, and was charged with providing material support to Al Qaeda. FBI information indicates that in the spring and summer of 2001, these subjects attended religious [Islamic group] Jamaat Tablighi training in Pakistan. They also attended an Al Qaeda training camp in Afghanistan where they received training in mountain climbing, and were instructed in the use of firearms, including assault rifles, handguns, and long range rifles. During their training, Usama bin Laden visited the camp and gave a speech to all of the trainees. At the guest houses where members stayed, some received lectures on jihad, prayers, and justification for using suicide as an operational tactic. All six defendants have pled guilty to providing material support to Al Qaeda.

• On December 22, 2001, Richard C. Reid was arrested after flight attendants on American Airlines Flight 63 observed him attempting to ignite an improvised explosive in his sneakers while onboard the Paris-to-Miami flight. Aided by passengers, the attendants overpowered and subdued Reid. The flight was diverted to Logan International Airport in Boston, Massachusetts. Reid, who was traveling on a valid British passport, was indicted on eight counts, including placing an explosive device on an aircraft and attempted murder. FBI investigation has determined that the explosives in Reid's shoes, if detonated in certain areas of the passenger cabin, could have blown a hole in the fuselage of the aircraft. Reid's indictment charged that he, too, trained in camps operated by Al Qaeda. Investigators continue to work to determine the extent of Reid's possible links to others in this plot. On October 4, 2002,

> *"While we know that Al Qaeda has focused on attacks that have economic impact, we believe that its goals still include the infliction of mass casualties."*

Reid pled guilty to all of the counts against him. On January 30, 2003, he was sentenced to life in prison.

• On December 11, 2001, Zacarias Moussaoui was indicted in the Eastern District of Virginia for his alleged role in the September 11, 2001 attacks on the World Trade Center and Pentagon. Moussaoui is charged with six counts, including conspiracy to commit an act of terrorism transcending national boundaries and conspiracy to use a weapon of mass destruction. He is awaiting trial.[1]

• Last week [June 2003], the Attorney General announced the guilty plea of Iyman Faris, an Ohio truck driver, who—as a key operative for Al Qaeda—conspired to provide, and did in fact provide, material support to a terrorist organi-

1. At press time, Moussaoui's trial was in progress.

zation. We believe he was tasked by Al Qaeda to assist in the identification of possible terrorist targets inside the United States and provided other logistical support to that organization.

• On Monday of this week [June 2003], Ali Saleh Kahlah Al-Marri was designated an enemy combatant and transferred to the control of the Department of Defense. Al-Marri is a Qatari national who was initially arrested on a material witness warrant following the September 11 attacks. He was subsequently indicted for credit card fraud and making false statements. Recent information from an Al Qaeda detainee identified Al-Marri as an Al Qaeda "sleeper" operative who was tasked with providing support to newly arriving Al Qaeda operatives inside the U.S. Two separate Al Qaeda detainees have confirmed that Al-Marri has been to Al Qaeda's Farook camp in Afghanistan where he pledged his service to bin Laden. The decision to designate Al-Marri as an enemy combatant has disrupted his involvement in terrorist planning and taken another Al Qaeda operative out of action.

> *"Islamic Shiite extremists . . . have been launching terrorist attacks against the U.S. and its allies for more than twenty years."*

• The FBI is also actively looking for suspected Al Qaeda operative Adnan G. El Shukrijumah. El Shukrijumah has been identified by numerous detainees as a key Al Qaeda operative who could possibly be used to plan and carry out acts of terrorism against the U.S. El Shukrijumah was in the United States prior to September 11th and his current whereabouts are unknown. The FBI has put out a "be on the look out" alert to law enforcement both inside the U.S. and overseas to locate and interview him regarding these reports.

## Preventing Funding of Terrorists

Additionally, the FBI has aggressively pursued the individuals and networks that provide financing for terrorism worldwide. Since September 11, 2001, our Terrorist Financing Operations Section (TFOS) has been involved in the financial investigations of over 3,195 individuals and groups suspected in financially supporting terrorist organizations. The FBI has also worked closely with the Treasury Department in developing targets for designation and blocking orders. This has resulted in the terrorist designation of some 250 individuals or entities by Executive Order, and the blocking or freezing of approximately $124.5 million in assets since September 11, 2001.

As I said at the outset, finding and rooting out Al Qaeda members and adherents once they have entered the U.S. is our most serious intelligence and law enforcement challenge. In addition to our focus on identifying individuals directly involved in launching terrorist attacks, we are also very concerned with identifying and locating persons engaged in terrorist support activities, such as fund-raising, recruiting, training and other logistical responsibilities. This is very important since these individuals are vital to the operation of terrorist networks. We also remain deeply concerned about Al Qaeda's efforts to recruit U.S. citizens to support its terrorist goals and, perhaps, to carry out attacks on American soil.

Al Qaeda is not our only concern. We know that many Islamic extremists are tied to terrorist activities. Islamic Shiite extremists, represented by such groups as Hizballah, have been launching terrorist attacks against the U.S. and its allies for more than twenty years. Islamic Sunni extremism, spearheaded by Al Qaeda, but which also includes HAMAS and other groups, continue to inflict casualties on innocent people worldwide. Hizballah and HAMAS in particular, also maintain a sizable presence in the U.S. While the activities of these U.S. cells have not involved actual attacks within the United States, we know that Hizballah and HAMAS have been involved in activities that support terrorism, such as fund-raising, recruiting, and spreading propaganda inside our country. Since they have been responsible for the deaths of Americans and our allies overseas, we continue to be concerned about their activities.

## A Wide Range of Threats

In conclusion, the United States faces threats from a wide range of international terrorist groups, although we assess Al Qaeda to be the greatest threat today [in 2003]. Their potential attacks could be large-scale, or smaller and more isolated. Since our understanding of terrorist groups and the underlying philosophy behind these movements continue to develop, the FBI's assessment of the overall threat continues to evolve. We remain, however, concerned about Al Qaeda's efforts to launch another major attack inside the U.S. Consequently, we continually work with the U.S. intelligence community and our foreign partners to assess Al Qaeda's intentions and capabilities, including their use of weapons of mass destruction in future attack scenarios.

That is why we remain as focused as we are on detecting and preventing terrorism. We will not stray from this purpose and intend to work closely with State and Local law enforcement and other federal agencies to improve our preventive capabilities. We sincerely appreciate your guidance and support as we carry out our mission.

# America Is Not Prepared for a Bioterrorist Attack

**by James Jay Carafano**

**About the author:** *James Jay Carafano is Senior Research Fellow for National Security and Homeland Security in the Kathryn and Shelby Cullom Davis Institute for International Studies at the Heritage Foundation, a conservative public policy institute.*

The proliferation of biotoxin threats, in all likelihood, will only grow with time. Of all the areas of emergency response, the federal government is least prepared to deal with catastrophic bioterrorism.

Before the creation of the Department of Homeland Security (DHS) in January 2002, numerous federal departments and agencies bore responsibility for assisting state and local governments in bioterrorism preparedness and response. There was little coordination. Today [in 2003], despite organizational changes, much expertise and capacity remains beyond the department. While the Secretary of Homeland Security is mandated to coordinate the federal response, planning and coordination are still inadequate, lines of operational control are unclear, and there is no coherent national preparedness program.

To address these shortfalls, further reforms are needed that cut across a range of federal departments and initiatives.

## Why Worry?

There is one simple reason why bioterrorist strikes will be attempted against the United States in the future: They can kill Americans on an unprecedented scale and spread unimaginable fear, panic, and economic disruption. A gram or less of many biotoxin weapons can kill or sicken tens of thousands. Weight for weight, they can be hundreds to thousands of times more lethal than the most deadly chemical agents and can, in some cases, be produced at much less cost.

Some biotoxin weapons are communicable and can be spread easily beyond the initial target. They are less difficult to obtain than nuclear arms and potentially more deadly than conventional explosives or radiological and chemical weapons. A terrorist could use a virulent, infectious biological agent to inflict catastrophic damage.

The technical procedures for biotoxin weapons production are available in open-source, scientific literature. Over 100 states have the capacity to manufacture biological weapons on a large scale. A basic facility can be constructed and operated for less than $10 million.

Biotoxin weapons programs, however, are not limited to state threats. Any non-state group might be capable of performing some form of biological or toxin warfare. A terrorist group, given a competent team of graduate students and a facility no larger than a few hundred square feet, could field a small-scale program for a few hundred thousand dollars or less. Individuals with some graduate-level science education or medical training could produce biotoxin weapons. In some cases, biological attacks can be mounted without any scientific skills or medical knowledge.

*"Of all the areas of emergency response, the federal government is least prepared to deal with catastrophic bioterrorism."*

Moreover, the proliferation of biological and toxin threats will only grow with time. Biotechnology is one of the fastest growing commercial sectors in the world. The number of biotechnology companies in the United States alone has tripled [between 1992 and 2003].

These firms are also research-intensive, bringing new methods and products to the marketplace every day, and many of the benefits of this effort are dual-use, increasing the possibility that knowledge, skills, and equipment could be adapted to a biological agent program. The pharmaceutical industry, for example, has invested enormous effort in making drugs more stable for oral or aerosol delivery and thus, unintentionally, is developing the tools for producing the next generation of easily deliverable biological weapons. As the global biotechnology industry expands, nonproliferation efforts will have a difficult time keeping pace with the opportunities available to field a bioweapon.

Equally troubling, the difficulties in effectively delivering biotoxins can be overcome with some forethought and ingenuity. For example, cruise missiles, unmanned aerial vehicles, or aircraft could perform sprayer attacks, but only if specialized spraying equipment was employed that ensured proper dispersal and prevented particle clumping. Clumping of agents can degrade the effectiveness of an attack. Large particles quickly drop to the ground or, if inhaled, do not easily pass into lung tissue, significantly lessening the potential for infection.

Mechanical stresses in the spraying system might also kill or inactivate a large percentage of particles—by some estimates up to 99 percent. However, if an enemy had a large supply (e.g., 50 kilograms of a virulent bioweapon) or was not terribly concerned about achieving maximum effects, crude dispensers might be adequate.

In creating bioweapons, terrorists might be limited only by their imagination. For example, a low-tech version of a bio–cruise missile attack could be attempted with a system like the Autonomous Helicopter, a 14-foot-long, pilotless, remote-controlled helicopter built by Yamaha for crop dusting in Japan. The $100,000 aircraft uses a GPS [global positioning system] system and video camera to allow its flight route to be preprogrammed and monitored.

Intentional contamination of food and water is another possible form of biological attack. Product tampering or contaminating food supplies is an ever-present danger. For instance, in 1984, the Rajneeshee cult contaminated local salad bars in an Oregon town with salmonella, demonstrating the ease of conducting small-scale, indiscriminate terrorist attacks.

Another means of bioattack is to spread infectious diseases through humans, animals, or insects. Infectious diseases are already the third leading cause of death in the United States, and battling them is an ongoing health issue. Foreign animal diseases also present a serious risk. Many diseases can infect multiple hosts. Three-quarters of emerging human pathogens are zoonotic—in other words, readily transmitted back and forth among humans, domesticated animals, and wildlife.

Biological dangers can threaten plants and animals as well as people. These are significant, even without the threat of terrorist strikes. Crop and livestock losses from contamination by mycotoxins (toxins produced by fungi), for example, cost the United States an average of $932 million per year. . . .

## Why the Current System Is Inadequate

The current federal response system is predicated on the thoughtful and systematic application of resources. Local communities are expected to deal with disasters and emergencies using their own resources. When they lack adequate capacity, they call on the assets from the state and neighboring jurisdictions. Federal resources are brought to bear only after state and local governments find they lack adequate capacity and request assistance from the federal government. In turn, FEMA [Federal Emergency Management Agency] then has to determine the level of required assistance and then coordinate the delivery of support with HHS [Department of Health and Human Services], the DOD [Department of Defense], the VA [Department of Veterans Affairs], and other federal agencies.

*"Bioterrorist strikes . . . can kill Americans on an unprecedented scale and spread unimaginable fear, panic, and economic disruption."*

The current approach could well prove totally inadequate in the event of a virulent biotoxin attack. Effectively negating threats in many cases requires a rapid response capability, and operating on compressed timelines leaves little room for delayed delivery of support or miscues in coordination.

One significant requirement, for example, is quickly emplacing an incident response structure that can detect and assess threats and mobilize appropriate resources. In particular, for a chemical or biological attack, actions taken in the first hours to identify, contain, and treat victims may significantly reduce the scope of casualties and reduce the prospects for the outbreak of an epidemic.

> *"The difficulties in effectively delivering biotoxins can be overcome with some forethought and ingenuity."*

Complicating any medical response is the plethora of federal, state, and local agencies that would play a role in consequence management. Orchestrating their efforts could be a major challenge. Some organizational chains of command are maximized for responding to infectious diseases, some for natural disasters, others for weapons of mass destruction incidents or investigating crime scenes, and still others for chronic health care issues or emergency or mass casualty treatment. A communicable biotoxin attack, however, could resemble elements of all these problems, requiring perhaps a more sophisticated and integrated response than any other form of terrorist weapon.

Virtually every large-scale exercise or response experiences problems in agency notification, mobilization, information management, communication systems, and administrative and logistical support. Emergency response operations are also frequently plagued by a lack of information sharing and confusion over responsibilities among policymakers, law enforcement, emergency managers, first responders, public health workers, physicians, nonprofit organizations, and federal agencies. The necessity for speed can exacerbate the coordination challenge.

Responders will also have to deal with the demanding conditions and requirements of any terrorist strike. One major command and control challenge is the problem of convergence, a phenomenon that occurs when people, goods, and services are spontaneously mobilized and sent into a disaster-stricken area. Although convergence may have beneficial effects, like rushing resources to the scene of a crisis, it can also lead to congestion, create confusion, hinder the delivery of aid, compromise security, and waste scarce resources. In the case of bioterrorist attack, responders could also become victims and unwittingly spread the contagion. . . .

## Improving the Federal Response

Preparing the federal government to deal more effectively with catastrophic bioterrorism requires developing a national system that can quickly move the right kind and level of assistance to local communities. The Administration and Congress need to take the following actions to streamline the current system, reduce bottlenecks, ensure adequate national surge capacity to respond to a catastrophic threat, and integrate and harmonize operational capabilities *before* a crisis ensues.

*Centralize medical response capabilities in HHS.* Bifurcating responsibility for medical response programs such as the National Strategic Stockpile between HHS and DHS was a mistake. Managing complex programs through interagency memoranda of understanding is bureaucratic, inefficient, and unnecessary. Clearly, efficiencies could be gained by transferring responsibility and budgetary oversight of these efforts into one department or the other.

The DHS lacks the expertise and experience to oversee large medical emergency response programs. Congress should amend the Homeland Security Act of 2002 to move responsibility for overseeing the National Strategic Stockpile, the Metropolitan Medical Response System, and the National Disaster Medical System to HHS.

*Create an Assistant Secretary for Bioterrorism in DHS.* To improve coordination of the national bioterrorism response effort and ensure that key biomedical response programs are seamlessly integrated into the overall national response system, the DHS requires a level of management commensurate with the assistant secretaries providing oversight for the DOD, VA, and HHS.

> *"Bioterrorism is a growing threat, but simply throwing more money at the problem or creating bigger and more complex bureaucracies is not the answer."*

Congress should establish an Assistant Secretary for Bioterrorism and Infectious Disease Response in the DHS Emergency Preparedness and Response Directorate. The Assistant Secretary should have responsibility for ensuring that plans and programs under development—including the National Response Plan, National Incident Management System, and HHS national preparedness plan—are consistent and provide for the rapid delivery of services and support in the event of biomedical emergency.

*Harmonize, simplify, and focus DHS and HHS grant programs for state and local governments.* The DHS and HHS need to work closely together to ensure that grant programs are operating as efficiently as possible to expand the capabilities of local communities to deal with a health disaster. Put simply, they need to ensure "the biggest bang for the buck." The departments need a common performance-based grant system that:

• Is based on national performance standards,

• Focuses most resources on major metropolitan areas and other critical high-risk targets,

• Simplifies the grant process so that states and local governments have to provide only one assessment of their needs and vulnerabilities,

• Encourages the development of regional response capabilities and mutual-support agreements, and

• Evaluates how effectively grant funds are being used to achieve the levels of performance set by the agencies.

Congress needs to act now to establish a framework for an effective national homeland security grant program.

*Focus federal resources on developing national surge capacity.* A significant portion of federal assistance (over one-third) contributes to developing local hospital surge capacity. This funding supports a questionable strategy and is perhaps wasteful spending. A fixed hospital-based national emergency response system is not the answer. It can be assumed that local hospitals will quickly be overwhelmed by a catastrophic bioterrorist attack. In addition, encouraging hospitals to maintain excess capacity, medical facilities, equipment, and staff that are not needed for normal operations only places further and perhaps unnecessary economic stresses on health care providers.

Federal aid should also strike the right balance in ensuring that the national, state, and local governments focus on their appropriate responsibilities. Assistance to the state and local level should focus on medical surveillance, detection, identification, and communication so that problems can be identified quickly and regional and national resources can be rushed to the scene.

This "national bioterrorism watch system" should include training and effective information and incorporate health clinics, hospitals, health care providers, public health officials, first responders, veterinary clinics and hospitals, and food and commodity distribution infrastructure. The Administration needs to develop an integrated national preparedness program that focuses the lion's share of assistance to state and local governments on helping to contribute to the "national bioterrorism watch system," while the federal government should focus on ensuring adequate regional and national surge capacity.

*Ensure appropriate DOD support for bioterrorism response.* Rather than building vast excess capacity in the national health care system at great cost, the Administration should focus on ensuring that the resources already available can be brought to bear as efficiently and effectively as possible. Two key issues that must be addressed are how quickly military capabilities can be brought to bear if needed and how the need for the armed forces to support homeland security and conduct missions overseas can be balanced. . . .

*Enhance federal expertise in emergency medical care.* The federal government lacks an integrated approach to emergency medicine, a key component for responding to a bioterrorist attack. HHS, for example, does not have a National Institute of Emergency Medicine. The Emergency Medical Services Division, tasked with developing the federal contribution to enhancing and guiding the emergency medical system, is a small office within the Department of Transportation's National Highway and Traffic Safety Administration, far removed from other key elements of the federal emergency medical response system in HHS and DHS.

Congress should amend the Public Health Security and Bioterrorism Preparedness and Response Act and address the shortfall in federal expertise in emergency medical services, including moving Emergency Medical Services Division functions to HHS and establishing an Institute for Emergency Medicine as part of the National Institutes of Health, dedicated to spearheading emergency medical research efforts. This institute should work closely with the CDC to devise more comprehensive emergency medical response strategies.

Bioterrorism is a growing threat, but simply throwing more money at the problem or creating bigger and more complex bureaucracies is not the answer. Providing sufficient resources for bioterrorism preparedness is important, but without the right organization, strategies, and programs, these efforts will be inefficient and wasteful. Congress and the Administration should move to ensure that the federal government is better organized to meet the challenge.

# Current Immigration Policies Are Failing to Protect the United States

**by Michelle Malkin, interviewed by Stephen Goode**

**About the authors:** *Michelle Malkin is a syndicated columnist and author of* Invasion: How America Still Welcomes Terrorists, Criminals, and Other Foreign Menaces to Our Shores. *Stephen Goode is a senior writer for* Insight on the News, *a national biweekly newsmagazine.*

*Stephen Goode: Some of your critics have described you as anti-immigrant. Do you think that is a fair assessment?*

*Michelle Malkin:* Many people on the open-border side of the issue have accused me of being anti-immigrant. I am not anti-immigrant. I think we've abandoned the basic principle that entry into this country is a privilege. What it is not is some sort of uncluttered "right" or entitlement.

Nor is it anti-immigrant to say that we should have certain standards and principles. And it is not anti-immigrant to say that when we set certain criteria for the people who come into this country they should be required to abide by those criteria.

Much to our detriment we have abandoned those standards and principles. It's part of the complete unravelling in many parts of the country of the common fabric, of the notion of America as a nation of laws.

*"Unravelling" is an apt word. In your columns and in your book you often take note of signs that indicate how unravelled our sense of ourselves has become.*

The last column I wrote before [the] Sept. 11 [2001 terrorist attacks] was called "The Devaluing of American Citizenship." It's creepy for me to go back and read it. In that column, I went through a litany of things that were going on across the country that showed the disintegration of America's assimilationist ethic.

The Little League World Series was going on at the time, for example. I think the Dominican Republic was in the finals. A lot of people from the Dominican

Republic who were in the United States had gone to the game, where they held Dominican Republic flags.

I mentioned too that the Bush White House had just introduced a Spanish version of the White House Website—the first time any administration had introduced any non-English Website. And I pointed out that [President George W.] Bush had met with Mexican President Vicente Fox and talked about yet another amnesty plan [for illegal aliens in the United States].

I said in that last column before Sept. 11 that it was a shame that we gave the keys of the republic to our enemies and that we were our own worst enemy because it is we who allowed this invasion of our country to take place. On Sept. 11, literally just a few hours after the attacks on America, people got in touch who had read that column because it took on a whole new meaning.

Another point: When I speak to groups about the oath of citizenship my parents took when they became citizens, I always point out that they took it in English. This always gets a rise out of people. You would be shocked to find out how many are pushing to allow people to become American citizens without speaking English and to take the oath in their own native language. We've gone nuts!

## Immigration Policy

*Why is it so difficult to come up with a consistent policy on immigration?*

I've simplified the problem to two driving factors. One is so-called "cheap labor" and the other is so-called "cheap votes."

Cheap votes involves the pandering by the Democratic Party to the illegal-alien lobby in anticipation of payback when they vote, and their calculations have been right for the most part. The Democratic Party does get votes by pandering to the illegal-alien lobby.

The cheap-labor argument comes from some of the influences that are brought to bear on the Republican Party. Those influences include corporate special interests that profit from open borders: the agricultural lobby, for example, the high-tech lobby, those that benefit from suppressed wages as a result of the massive immigration that we tolerate.

*"We've abandoned the basic principle that entry into [America] is a privilege. What it is not is some sort of uncluttered 'right' or entitlement."*

*You are very unhappy with the Bush White House and its support for amnesty for illegal aliens.*

The new factor that I find completely alarming is that there's a very formidable influence on the White House—namely [chief campaign strategist for George W. Bush] Karl Rove—who thinks the GOP [Republican Party] can capitalize on the illegal-alien lobby and those cheap votes the way the Democrats have.

I cannot read their psyches, but I think it is self-delusion. It has never been the case that large numbers of illegal aliens who were amnestied by the GOP then voted Republican. In fact, there's going to be a huge backlash against this pandering to the illegals in the long term.

*What kind of backlash?*

It will be a backlash from those who see it as a reward for massive undermining of the rule of law. It's not just Americans born in America who feel that way. One of the most remarkable things I've experienced in the past several months [early 2003] in going out and talking about my book is meeting naturalized Americans who are longtime Republican Party supporters but are totally put off by amnesty for illegals. They don't like the fact that people such as my parents, the naturalized Americans to whom I've been talking, are made to seem like chumps for having followed the rules in becoming American citizens.

## Immigration and Security

*In your writing, you consistently make a very important connection between immigration policy and national security.*

More than anything else, that's the theme of my book *Invasion*. We have to treat immigration as a national-security issue first and foremost. It's not just terrorism we have to think about, it's all the public-safety consequences that people have been ignoring. That's why I included all the individual case studies where Americans have died because of lax immigration enforcement.

*The title of the first chapter is an eye-opener, "What Would Mohammed Do?" meaning Mohammed Atta, the Egyptian who was the leader of the 19 hijackers who flew the planes into the World Trade Center twin towers and the Pentagon* [on September 11, 2001].

> *"We are not bound to protect each and every piece of 'wretched refuse' that washes up on our shores."*

I saved that first chapter to write last because I wanted to shake people by the shoulders. I wanted to make it as jarring as possible with up-to-date information about how open every doorway is to this country.

Anybody who wants to come into the country now can enter, even after Operation Liberty Shield[1] has been introduced. Some of these foreign nationals even have infiltrated our military. In one case, you have a guy who was of ethnic Lebanese extraction, who came in by way of Sierra Leone and obtained American citizenship through fraudulent marriage. He was fingered in the investigation of the Seattle-based al-Qaeda cell.

What annoyed me particularly about this case was that they dropped the immigration charges against him. This is typical and sends the message that we don't care whether you break these laws.

---

1. Operation Liberty Shield is a comprehensive national plan implemented in 2003. The plan, designed to increase homeland security, includes increased border security.

*What can be done about the foreign nationals in our military?*

We certainly can increase scrutiny of foreign nationals who are serving in the military. There are as many as 31,000 of these, and President Bush has promised them citizenship. At least those people are doing something to serve our country. But I don't think there's nearly enough scrutiny as there should be.

## A "Nation of Laws"

*But hasn't America traditionally smiled on immigrants? The lines from [American poet] Emma Lazarus' famous sonnet inscribed at the Statue of Liberty declare, "Give me your tired, your poor, / Your huddled masses yearning to breathe free, / The wretched refuse of your teeming shore." That's strong stuff!*

One of the arguments I've met repeatedly is, "But we're a nation of immigrants!" I have a couple of things to say about that. We're also a nation of laws. One of the things that's significant about the title of my book is that the word "invasion" appears in Article IV, Section 4 of the U.S. Constitution, which requires that our federal government protect each of the individual states "against Invasion."

> *"You're not going to have any immigration laws on the books that matter if there are no consequences for breaking them."*

I think that the ability to do that and the ability to protect our national sovereignty should be the foremost concern of any immigration or entrance policy. We are not bound to protect each and every piece of "wretched refuse" that washes up on our shores.

But let me concentrate on the homeland-security aspect of immigration policy. While this war [against Iraq in 2003] is going on overseas, we continue to have a war here at home. You can reorganize the Immigration and Naturalization Service, put up new acronyms, give everybody a new title and hire new people. But if those people are not committed to enforcing the law, you're not any better off than you were on Sept. 11, 2001.

*You are especially concerned about laxness on our southern border.*

There was a story recently that we had fortunately caught a handful of Iraqis who were trying to cross the border from Mexico to reach the president's ranch in Texas. They tried to pay a couple of coyotes [smugglers] to get them across.

I keep pressing the federal government to release the figures on the origins of illegal aliens, but they remain totally mum on the breakdown of the ethnic background of people who are crossing the border from Mexico. From the reports I get from rank-and-file U.S. Border Patrol agents and immigration inspectors, there are untold numbers of them that are Yemeni, Pakistani and Saudi Arabian. Are we supposed to buy the open-borders line that they are here only to do the jobs that no one else is willing to do? What if that job includes terrorism?

*If tomorrow you got a call from George W. Bush and he asked you to take over Tom Ridge's job and become secretary of homeland security, what would you do first?*

The first thing I would do would be to end the catch-and-release policy, which is fine for fish but not for immigrants. That would mean lobbying for more detention space. You're not going to have any immigration laws on the books that matter if there are no consequences for breaking them.

For Tom Ridge or for anyone who heads the Department of Homeland Security, the main thing is to use what he already has and enforce the laws already on the books. You go after the employers who are employing illegal aliens instead of giving the illegal aliens amnesty or offering them the chance to get a driver's license, as we do now.

The open-borders people say to me, "There are 11 million illegal aliens in this country. Are you saying we should deport every single one?" I say, "Yes, we should try!"

# Security Lapses at Nuclear Plants Threaten America

## by Alexander Cockburn

**About the author:** *Columnist Alexander Cockburn contributes to many publications, including the* New York Review of Books, Harper's Magazine, *the* Atlantic Monthly, *and the* Wall Street Journal.

Snoozing guards at Los Alamos [nuclear laboratory], missing vials of plutonium oxide . . . Yes, the headlines in late June [2003] were announcing "security lapses" again at national labs and nuclear weapons plants.[1] It seems that an Al Qaeda terrorist could roll up to the gates of the Sandia National Laboratories [government-owned laboratory that develops technology to support national security], haul out an RPG [rocket-propelled grenade] and catch America napping yet again. Sounding all brisk and efficient, Energy Secretary Spencer Abraham acknowledged a recent critical report from the General Accounting Office and has taken standard evasive action, in the form of that whiskered veteran of bureaucratic ass-covering, the "security review." At Sandia, Dave Nokes, vice president for national security, was picked as the sacrificial goat and forced to resign.

The mess at Los Alamos has had its humorous side. Lillian Anaya, a Los Alamos equipment buyer, thought she was ordering $30,000 worth of transducers. But the number she called had been changed from an industrial equipment dealer to an auto parts shop, so she wound up buying a Mustang instead—with government money. Or so say Los Alamos and University of California investigators, who recently cleared Anaya of any wrongdoing (though I still don't quite understand why she got the Mustang).

Let's get back to the larger picture and the obvious question: Whom do they think they're kidding? To talk about terrorist opportunity offered by slack security just at Los Alamos and Livermore [a nuclear laboratory in California] is

1. In June 2003 there were reports of a number of security lapses at Los Alamos National Laboratory, including sleeping guards and two missing vials of plutonium oxide.

like saying that hijackers would try to board planes only at Logan and Atlanta [airports]. There's scarcely a state in the union that hasn't got tanks or barrels of nuclear waste, or decommissioned reactors saturated with radioactive materials. Most Interstates carry trucks hauling mobile Chernobyls[2] around the country.

We're talking sixty years of US nuclear weapons research, development, testing and production, which has left us with staggering amounts of some of the most dangerous substances on the planet. And that's not even to mention the nuclear utilities.

The "security" scene doesn't change rapidly when it comes to nuclear materials and waste. All you can do is try to store radioactivity safely and wait for the millennia to roll by until it naturally decays. But of course it's mostly stored in extremely unsafe and vulnerable conditions.

You live in Texas? There's the Pantex plant, producing nuclear weapons. In Colorado? You've got Rocky Flats. Flee to the clean breezes of the Pacific Northwest? Whoa! Here's the Hanford nuclear reservation, with 177 tanks, each containing a million gallons of radioactive waste, of which sixty-seven are known to have leaked at some point. How about Idaho? Camp in the hills, cheek by jowl with the militia holdouts. Sorry, you've got the National Engineering lab up the road, where intensely radioactive waste was converted to dry form for "permanent" storage nearly forty years ago but now has to be extracted and repackaged.

> *"There's scarcely a state in the union that hasn't got tanks or barrels of nuclear waste, or decommissioned reactors saturated with radioactive materials."*

Head for the heartland, and you find the Fernald plant in Ohio, whose career history includes cumulative "release" of at least 500 tons of toxic uranium dust, kept secret for many years. Turn south into Kentucky, and there, across the horizon, is the Paducah Gaseous Diffusion Plant. Watch where you drink. A 1,300-acre underground plume of Technetium-99 (a uranium-decay product) is migrating toward the Ohio River at the rate of several inches a day. The DOE [Department of Energy] has identified more than 5,700 such plumes of various kinds of contamination under or near its sites across the country.

Go to the densely populated research triangle of North Carolina. Walk along the railroad tracks, and in the end you come to the Shearon Harris plant, a nuclear power generating station where they take spent fuel rods from two other nuclear plants, owned by Progress Energy, storing them in four densely packed pools filled with circulating cold water to keep the waste from heating up. They're the largest radioactive waste storage pools in the country.

Even the Department of Homeland Security acknowledges Shearon Harris as a ripe terror target. If your Al Qaeda operative found a way to interrupt the flow

---

2. Chernobyl is the site of a severe nuclear accident in 1986.

of cooling water, you'd have unstoppable pool fires and possibly a plant melt-down, with consequent peril for 2 million people residing in that part of the state. The Nuclear Regulatory Commission reckons that on a best-case basis there's a 1 in 100 chance of a pool fire. And needless to say, there have been scores of terrifying screw-ups at Shearon Harris.

## A Deadly Threat

Get the picture? Shearon Harris is a really dangerous place, and if you read all the security assessments and reports of past lapses, plus [Secretary of Home-land Security] Tom Ridge's bleak warning, no doubt monitored by America's foes, you can see that—as with Hanford and all the other nuclear waste dumps—it wouldn't take much for a dedicated little crew of terrorists to inflict monstrous disaster, disaster that might well come anyway through native in-competence, without Al Qaeda having to lift a finger.

And don't forget, we're heading for a new phase in the itinerary to Armaged-don. The DOE now proposes building a new plant to manufacture 450 pluto-nium "pits" (nuclear triggers) a year. Function? To arm the mini-nuke bunker-busters scheduled under the Bush Administration's new nuclear strategy. Los Alamos is bidding for it, as is Carlsbad, New Mexico; Savannah River in South Carolina; the Nevada Test Site; and Pantex.

Since the government has been doing its best down the years to damp trouble-some public discussion of these dangers, concerned citizens should take advan-tage of the current sensitivity to weapons of mass destruction [WMD], which places like Shearon Harris most certainly are. There are dedicated groups across the United States that have been active for decades on issues of nuclear safety, and have generated the information offered here.

Now that he's stepped down from his UN [United Nations] job, why not have a nonprofit foundation invite [former UN weapons inspector] Hans Blix and a few other veteran inspectors to start touring the United States, assessing the risks posed by WMDs here? They could make well-publicized "surprise inspec-tions," hold hearings, take evidence from local groups, issue public reports, build up pressure on the Department of Homeland Security to force the govern-ment to get serious about containing America's gravest and most deadly inter-nal threat.

# Reliance on Technology May Make America Less Secure from Terrorism

**by Charles C. Mann**

**About the author:** *Charles C. Mann is a contributing editor for both* Science *and the* Atlantic Monthly. *He also writes for the* New York Times Magazine, *the* Sciences, *and* Smithsonian. *He is the recipient of an Alfred P. Sloan Foundation Science Writing Prize.*

To stop the rampant theft of expensive cars, manufacturers in the 1990s began to make ignitions very difficult to hot-wire. This reduced the likelihood that cars would be stolen from parking lots—but apparently contributed to the sudden appearance of a new and more dangerous crime, carjacking.

After a vote against management [global media and communications company] Vivendi Universal announced earlier this year [2002] that its electronic shareholder-voting system, which it had adopted to tabulate votes efficiently and securely, had been broken into by hackers. Because the new system eliminated the old paper ballots, recounting the vote—or even independently verifying that the attack had occurred—was impossible.

To help merchants verify and protect the identity of their customers, marketing firms and financial institutions have created large computerized databases of personal information: Social Security numbers, credit-card numbers, telephone numbers, home addresses, and the like. With these databases being increasingly interconnected by means of the Internet, [they] have become irresistible targets for criminals. From 1995 to 2000 the incidence of identity theft tripled. . . .

## Thinking About Consequences

[According to ex-cryptographer Bruce Schneier], the way people think about security, especially security on computer networks, is almost always wrong. All too often planners seek technological cure-alls, when such security measures at best limit risks to acceptable levels. In particular, the consequences of going wrong—and all these systems go wrong sometimes—are rarely considered. For these reasons Schneier believes that most of the security measures envisioned after [the September 11, 2001, terrorist attacks] will be ineffective, and that some will make Americans less safe. . . .

Legislators, the law-enforcement community, and the Bush Administration are embroiled in an essential debate over the measures necessary to prevent future attacks. To armor-plate the nation's security they increasingly look to the most powerful technology available: retina, iris, and fingerprint scanners; "smart" driver's licenses and visas that incorporate anti-counterfeiting chips; digital surveillance of public places with face-recognition software; huge centralized databases that use data-mining routines to sniff out hidden terrorists. Some of these measures have already been mandated by Congress, and others are in the pipeline. State and local agencies around the nation are adopting their own schemes. More mandates and more schemes will surely follow.

> *"The way people think about security . . . is almost always wrong."*

Schneier is hardly against technology—he's the sort of person who immediately cases public areas for outlets to recharge the batteries in his laptop, phone, and other electronic prostheses. "But if you think technology can solve your security problems," he says, "then you don't understand the problems and you don't understand the technology." Indeed, he regards the national push for a high-tech salve for security anxieties as a reprise of his own early and erroneous beliefs about the transforming power of strong crypto. The new technologies have enormous capacities, but their advocates have not realized that the most critical aspect of a security measure is not how well it works but how well it fails. . . .

## Stealing Your Thumb

A couple of months after September 11, I flew from Seattle to Los Angeles to meet Schneier. As I was checking in at Sea-Tac Airport, someone ran through the metal detector and disappeared onto the little subway that runs among the terminals. Although the authorities quickly identified the miscreant, a concession stand worker, they still had to empty all the terminals and re-screen everyone in the airport, including passengers who had already boarded planes. Masses of unhappy passengers stretched back hundreds of feet from the checkpoints. Planes by the dozen sat waiting at the gates. I called Schneier on a cell phone to report my delay. I had to shout over the noise of all the other people on their cell phones making similar calls. "What a mess," Schneier said. "The problem with airport security, you know, is that it fails badly."

For a moment I couldn't make sense of this gnomic utterance. Then I realized he meant that when something goes wrong with security, the system should recover well. In Seattle a single slip-up shut down the entire airport, which delayed flights across the nation. Sea-Tac, Schneier told me on the phone, had no adequate way to contain the damage from a breakdown—such as a button installed near the x-ray machines to stop the subway, so that idiots who bolt from checkpoints cannot disappear into another terminal. The shutdown would inconvenience subway riders, but not as much as being forced to go through security again after a wait of several hours. An even better idea would be to place the x-ray machines at the departure gates, as some are in Europe, in order to scan each group of passengers closely and minimize inconvenience to the whole airport if a risk is detected—or if a machine or a guard fails. . . .

[Schneier believes that] security measures are characterized less by their manner of success than by their manner of failure. All security systems eventually miscarry. But when this happens to the good ones, they stretch and sag before breaking, each component failure leaving the whole as unaffected as possible. Engineers call such failure-tolerant systems "ductile." One way to capture much of what Schneier told me is to say that he believes that when possible, security schemes should be designed to maximize ductility, whereas they often maximize strength.

Since September 11 the government has been calling for a new security infrastructure—one that employs advanced technology to protect the citizenry and track down malefactors. Already the USA PATRIOT Act,

> *"The most critical aspect of a security measure is not how well it works but how well it fails."*

which Congress passed in October [2001], mandates the establishment of a "cross-agency, cross-platform electronic system . . . to confirm the identity" of visa applicants, along with a "highly secure network" for financial-crime data and "secure information sharing systems" to link other, previously separate databases. Pending legislation demands that the Attorney General employ "technology including, but not limited to, electronic fingerprinting, face recognition, and retinal scan technology." The . . . Department of Homeland Security is intended to oversee a "national research and development enterprise for homeland security comparable in emphasis and scope to that which has supported the national security community for more than fifty years"—a domestic version of the high-tech R&D [research and development] juggernaut that produced stealth bombers, smart weapons, and anti-missile defense.

Iris, retina, and fingerprint scanners; hand-geometry assayers; remote video-network surveillance; face-recognition software; smart cards with custom identification chips; decompressive baggage checkers that vacuum-extract minute chemical samples from inside suitcases; tiny radio implants beneath the skin that continually broadcast people's identification codes; pulsed fast-neutron analysis of shipping containers ("so precise," according to one manufacturer, "it can determine within inches the location of the concealed target"); a vast national network of interconnected databases—the list goes on and on. In the first five months after the terrorist attacks the Pentagon liaison office that works with technology companies received more than 12,000 proposals for high-tech security measures.

Credit-card companies expertly manage credit risks with advanced information-sorting algorithms. Larry Ellison, the head of Oracle, the world's biggest database firm, told *The New York Times* in April [2002]: "We should be managing security risks in exactly the same way." To "win the war on terrorism," a former deputy undersecretary of commerce, David J. Rothkopf, explained in the May/June [2002] issue of *Foreign Policy*, the nation will need "regiments of geeks"—"pocket-protector brigades" who "will provide the software, systems, and analytical resources" to "close the gaps [terrorist] Mohammed Atta and his associates revealed [in the September 11, 2001, terrorist attack]."

Such ideas have provoked the ire of civil-liberties groups, which fear that governments, corporations, and the police will misuse the new technology. Schneier's concerns are more basic. In his view, these measures can be useful, but their large-scale application will have little effect against terrorism. Worse, their use may make Americans less safe, because many of these tools fail badly—they're "brittle," in engineering jargon. Meanwhile, simple, effective, ductile measures are being overlooked or even rejected.

## Kerckhoffs's Principle

The distinction between ductile and brittle security dates back, Schneier has argued, to the nineteenth-century linguist and cryptographer Auguste Kerckhoffs, who set down what is now known as Kerckhoffs's principle. In good crypto systems, Kerckhoffs wrote, "the system should not depend on secrecy, and it should be able to fall into the enemy's hands without disadvantage." In other words, it should permit people to keep messages secret even if outsiders find out exactly how the encryption algorithm works.

At first blush this idea seems ludicrous. But contemporary cryptography follows Kerckhoffs's principle closely. The algorithms—the scrambling methods—are openly revealed; the only secret is the key. Indeed, Schneier says, Kerckhoffs's principle applies beyond codes and ciphers to security systems in general: every secret creates a potential failure point. Secrecy, in other words, is a prime cause of brittleness—and therefore something likely to make a system prone to catastrophic collapse. Conversely, openness provides ductility.

> *"When possible, security schemes should be designed to maximize ductility, whereas they often maximize strength."*

From this can be drawn several corollaries. One is that plans to add new layers of secrecy to security systems should automatically be hewed with suspicion. Another is that security systems that utterly depend on keeping secrets tend not to work very well. Alas, airport security is among these. Procedures for screening passengers, for examining luggage, for allowing people on the tarmac, for entering the cockpit, for running the autopilot software—all must be concealed and all seriously compromise the system if they become known. As a result, Schneier wrote in the May [2002] issue of *Crypto-Gram*, brittleness "is an inherent property of airline security."

*"Secrecy . . . is a prime cause of brittleness—and therefore something likely to make a system prone to catastrophic collapse."*

Few of the new airport-security proposals address this problem. Instead, Schneier told me in Los Angeles, they address problems that don't exist. "The idea that to stop bombings cars have to park three hundred feet away from the terminal, but meanwhile they can drop off passengers right up front like they always have. . . ." He laughed. "The only ideas I've heard that make any sense are reinforcing the cockpit door and getting the passengers to fight back." Both measures test well against Kerckhoffs's principle: knowing ahead of time that law-abiding passengers may forcefully resist a hijacking en masse, for example, doesn't help hijackers to fend off their assault. Both are small-scale, compartmentalized measures that make the system more ductile, because no matter how hijackers get aboard, beefed-up doors and resistant passengers will make it harder for them to fly into a nuclear plant. And neither measure has any adverse effect on civil liberties.

Evaluations of a security proposal's merits, in Schneier's view, should not be much different from the ordinary cost-benefit calculations we make in daily life. The first question to ask of any new security proposal is, What problem does it solve? The second: What problems does it cause, especially when it fails?

## Types of Failures

Failure comes in many kinds, but two of the more important are simple failure (the security measure is ineffective) and what might be called subtractive failure (the security measure makes people less secure than before). An example of simple failure is face-recognition technology. In basic terms, face-recognition devices photograph people; break down their features into "facial building elements"; convert these into numbers that, like fingerprints, uniquely identify individuals; and compare the results with those stored in a database. If someone's facial score matches that of a criminal in the database, the person is detained. Since September 11 face-recognition technology has been placed in an increasing number of public spaces: airports, beaches, nightlife districts. Even visitors to the Statue of Liberty now have their faces scanned.

Face-recognition software could be useful. If an airline employee has to type in an identifying number to enter a secure area, for example, it can help to confirm that someone claiming to be that specific employee is indeed that person.

But it cannot pick random terrorists out of the mob in an airline terminal. That much-larger-scale task requires comparing many sets of features with the many other sets of features in a database of people on a "watch list." Identix, of Minnesota, one of the largest face-recognition-technology companies, contends that in independent tests its FaceIt software has a success rate of 99.32 percent—that is, when the software matches a passenger's face with a face on a list of terrorists, it is mistaken only 0.68 percent of the time. Assume for the moment that this claim is credible; assume, too, that good pictures of suspected terrorists are readily available. About 25 million passengers used Boston's Logan Airport in 2001. Had face-recognition software been used on 25 million faces, it would have wrongly picked out just 0.68 percent of them—but that would have been enough, given the large number of passengers, to flag as many as 170,000 innocent people as terrorists. With almost 500 false alarms a day, the face-recognition system would quickly become something to ignore.

## Biometrics

The potential for subtractive failure, different and more troublesome, is raised by recent calls to deploy biometric identification tools across the nation. Biometrics—"the only way to prevent identity fraud," according to the former senator Alan K. Simpson, of Wyoming—identifies people by precisely measuring their physical characteristics and matching them up against a database. The photographs on driver's licenses are an early example, but engineers have developed many high-tech alternatives, some of them already mentioned: fingerprint readers, voiceprint recorders, retina or iris scanners, face-recognition devices, hand-geometry assayers, even signature-geometry analyzers, which register pen pressure and writing speed as well as the appearance of a signature.

Appealingly, biometrics lets people be their own ID cards—no more passwords to forget! Unhappily, biometric measures are often implemented poorly. This past spring [2002] three reporters at *c't*, a German digital-culture magazine, tested a face-recognition system, an iris scanner, and nine fingerprint readers. All proved easy to outsmart. Even at the highest security setting, Cognitec's FaceVACS-Logon could be fooled by showing the sensor a short digital movie of someone known to the system—the president of a company, say—on a laptop screen. To beat Panasonic's Authenticam iris scanner, the German journalists photographed an authorized user, took the photo and created a detailed, life-size image of his eyes, cut out the pupils, and held the image up before their faces like a mask. The scanner read the iris, detected the presence of a human pupil—and accepted the imposture. Many of the fingerprint readers could be tricked simply by breathing on them, reactivating the last user's fingerprint. Beating the more sophisticated Identix Bio-Touch fingerprint reader required a trip to a hobby shop. The journalists used graphite powder to dust the latent fingerprint—the kind left on glass—of a previous, authorized user; picked up the image on adhesive tape; and pressed the tape on the reader. The Identix reader, too, was fooled. Not all biometric devices are so poorly put together, of course. But all of them fail badly.

Consider the legislation introduced in May [2002] by Congressmen Jim Moran and Tom Davis, both of Virginia, that would mandate biometric data chips in driver's licenses—a sweeping, nationwide data-collection program, in essence. . . .[1] Although Moran and Davis tied their proposal to the need for tighter security after [the 9/11] attacks, they also contended that the nation could combat fraud by using smart licenses with bank, credit, and Social Security cards, and for voter registration and airport identification. Maybe so, Schneier says. "But think about screw-ups, because the system will screw up."

> *"Good security is built in overlapping, cross-checking layers, to slow down attacks. . . . Its most important components are almost always human."*

Smart cards that store non-biometric data have been routinely cracked in the past, often with inexpensive oscilloscope-like devices that detect and interpret the timing and power fluctuations as the chip operates. An even cheaper method, announced in May [2002] by two Cambridge security researchers, requires only a bright light, a standard microscope, and duct tape. Biometric ID cards are equally vulnerable. Indeed, as a recent National Research Council study points out, the extra security supposedly provided by biometric ID cards will raise the economic incentive to counterfeit or steal them, with potentially disastrous consequences to the victims. "Okay, somebody steals your thumbprint," Schneier says. "Because we've centralized all the functions, the thief can tap your credit, open your medical records, start your car, any number of things. Now what do you do? With a credit card, the bank can issue you a new card with a new number. But this is your thumb—you can't get a new one."

The consequences of identity fraud might be offset if biometric licenses and visas helped to prevent terrorism. Yet smart cards would not have stopped the terrorists who attacked the World Trade Center and the Pentagon. According to the FBI [Federal Bureau of Investigation], all the hijackers seem to have been who they said they were; their intentions, not their identities, were the issue. Each entered the country with a valid visa, and each had a photo ID in his real name (some obtained their IDs fraudulently, but the fakes correctly identified them). "What problem is being solved here?" Schneier asks.

Good security is built in overlapping, cross-checking layers, to slow down attacks; it reacts limberly to the unexpected. Its most important components are almost always human. "Governments have been relying on intelligent, trained guards for centuries," Schneier says. "They spot people doing bad things and then use laws to arrest them. All in all, I have to say, it's not a bad system.". . .

1. As this volume went to press, the legislation had not passed.

*Chapter 1*

## Insecurity of Networked Computers

In security terms, [Schneier] explained, cryptography is classed as a protective countermeasure. No such measure can foil every attack, and all attacks must still be both detected and responded to. This is particularly true for digital security. . . . Countless [networked computers] are broken into every year, including machines in people's homes. Taking over computers is simple with the right tools, because software is so often misconfigured or flawed. In the first five months of this year, for example, Microsoft released five "critical" security patches for Internet Explorer, each intended to rectify lapses in the original code.

Computer crime statistics are notoriously sketchy, but the best of a bad lot come from an annual survey of corporations and other institutions by the FBI and the Computer Security Institute, a research and training organization in San Francisco. In the most recent survey, released in April [2002], 90 percent of the respondents had detected one or more computer-security breaches within the previous twelve months—a figure that Schneier calls "almost certainly an underestimate." His own experience suggests that a typical corporate network suffers a serious security breach four to six times a year—more often if the network is especially large or its operator is politically controversial.

Given the pervasive insecurity of networked computers, it is striking that nearly every proposal for "homeland security" entails the creation of large national databases. The Moran-Davis proposal, like other biometric schemes, envisions storing smart-card information in one such database; the USA PATRIOT Act effectively creates another; the . . . Department of Homeland Security would "fuse and analyze" information from more than a hundred agencies, and would "merge under one roof" scores or hundreds of previously separate databases. (A representative of the new department told me no one had a real idea of the number. "It's a lot," he said.) Better coordination of data could have obvious utility, as was made clear by recent [2002] headlines about the failure of the FBI and the CIA [Central Intelligence Agency] to communicate. But carefully linking selected fields of data is different from creating huge national repositories of information about the citizenry, as is being proposed. Larry Ellison, the CEO of Oracle, has dismissed cautions about such databases as whiny cavils that don't take into account the existence of murderous adversaries. But murderous adversaries are exactly why we should ensure that new security measures actually make American life safer.

## Large-Scale Federal Databases

Any new database must be protected, which automatically entails [a] new layer of secrecy. As Kerckhoffs's principle suggests, the new secrecy introduces a new failure point. Government information is now scattered through scores of databases; however inadvertently, it has been compartmentalized—a basic security practice. (Following this practice, tourists divide their money between their wallets and hidden pouches; pickpockets are less likely to steal it all.) Many

65

new proposals would change that. An example is Attorney General John Ashcroft's plan, announced in June [2002], to fingerprint and photograph foreign visitors "who fall into categories of elevated national security concern" when they enter the United States ("approximately 100,000" will be tracked this way in the first year). The fingerprints and photographs will be compared with those of "known or suspected terrorists" and "wanted criminals" Alas, no such database of terrorist fingerprints and photographs exists. Most terrorists are outside the country, and thus hard to fingerprint, and latent fingerprints rarely survive bomb blasts. The databases of "wanted criminals" in Ashcroft's plan seem to be those maintained by the FBI and the [former] Immigration and Naturalization Service. But using them for this purpose would presumably involve merging computer networks in these two agencies with the visa procedure in the State Department—a security nightmare, because no one entity will fully control access to the system.[2]

Equivalents of the big, centralized databases under discussion already exist in the private sector: corporate warehouses of customer information, especially credit-card numbers. The record there is not reassuring. "Millions upon millions of credit-card numbers have been stolen from computer networks," Schneier says. So many, in fact, that Schneier believes that everyone reading this article "has, in his or her wallet right now, a credit card with a number that has been stolen," even if no criminal has yet used it. Number thieves, many of whom operate out of the former Soviet Union, sell them in bulk: $1,000 for 5,000 credit-card numbers, or twenty cents apiece. In a way, the sheer volume of theft is fortunate: so many numbers are floating around that the odds are small that any one will be heavily used by bad guys.

Large-scale federal databases would undergo similar assaults. The prospect is worrying, given the government's long-standing reputation for poor information security. Since September 11 at least forty government networks have been publicly cracked by typographically challenged vandals with names like "CriminalS," "S4t4n1c SOuls" "cr1m3 Org4n1z4dO" and

> *"The most important element of any security measure . . . is people, not technology— and the people need to be at the scene."*

"Discordian Dodgers." Summing up the problem, a House subcommittee last November [2001] awarded federal agencies a collective computer-security grade of F. According to representatives of Oracle, the federal government has been talking with the company about employing its software for the new central databases. But judging from the past, involving the private sector will not greatly improve security. In March [2002], CERT/CC, a computer-security watchdog based at Carnegie Mellon University, warned of thirty-eight vulnerabilities in

2. As of April 2004, this system was being implemented at border checkpoints.

Oracle's database software. Meanwhile, a centerpiece of the company's international advertising is the claim that its software is "unbreakable." Other software vendors fare no better: CERT/CC issues a constant stream of vulnerability warnings about every major software firm.

Schneier, like most security experts I spoke to, does not oppose consolidating and modernizing federal databases per se. To avoid creating vast new opportunities for adversaries, the overhaul should be incremental and small-scale. Even so, it would need to be planned with extreme care—something that shows little sign of happening.

## Improving Computer Security

One key to the success of digital revamping will be a little-mentioned, even prosaic feature: training the users not to circumvent secure systems. The federal government already has several computer networks—INTELINK, SIPRNET, and NIPRNET among them—that are fully encrypted, accessible only from secure rooms and buildings, and never connected to the Internet. Yet despite their lack of Net access the secure networks have been infected by e-mail perils such as the Melissa and I Love You viruses, probably because some official checked e-mail on a laptop, got infected, and then plugged the same laptop into the classified network. Because secure networks are unavoidably harder to work with, people are frequently tempted to bypass them—one reason that researchers at weapons labs sometimes transfer their files to insecure but more convenient machines.

Schneier has long argued that the best way to improve the very bad situation in computer security is to change software licenses. If software is blatantly unsafe, owners have no such recourse, because it is licensed rather than bought, and the licenses forbid litigation. It is unclear whether the licenses can legally do this (courts currently disagree), but as a practical matter it is next to impossible to win a lawsuit against a software firm. If some big software companies lose product-liability suits, Schneier believes, their confreres will begin to take security seriously.

Computer networks are difficult to keep secure in part because they have so many functions, each of which must be accounted for. For that reason Schneier and other experts tend to favor narrowly focused security measures—more of them physical than digital—that target a few precisely identified problems. For air travel, along with reinforcing cockpit doors and teaching passengers to fight back, examples include armed uniformed—not plainclothes—guards on select flights; "dead-man" switches that in the event of a pilot's incapacitation force planes to land by autopilot at the nearest airport; positive bag matching (ensuring that luggage does not get on a plane unless its owner also boards); and separate decompression facilities that detonate any altitude bombs in cargo before takeoff. None of these is completely effective; bag matching, for instance, would not stop suicide bombers. But all are well tested, known to at least impede hijackers, not intrusive to passengers, and unlikely to make planes less secure if they fail.

It is impossible to guard all potential targets, because anything and everything can be subject to attack. Palestinian suicide bombers have shown this by murdering at random the occupants of pool halls and hotel meeting rooms. Horrible as these incidents are, they do not risk the lives of thousands of people, as would attacks on critical parts of the national infrastructure: nuclear-power plants, hydroelectric dams, reservoirs, gas and chemical facilities. Here a classic defense is available: tall fences and armed guards. Yet this past spring [2002] the Bush Administration cut by 93 percent the funds requested by the Energy Department to bolster security for nuclear weapons and waste; it denied completely the funds requested by the Army Corps of Engineers for guarding 200 reservoirs, dams, and canals, leaving fourteen large public-works projects with no budget for protection. A recommendation by the American Association of Port Authorities that the nation spend a total of $700 million to inspect and control ship cargo (today less than two percent of container traffic is inspected) has so far resulted in grants of just $92 million. In all three proposals most of the money would have been spent on guards and fences.

## The Importance of People

The most important element of any security measure, Schneier argues, is people, not technology—and the people need to be at the scene. Recall the German journalists who fooled the fingerprint readers and iris scanners. None of their tricks would have worked if a reasonably attentive guard had been watching. Conversely, legitimate employees with bandaged fingers or scratched corneas will never make it through security unless a guard at the scene is authorized to overrule the machinery. Giving guards increased authority provides more opportunities for abuse, Schneier says, so the guards must be supervised carefully. But a system with more people who have more responsibility "is more robust," he observed in the June *Crypto-Gram*, "and the best way to make things work. (The U.S. Marine Corps understands this principle; it's the heart of their chain of command rules.)"

"The trick is to remember that technology can't save you," Schneier says. "We know this in our own lives. We realize that there's no magic anti-burglary dust we can sprinkle on our cars to prevent them from being stolen. We know that car alarms don't offer much protection. The Club [car security device] at best makes burglars steal the car next to you. For real safety we park on nice streets where people notice if somebody smashes the window. Or we park in garages, where somebody watches the car. In both cases people are the essential security element. You always build the system around people."

# Chapter 2

# Is the Department of Homeland Security Effective?

CURRENT CONTROVERSIES

# The Department of Homeland Security: An Overview

**by the U.S. Department of Homeland Security**

**About the author:** *The U.S. Department of Homeland Security, created in 2003, is the federal department responsible for ensuring the safety of the American homeland.*

In January 2003, the Department of Homeland Security became the Nation's 15th and newest Cabinet department, consolidating 22 previously disparate agencies under one unified organization. In 2002, no single federal department had homeland security as its primary objective. Now it is our mission. We are integrating our resources to meet a common goal. Our most important job is to protect the American people and our way of life from terrorism. We have a single, clear line of authority to get the job done. While we can never eliminate the potential for attack, particularly in a society that's as open, as diverse, and as large as ours, we will significantly reduce the Nation's vulnerability to terrorism and terrorist attack over time. Through partnerships with state, local and tribal governments and the private sector, we are working to ensure the highest level of protection and preparedness for the country and the citizens we serve. . . .

The [terrorist] attack on our homeland of September 11, 2001, was an assault on the ideals that make our nation great. We were reminded that the values we hold dear must not be taken for granted. From these tragic events, a stronger union has emerged. Our citizens, and those of countries around the world, renewed their commitment to this nation and to the values for which it stands. In January of 2003, the United States Government established the Department of Homeland Security to focus America's efforts to thwart those who seek to do us harm. The Department has an overriding and urgent mission: secure the American homeland and protect the American people. . . .

The Department of Homeland Security was created not to increase the size of

U.S. Department of Homeland Security, "Securing Our Homeland: U.S. Department of Homeland Security Strategic Plan," 2004.

the government, but to focus and integrate our collective efforts. Employees of this new organization come to work every day knowing their most important job is to protect their fellow citizens. We are stronger and better prepared today than we were in the past, and in the future will be stronger still. We have learned a great deal since September 11, 2001, and will act on every lesson to ensure the security of the American people. . . .

## Guiding Principles

The philosophy that informs and shapes decision making and provides normative criteria that governs the actions of policy makers and employees in performing their work.

*Protect Civil Rights and Civil Liberties.*

We will defend America while protecting the freedoms that define America. Our strategies and actions will be consistent with the individual rights and liberties enshrined by our Constitution and the Rule of Law. While we seek to improve the way we collect and share information about terrorists, we will nevertheless be vigilant in respecting the confidentiality and protecting the privacy of our citizens. We are committed to securing our nation while protecting civil rights and civil liberties.

*Integrate Our Actions.*

We will blend 22 previously disparate agencies, each with its employees, mission and culture, into a single, unified Department whose mission is to secure the homeland. The Department of Homeland Security will be a cohesive, capable and service-oriented organization whose cross-cutting functions will be optimized so that we may protect our nation against threats and effectively respond to disasters.

*Build Coalitions and Partnerships.*

Building new bridges to one another are as important as building new barriers against terrorism. We will collaborate and coordinate across traditional boundaries, both horizontally (between agencies) and vertically (among different levels of government). We will engage partners and stakeholders from federal, state, local, tribal and international governments, as well as the private sector and academia. We will work together to identify needs, provide service, share information and promote best practices. We will foster inter-connected systems, rooted in

> *"Our most important job is to protect the American people and our way of life from terrorism."*

the precepts of federalism that reinforce rather than duplicate individual efforts. Homeland security is a national effort, not solely a federal one.

*Develop Human Capital.*

Our most valuable asset is not new equipment or technology, but rather our dedicated and patriotic employees. Their contributions will be recognized and valued by this Department. We will hire, train and place the very best people in jobs to which they are best suited. We are committed to personal and professional growth and will create new opportunities to train and to learn. We will create a model human resources management system that supports equally the mission of the Department and the people charged with achieving it.

*Innovate.*

We will introduce and apply new concepts and creative approaches that will help us meet the challenges of the present and anticipate the needs of the future. We will support innovation and agility within the public and private sector, both by providing resources and removing red tape so that new solutions reach the Department and the marketplace as soon as possible. We will harness our nation's best minds in science, medicine and technology to develop applications for homeland security. Above all, we will look for ways to constantly improve—we will recognize complacency as an enemy.

*Be Accountable.*

We will seek measurable progress as we identify vulnerabilities, detect evolving threats to the American homeland and prioritize our homeland security resources. We will assess our work, evaluate the results and incorporate lessons learned to enhance our performance. We will reward excellence and fix what we find to be broken. We will communicate our progress to the American people, operating as transparently as possible and routinely measuring the success of our progress.

## Summary of the National Security Strategy

The *National Strategy for Homeland Security* and the *Homeland Security Act of 2002* served to mobilize and organize our nation to secure the homeland from terrorist attacks. This is an exceedingly complex mission that requires coordinated and focused effort from our entire society. To this end, the Department of Homeland Security was established to provide the unifying core of the vast national network of organizations and institutions involved in efforts to secure our homeland. Our first priority is to prevent further terrorist attacks within the United States. To reduce vulnerability without diminishing economic security, we gather intelligence and analyze threats, guard our nation's borders and airports, protect our critical infrastructure and coordinate response to the American people during times of disaster. The goals guide the full breadth of our activities (both terrorism and non-terrorism related):

> *"The Department of Homeland Security was created not to increase the size of the government, but to focus and integrate our collective efforts."*

1. Awareness: Identify and understand threats, assess vulnerabilities, determine potential impacts and disseminate timely information to our homeland security partners and the American public.

2. Prevention: Detect, deter and mitigate threats to our homeland.

3. Protection: Safeguard our people and their freedoms, critical infrastructure, property and the economy of our nation from acts of terrorism, natural disasters, or other emergencies.

4. Response: Lead, manage and coordinate the national response to acts of terrorism, natural disasters, or other emergencies.

5. Recovery: Lead national, state, local and private sector efforts to restore services and rebuild communities after acts of terrorism, natural disasters, or other emergencies.

6. Service: Serve the public effectively by facilitating lawful trade, travel and immigration.

7. Organizational Excellence: Value our most important resource, our people. Create a culture that promotes a common identity, innovation, mutual respect, accountability and teamwork to achieve efficiencies, effectiveness and operational synergies. . . .

> *"While we seek to improve the way we collect and share information about terrorists, we will nevertheless be vigilant in . . . protecting the privacy of our citizens."*

## A Day in the Life of Homeland Security

The Department of Homeland Security has one mission but uses many tools and areas of expertise to accomplish our goal of securing the homeland. On any given day, we perform a variety of different tasks and functions to make America safer and our citizens more secure. Although our responsibilities are varied, we are united in a common purpose—24 hours a day, 7 days a week.

Below is a sampling of what the men and women of the Department of Homeland Security do in an average day.

*Today, United States Customs and Border Protection agents will:*

• Process over 1.1 million passengers arriving into our nation's airports and seaports;

• Inspect over 57,006 trucks and containers, 580 vessels, 2,459 aircraft and 323,622 vehicles coming into this country;

• Execute over 64 arrests;

• Seize 4,639 pounds of narcotics in 118 narcotics seizures;

• Seize an average of $715,652 in currency in 11 seizures;

• Seize an average of $23,083 in arms and ammunition and $467,118 in merchandise;

• Deploy 1,200 dog teams to aid inspections;

• Make 5,479 pre-departure seizures of prohibited agricultural items;

• Apprehend 2,617 people crossing illegally into the United States;

• Rescue 3 people illegally crossing the border in dangerous conditions;

• Deploy 350,000 vehicles, 108 aircraft, 118 horses on equestrian patrol and 480 all-terrain vehicles;

• Utilize 238 Remote Video Surveillance Systems, each system using 1–4 cameras to transmit images to a central location; and

• Maintain the integrity of 5,525 miles of border with Canada and 1,989 miles of border with Mexico.

*Today, United States Immigration and Customs Enforcement agents will:*

• Make 217 arrests on immigration-related violations;

• Make 41 arrests on customs violations;

• Remove 407 criminal aliens and other illegal aliens;

• Investigate 12 cases involving unauthorized employment threatening critical infrastructure;

• Participate in 24 drug seizures resulting in the seizure of 5,511 pounds of marijuana, 774 pounds of cocaine and 16 pounds of heroin;

• Make seven currency seizures, totaling $478,927;

• Make grand jury appearances resulting in the indictment of a combination of 32 people and companies;

• Launch 20 vessels in support of marine operations protecting the territorial seas of Puerto Rico, South Florida, the Gulf of Mexico and Southern California;

• Fly 25 surveillance flights supporting criminal investigations in Puerto Rico and the Continental United States;

• Disseminate 80 criminal investigative leads to field offices;

• Review 1,200 classified intelligence cables;

• Protect over 8,000 federal facilities;

• Screen over 1 million federal employees and visitors entering federal facilities;

• Make 6 arrests for criminal offenses on federal property; and

• Intercept 18 weapons from entering federal facilities to include firearms, knives and box cutters.

*Today, Transportation Security Agency employees will:*

• Screen approximately 1.5 million passengers before they board commercial aircraft;

• Intercept 2 firearms; and

• Deploy thousands of federal air marshals to protect the skies.

> *"We are establishing a foundation of national policies and initiatives that will further secure our homeland in the face of evolving external trends."*

*Today, the Federal Law Enforcement Training Center will:*

• Provide law enforcement training for more than 3,500 federal officers and agents from 75 different federal agencies.

*Today, the Office of Domestic Preparedness will:*

• Disburse millions of dollars to states and cities across the country.

*Today, United States Coast Guard units will:*

• Save 10 lives;

• Assist 192 people in distress;

• Protect $2.8 million in property;
• Interdict 14 illegal migrants at sea;
• Conduct 109 search and rescue cases;
• Seize $9.6 million of illegal drugs;
• Respond to 20 oil and hazardous chemical spills;
• Conduct 50 Port Security Patrols;
• Conduct 20 Homeland Security Air Patrols;
• Board 2 high interest vessels;
• Escort 8 vessels, such as cruise ships or high interest ships, in and out of port;
• Embark Sea Marshals on 2 vessels;
• Maintain over 90 security zones around key infrastructure in major ports or coastal areas; and
• Educate 502 people in Boating Safety Courses.

*Today, the United States Citizenship and Immigration Services will:*
• Provide information and services to approximately 225,000 customers in one of its 250 field locations;
• Respond to 75,000 calls to its 1-800 customer service number;
• Naturalize approximately 1,900 new citizens; and
• Process approximately 19,000 applications for a variety of immigration related benefits.

> *"Through continuous program assessment and evaluation we will identify gaps that are formed by developing issues and changing circumstances."*

*Today, Federal Emergency Management Agency (FEMA) employees will:*
• Provide 11,035 fire education publications through FEMA's United States Fire Administration to help Americans better prevent and respond to fires;
• Improve the effectiveness of 220 fire service personnel through courses offered by FEMA's National Fire Academy;
• Help protect 1,000 students at risk for tornadoes by providing their school administrators with information about how to properly construct tornado shelters;
• Provide critical preparedness, prevention, response and recovery information to 2.5 million Americans who access the FEMA website, www.FEMA.gov, each day;
• Provide 4,000 people volunteer opportunities to help better prepare their communities through Citizen Corps at its website, www.citizencorps.gov. The site receives 36,000 hits per day;
• Help save $2.7 million in damages from flooding across the country through the Department's flood plain management;
• Spend $10.6 million to help communities respond and recover from disasters;
• Help protect an additional 104 homes from the devastating effects of flooding through flood insurance policies issued by the National Flood Insurance Program;

• Help 224 Americans recover from disasters by providing direct federal disaster relief assistance in the forms of low-interest loans, unemployment insurance, crisis counseling and temporary housing;

• Partner with the Small Business Administration to provide almost 60 low-interest loans worth approximately $3.6 million to help America's businesses recover from disasters;

• Distribute $45,243 to state and local governments through FEMA's Emergency Management Performance Grants to help develop, maintain and improve their emergency management capabilities;

• Distribute $51,506 through FEMA's Community Emergency Response Team grants to help state emergency managers initiate, organize, train and maintain teams of citizens who are qualified to assist in responding to disasters;

• Provide an average of $917,808 in grants to America's fire departments through the Assistance to Firefighters Grant program;

• Distribute $221,917 through FEMA's Emergency Operations Center grants to state governments to help them develop and improve emergency management facilities; and

• Distribute $218,493 through FEMA's Interoperable Communications Equipment grants to help develop and support communications interoperability among first responders and public safety emergency officials.

*Today, Department of Homeland Security Science and Technology employees will:*

• Receive approximately 27 new home and security technology proposals from large and small businesses;

• Receive an average of 6 Homeland Security technology proposals submitted via the science.technology@dhs.gov email address; and

• Meet with an average of 4 industry leaders to discuss new technologies to protect the homeland.

*Today, Department of Homeland Security Information Analysis and Infrastructure Protection employees will:*

• Receive and review 500 cyber security reports from Internet security firms, government organizations, private companies and foreign governments;

• Review more than a 1,000 pieces of intelligence from the intelligence community and law enforcement agencies; and

• Distribute 4 information bulletins or warning products to critical infrastructure about vulnerability assessments, risk reduction and protective measures.

*Today, the United States Secret Service will:*

• Protect high profile government officials including the President, the Vice President, visiting heads of state and former Presidents;

• Provide protection to traveling protectees in 17 different cities;

• Screen over 4,000 people entering protective sites;

• Examine 1,500 protective intelligence reports to assess potential threats to protectees;

• Complete 11 protective intelligence investigations to assess potential risk to protectees from individuals or groups;

• Open over 90 new cases involving financial and electronic crime, identity theft, counterfeiting and personnel security investigations;

• Prevent over $6 million in financial crime losses to the American public; and

• Seize $172,000 in counterfeit currency. . . .

## Continual Improvement

As a newly formed department, we are in a period of profound transition. We are establishing a foundation of national policies and initiatives that will further secure our homeland in the face of evolving external trends that include diverse security threats and increasing global interdependence. While we face an array of challenges, we have an unprecedented opportunity to restructure the operation of the Federal Government to address the needs of our society and enhance collective performance. . . .

Through continuous program assessment and evaluation we will identify gaps that are formed by developing issues and changing circumstances. We will refine performance goals based on measures of effectiveness. We will continuously evaluate results-oriented performance information as a routine part of decision making, at all levels, to address evolving trends and emerging threats. To remain agile and enhance daily performance, we will reorient our direction as conditions warrant, immediately or more deliberately.

# The Department of Homeland Security Is the Best Way to Protect America

**by Todd Tiahrt**

**About the author:** *Todd Tiahrt was first elected to the U.S. House of Representatives in 1994, representing the state of Kansas. He serves on the Appropriations Committee.*

*Editor's Note: The following viewpoint was originally given in July 2002 as part of a debate in the House of Representatives over HR 5005, the proposed Homeland Security Act of 2002. Following the debate the act was passed, and the U.S. Department of Homeland Security was created on March 1, 2003.*

I rise today in support of H.R. 5005, the Homeland Security Act of 2002. This important legislation will bring more than 100 different security and safety units from around the Nation together into a newly created Cabinet department.

This new department will work to control movement at the borders, emphasize coordination with State and local emergency responders, merge intelligence units to identify and map threats, address vulnerabilities, and develop technologies to protect the homeland.

The [terrorist] attacks on September 11th [2001] changed the everyday lives of Americans. As a result of these attacks, our country is now at war with an invisible enemy that lurks in the shadows. We face the real possibility of additional attacks of a similar or even greater magnitude. Terrorists around the world are conspiring to obtain chemical, biological, and nuclear weapons with the express intent of killing large numbers of Americans. We saw on September 11th that terrorists will use unconventional means to deliver their terror.

Todd Tiahrt, address before the U.S. House of Representatives, Washington, DC, July 26, 2002.

These new times require new thinking. Creating a Department of Homeland Security will give the government the flexibility necessary to make the right decisions that are needed to protect the American people.

## A More Effective Organization

Consolidating these agencies into one Cabinet-level department will support the President's National Strategy for Homeland Security, it will facilitate the ability of the private sector to more effectively communicate and coordinate threat and vulnerability management, and it will centralize response and recovery management with the Federal Government.

The Department of Homeland Security will have three mission functions. They are (1) to prevent terrorist attacks within the United States, (2) to reduce America's vulnerability to terrorism, and (3) to minimize the damage and recover from attacks that do occur.

*"Reorganization of America's homeland security functions is critical to defeating the threat of terrorism and is vital to the Nation's long-term security."*

H.R. 5005 transforms many government functions into a twenty-first century department. In order to protect the freedom of our citizens, we must protect America's borders from those who seek to cause us harm.

Under this legislation, protection of our borders is a primary function. This legislation will encompass INS [Immigration and Naturalization Service] enforcement functions, the Customs service, the border functions of the Animal and Plant Health Inspections Service, and the Coast Guard all together in the new Department of Homeland Security.

H.R. 5005 will also ensure that our neighborhoods and communities are prepared to address any threat or attack we may face. The Federal Emergency Management Agency will also be included in the Department of Homeland Security. Thus, if an attack should occur, it will be clear who is responsible for consequence management and whom our first responders can quickly communicate with.

Additionally, H.R. 5005 places a high priority on transportation safety. The Transportation Security Agency [TSA] is transferred entirely to the Department of Homeland Security. TSA has the statutory responsibility for security of all modes of transportation and it directly employs transportation security personnel.

These are just a few of the agencies that will encompass the Department of Homeland Security. Only those agencies whose principal missions align with the Department's mission of protecting the homeland are included in this proposal.

The current unfocused confederation of government agencies is not the best way to organize if we are to effectively protect our homeland, as responsibility is too scattered across the Federal Government. This has led to confusion, redundancy, and ineffective communication.

Even though this legislation addresses issues concerning personal privacy, government disclosure, and individual rights, lawmakers and citizens alike must be vigilant against government encroachment of traditional liberties. . . .

## The Best Way to Protect America

I believe an unaccountable government is an irresponsible government and in addition to a vigilant watch against abuses of individual rights, we must be accountable to tax-payers and not allow the department to expand beyond its fiscal and bureaucratic parameters.

The new Department of Homeland Security will be the one department whose primary mission is to protect the American homeland.

It will be the one department to secure our borders, transportation sector, ports, and critical infrastructure. One department to synthesize and analyze homeland security intelligence. One department to coordinate communications with State and local governments, private industry, and first responders. And one department to manage our Federal emergency response activities.

We owe the American people nothing less than the absolute best to protect our citizens. Reorganization of America's homeland security functions is critical to defeating the threat of terrorism and is vital to the Nation's long-term security.

# The Department of Homeland Security Is Making America Safer

**by George W. Bush**

**About the author:** *George W. Bush was elected the forty-third president of the United States in November 2000. Prior to that he was governor of Texas.*

*Editor's Note: The following viewpoint was originally given as a speech to the employees of the U.S. Department of Homeland Security on March 2, 2004, the department's one-year anniversary.*

I'm honored to join the proud men and women of the Department of Homeland Security in celebrating this agency's first anniversary [March 2, 2004].

Many of you were here from day one. Others have come aboard in the days since. Yet, from the President to the Secretary to the newest employee, all of us here are tasked with a single, vital mission: to secure the American homeland and to protect the American people. There is no duty more important. We're meeting that duty together, and on behalf of a grateful nation, I thank you all for what you do to defend our country.

I appreciate Secretary [of Homeland Security Tom] Ridge's leadership. I plucked him out of the ranks of the governors because I knew he knew how to manage and to set an agenda. He has not let me down. Along with the other leaders here, he and the team are doing a fantastic job of leading this Department. I appreciate Deputy Secretary Jim Loy, as well, for his outstanding leadership. . . .

I appreciate all the employees who are here. I appreciate you working hard for the American people. I'm sure people don't thank you enough. Well, I'm here to thank you as much as an individual possibly can, for working the long hours, for taking the risks on behalf of the security of this country.

Today [March 2, 2004] I had the honor of meeting the family of Agent Jimmy Epling. Jimmy was the first Department of Homeland Security employee to be

George W. Bush, address to the U.S. Department of Homeland Security, Washington, DC, March 2, 2004.

killed in the line of duty. He did so rescuing an individual. He risked his life to save a life. And on behalf of our nation, Monica and Seth and Shaine and Sean and James, and his loving parents, Ken and Amy, thank you for raising such a good son and thank you for having such a good husband; boys, you need to be proud of your daddy. . . .

## Success in Protecting America

Two-and-a-half years ago [on September 11, 2001], our nation saw war and grief arrive on a quiet September morning. From that day to this, we have pursued a clear strategy: We are taking the offensive against the terrorists abroad. We're taking unprecedented measures to protect the American people here at home. The goal of the terrorists is to kill our citizens—that's their goal—and to make Americans live in fear. This nation refuses to live in fear. We will stand together until this threat to our nation and to the civilized world is ended.

We have been called to service. We've been called to action. And we accept that responsibility. With fine allies, we are winning the war against the terrorists. We're disrupting terrorist operations. We're cutting off their funding. We are chasing down their leaders one person at a time. We are relentless. We are strong. We refuse to yield. Some two-thirds of . . . al Qaeda's key leaders have been captured or killed. The rest of them hear us breathing down their neck. We're after them. We will not relent. We will bring these killers to justice. . . .

We will stay on the offensive. We will not relent. And as we wage this war abroad, we must remember where it began, here in our homeland. Life in America, in many ways, has returned to normal, and that's positive. It means we're doing our jobs. But life will really never return to normal so long as there's an enemy that lurks in the shadows, that aims to destroy and kill. The enemies are wounded, but they're not broken. They still have desires to strike America again. That's the reality with which we live. The reality is, vast oceans can no longer protect us, and therefore we must have, and we do have, a clear strategy to defend our homeland. Oh, we'll do everything we can to prevent attacks on America. As we do so, we'll reduce our vulnerabilities and prepare for any attack that might come; that's our duty; that is our collective mission.

> *"Vast oceans can no longer protect us, and therefore we must have, and we do have, a clear strategy to defend our homeland."*

To meet the goals, we have tripled federal funding for homeland security since 2001, to some $30.5 billion. I want to thank the Congress for working with the administration to make sure these good folks have got the ability to implement the strategy to protect our country.

We've undertaken the most sweeping reorganization of the federal government since the beginning of the Cold War. The FBI has transformed itself into an agency dedicated primarily to the prevention of future terrorist attacks. The Department of Defense has established a new top level command whose priority is to protect the American homeland. We established the Terrorist Threat Integration Center, to merge and analyze in a single place all vital intelligence on global terror. We created the Homeland Security Council within the White House . . . to help coordinate all homeland security activities across our government.

## The Department of Homeland Security

We'll face the terrorist threat for years to come. Our government is prepared to meet that threat. One of the most important steps we've taken is creating the Department of Homeland Security [DHS], combining under one roof, with a clear chain of command, many agencies responsible for protecting our nation. All of you go to work every day with a single, overriding responsibility: to make this nation more secure.

Creating the newest department of our federal government was a tough task. It required a lot of hard work, changing some old habits, in order to merge into a new strategy and a new department. You've accomplished an historic task. In just 12 months, under the leadership of your President, you have made air travel safer, you've strengthened the security of our borders and infrastructure, you've taken steps to protect the American people from dangerous weapons, and you helped prepare our first responders for any emergency. You faced the challenges standing up this new Department and you get a gold star for a job well done.

> *"We've undertaken the most sweeping reorganization of the federal government since the beginning of the Cold War."*

Since the September 11th attacks, we've taken significant steps to ensure the safety of air travel. DHS is completing a massive overhaul of security at our nation's airports. Federal air marshals are flying on hundreds of commercial flights every day. We are determined to protect Americans who travel by plane. We're determined to prevent those planes from being used as weapons against us.

The Department of Homeland Security is strengthening control of all our borders and ports of entry, to keep out terrorists and criminals and dangerous materials. We're using technology to allow law abiding travelers to cross the border quickly and easily, while our officials concentrate on stopping possible threats. We've increased the number of border inspectors and improved access to sophisticated data bases.

DHS personnel are checking ships and analyzing manifests to prevent high risk cargo from entering our nation by sea. DHS officials are also posted at foreign ports, working with other governments to inspect shipments before they're loaded and shipped to America. America welcomes tourists and students and business people, legitimate cargo. Yet, we're working hard, you're working hard, to make sure our border is closed to terrorists and criminals and weapons and illegal drugs.

Third, we've worked with state and local governments and the private sector to strengthen the defenses of our key infrastructure, communication systems and power grids and transportation networks. DHS is helping the operators of chemical facilities improve security.

We're working with Congress on new legislation that establishes uniform standards for securing chemical sites, and gives DHS the power to enforce those standards. We've established a national cyber security division to examine cyber security incidents and track attacks and coordinate nationwide responses. America's infrastructure drives our economy and serves our people. We're determined to provide the infrastructure with the best possible protection.

> *"For the men and women of the Department of Homeland Security, the past year has been one of progress and achievement."*

Fourth, we're bringing the best technologies to bear against the threat of chemical and biological weapons; we placed sophisticated equipment to detect biological agents in many metropolitan areas. We've greatly expanded the strategic national stockpile for drugs and vaccines and medical supplies. We now have on hand, for instance, enough smallpox vaccine to immunize every American in the case of an emergency. . . .

Even with all these measures, there's no such thing as perfect security in a vast and free country. So as a fifth step, we've worked to improve the ability of state and local authorities to respond quickly and effectively to emergencies. My administration has provided over $13 billion to equip and train local officials, such as firefighters and police officers and EMS [Emergency Medical Services] workers and health professionals. I thank the Congress for their work on this important measure.

The new budget proposes additional money, $5 billion, to continue to help the first responders. We're focusing more of our resources on the areas of greatest risk. It's essential we set priorities with the taxpayer's money, to better protect the American people. And so DHS is creating a national incident management plan, a strategy to make sure taxpayer's money is wisely spent. Under this plan, first responders at all levels of government will know their responsibilities, will follow a clear chain of command, and will be able to work with each other effectively in a time of crisis.

## A Year of Progress

Your hard work is already paying off. The system has proven its worth in coordinating responses to such emergencies as Hurricane Isabel and the California wildfires. America's first responders are the first on the scene of danger. They need a strategy. They need coordination. They need training. And they will get our help. . . .

*Chapter 2*

For the men and women of the Department of Homeland Security, the past year has been one of progress and achievement. You have risen to confront a new threat and to meet unprecedented challenges. You have responded to hurricanes and tornadoes and wildfires with incredible skill and speed. You've worked hard to protect our borders, you've saved lives. You're prepared for greater dangers. You've passed every single test. You should be proud of all you've accomplished, and you need to know America is proud of you.

We have done a lot in a year. It's been an incredible year of accomplishment, but none of us charged with defending this nation can rest. We must never forget the day when the terrorists left their mark of murder on our nation. We must never forget that day. We will remember the sorrow and the anger. We'll also remember the resolve we felt that day. All of us have a responsibility that goes on. We will protect this country, whatever it takes.

# The Homeland Security Advisory System Is Effective

## by Tom Ridge

**About the author:** *On January 24, 2003, Tom Ridge was appointed as the first secretary of the Department of Homeland Security.*

*Editor's Note: The following viewpoint was originally given as a speech on March 12, 2002, to announce the implementation of the Homeland Security Advisory System.*

Sixty years ago [during World War II], this building, Constitution Hall [in Washington, D.C.], was used by the American Red Cross to help the war effort. It was a time when the civilized world fought enemies bent on our destruction, when civilization itself hung in the balance, when Americans united to support the war effort and took new measures to guard ourselves from attack here at home. In short, a time very much like our own.

We, too, must take new measures to protect our cities, our resources and people from the threat we face today, the threat of terrorism. That is why today [March 12, 2002] we announce the Homeland Security Advisory System. The Homeland Security Advisory System is designed to measure and evaluate terrorist threats and communicate them to the public in a timely manner. It is a national framework; yet it is flexible to apply to threats made against a city, a state, a sector, or an industry. It provides a common vocabulary, so officials from all levels of government can communicate easily with one another and to the public. It provides clear, easy-to-understand factors which help measure threat.

And most importantly, it empowers government and citizens to take actions to address the threat. For every level of threat, there will be a level of preparedness. It is a system that is equal to the threat.

Here's how it works. The advisory system is based on five threat conditions

Tom Ridge, address, Washington, DC, March 12, 2002.

or five different alerts: low, guarded, elevated, high and severe. They're going to be represented by five colors: green, blue, yellow, orange and red. . . .

Now, a number of factors will be used to analyze the threat information: Is it credible? Is it a credible source? Have we been able to corroborate this threat? Is it specific as to time or place or method of attack? What are the consequences if the attack is carried out? Can the attack be deterred? Many factors go into the value judgment; many factors go into the assessment of the intelligence.

Now, the American people want to know what is behind these alerts and,

> *"[The Homeland Security Advisory System] provides clear, easy-to-understand factors which help measure threat."*

to them, perhaps even more importantly, what shall we do in response to them. I believe this system, when in full force and effect, will provide those answers. For the first time, threat conditions will be coupled with protective measures. . . .

## Five Levels of Threat

Now, for example, under a guarded or blue condition—that's a general risk of terrorist attack—federal agencies may review and update their emergency response procedures. We want them to test their emergency communication systems. They may also share with the public any information that would strengthen our response.

The next threat condition is yellow or elevated, a significant risk of terrorist attacks. Agencies under yellow condition may increase their surveillance of critical locations, and implement contingency plans where appropriate. Again, we have a level of threat, a level of preparedness, and the recommendation that we give with regard to preparedness is a floor, it's not the ceiling. And this is the same procedure and the same process and engagement that we want the state and local communities to deal with. Take a look at a level of threat, and then assess where your level of preparedness should be. Now, obviously, we're going to be working with the state and local communities in that assessment and in that effort, as well.

Now, presently [in March 2002], the nation currently stands in the yellow condition, in elevated risk. Chances are we will not be able to lower the condition to green until, as the President [George W. Bush] said yesterday, the terror networks of global reach have been defeated and dismantled. And we are far from being able to predict that day.

And again, this is an information-based system. Based on the information we know—there may be some information and some things going on in the world or in this country that we will know about. But when we get information, and it is credible information, and corroborated, this system will kick into effect.

The fourth is the orange condition, which indicates a very high, high risk of attack. And finally, the red condition, the highest or most severe risk of attack.

Under red you might see actions similar to the ones taken on 9/11 [after the terrorist attacks], when we basically grounded most or all of air traffic for an extended period of time.

We anticipate and hope that businesses and hospitals and schools, even individuals working with their community leaders to develop the local plan, will develop their own protective measures for each threat condition. This system is designed to encourage them to do just that.

The Homeland Security Advisory System also allows us to designate a threat condition for the entire nation or a portion of this country. If we received a credible threat at one of our national monuments, . . . it could be designated orange, while the rest of the country remained at yellow. But that would simply mean that the Department of Interior, based on that assessment and the elevation of the risk, would have to elevate or extend the conditions that she had prepared in advance, in response to the higher risk. Again, level of risk, level of preparedness. . . .

Finally, I think it is very important to underscore . . . the system will not eliminate risk; no system can. We face an enemy as ruthless and as cunning and as unpredictable as any we have ever faced. Our intelligence

> *"We anticipate and hope that businesses and hospitals and schools, even individuals . . . will develop their own protective measures for each threat condition."*

may not pick up every threat. And unlike natural disasters, as hurricanes, terrorists can change their patterns and their plans based on our response, based on what they see that we're doing. But the President has certainly pledged to bring every possible human and technological resource to the task of implementing this advisory system.

## Working Together to Prevent Terrorism

The Homeland Security Advisory System is designed to encourage partnerships. And this can't be emphasized and reiterated enough. The system is designed to encourage partnerships between the public and the private sectors, between all levels of law enforcement and public safety officials, and between—and among all levels of government.

Our emerging national homeland security strategy will rely on the antiterrorism plans of all 50 states and the territories. But there are 3,300 counties and parishes, and there are about 18,000 cities. So we all need to work together to coordinate and collaborate our effort to be prepared. Working together is the only way this system will work. It's the only way we can have a national system.

The system is the end result of countless conversations with first responders, local and state officials, business leaders and concerned citizens. And I certainly express our appreciation for their input and their participation. . . .

With a Homeland Security Advisory System, we hope to make America safer and more aware. But we also hope to make America better and stronger. Attorney General [John] Ashcroft has said that information is the best friend of prevention. But not just prevention of terrorism, information is also the best friend of crime prevention, fire prevention and disease prevention. It often starts with one doctor, one police officer, one eyewitness. They are America's eyes and ears. And we must work to get that information from the grass roots to government in as quick a time as possible.

Six months after September 11th [2001], our resolve is stronger than ever. Our fight against terrorism is making real progress on both fronts, thanks to the leadership of our President, the strong bipartisan support of these initiatives in Congress, and the extraordinary work that our military has done overseas.

However, we should not expect a V-T day, a victory over terrorism day anytime soon. But that does not mean Americans are powerless against the threat. On the contrary, ladies and gentlemen, we are more powerful than the terrorists. We can fight them not just with conventional arms, but with information and expertise and common sense; with freedom and openness and truth; with partnerships born from our cooperation. If we do, then like the men and women who fought Nazism and Fascism 60 years ago, our outcome will be equally certain: victory for America, and safety for Americans.

# The Department of Homeland Security Is Not the Best Way to Protect America

**by Ivan Eland**

**About the author:** *Ivan Eland is director of defense policy studies at the Cato Institute, a public policy research foundation.*

*Editor's Note: The following viewpoint was originally given as a statement before the Senate in June 2002 while the proposed Department of Homeland Security was being debated.*

The [terrorist] attacks of September 11, 2001, illustrated dramatically that the U.S. governmental security apparatus has paid too much attention to the defense of other nations and too little to the security of the U.S. homeland. But in the wake of this horrible event, Washington policymakers in the Executive Branch and Congress may feel so much pressure to act that they will make hasty decisions on policies that actually might reduce U.S. homeland security further.

Specifically, I believe that the Bush administration's plan to merge disparate agencies into a new Department of Homeland Security will do nothing to enhance homeland security and may actually reduce it. The threat we face from al Qaeda and other terrorist groups is one of agile, non-bureaucratic adversaries who have the great advantage of being on the offense—knowing where, when and how they will attack. Terrorists take advantage of the sluggishness and poor coordination among military, intelligence, law enforcement, and domestic response bureaucracies to attack gaps in the defenses. Yet the Bush administration has rushed, before the congressional intelligence panels have completed their work to determine the exact nature of the problem prior to September 11, to

Ivan Eland, testimony before the Subcommittee on Technology, Terrorism, and Government Information, Senate Judiciary Committee, Washington, DC, June 25, 2002.

propose a solution that does not seem to deal with preliminary indications of what the major problem seems to have been—lack of coordination between and inside the intelligence agencies making up the vast U.S. intelligence bureaucracy. Instead, the president has proposed reorganizing other agencies into a new super bureaucracy, while leaving out the CIA and FBI. Furthermore, although seeming to consolidate federal efforts at homeland defense, the new department may actually reduce U.S. security by adding bureaucracy rather than subtracting it. More bureaucracy means more coordination problems of the kind that seem to have been prevalent in the intelligence community prior to September 11.

## A Nontraditional Strategic Threat

The intelligence community and other agencies involved in security have traditionally battled nation-states. Fortunately, those states have governments with bureaucracies that are often more sluggish than our own government's agencies. In contrast, terrorist groups have always been nimble opponents that were difficult to stop, but they were not a strategic threat to the U.S. homeland. As dramatically illustrated by the attack on September 11, terrorists willing to engage in mass slaughter (with conventional weapons or weapons of mass destruction) and commit suicide now pose a strategic threat to the U.S. territory and population.

> *"Although consolidating federal efforts is not a bad idea in itself, it does not ensure that the bureaucracy will be more streamlined."*

No security threat to the United States matches this one. To fight this nontraditional threat, we must think outside the box and try to be as nimble as the opponent (a difficult task). The Bush administration is correct that the current [in June 2002] U.S. government structure—with more than 100 federal entities involved in homeland security—is not optimal for defending the nation against the new strategic threat. Although consolidating federal efforts is not a bad idea in itself, it does not ensure that the bureaucracy will be more streamlined, experience fewer coordination problems, or be more effective in the fight against terrorism.

## Proposal May Make Government Less Agile

The Bush administration's merging of parts of other agencies into a Department of Homeland Security will add yet another layer of bureaucracy to the fight against terrorism. In his message to Congress urging the passage of his proposal to create the new department, the President made a favorable reference to the National Security Act of 1947, which merged the departments of War and the Navy to create the Department of Defense (DoD) and created an Office of the Secretary of Defense (OSD) to oversee the military services. But today, 55 years after the act's passage, OSD is a bloated bureaucracy that exercises comparatively weak oversight of military services whose failure to coordinate and cooperate even during wartime is legion. Even Secretary of Defense Donald Rumsfeld has compared the efficiency and responsiveness of the DoD bureaucracy to Soviet central planning.

Fifty-five years from today, I hope we will not have created another organization like today's Department of Defense. Yet the new . . . department is similar to DoD because it will bring together agencies with very different missions and methods of operation and create a large new departmental bureaucracy to try to rein them all in. As was the case when DoD was created, consolidation of the government's efforts is not a bad idea, but it may be

> *"Merging of parts of other agencies into a Department of Homeland Security will add yet another layer of bureaucracy to the fight against terrorism."*

unhelpful or even counterproductive to establish another layer of bureaucracy without cutting out layers of management from the agencies being merged or removing some agencies entirely from the homeland security arena and giving their functions to existing agencies. Interagency coordination problems may just become intra-agency coordination problems—agencies with each other and with the secretary's office.

A good analogy to use may be the creation of the European Union [EU]. Creating a consolidated market for goods, services and financial transactions was a good idea. But a bloated EU bureaucracy has now been superimposed over the already intrusive national governments in Europe. It is yet another layer of bureaucracy for people living in Europe to deal with.

In short, consolidation is fine as long as we cut before pasting rather than paste before cutting. In other words, agencies should be trimmed and reformed (and some totally eliminated) before consolidating them. If the agencies are consolidated with the pledge of cuts or savings to come later, that promise is not likely to be fulfilled. Once the new, large consolidated department is created—it will be one of the largest departments in the government—the new department head will be a powerful advocate for more money and people rather than the opposite. Yet the Bush administration proposes pasting agencies together first, but does not even promise savings. At best, policymakers in the administration have promised that a consolidated department will not increase costs. But it is telling that the president's [George W. Bush] plan had no cost estimates accompanying it. Historically, mergers of government agencies have increased costs rather than decreased them. Although some longer term savings by consolidation of payroll and computer systems may occur, creating the new secretary's bureaucracy to ride herd over all of the agencies will likely increase net costs. The president's proposal calls for adding one deputy secretary, five undersecretaries, and up to 16 assistant secretaries.

So the president's plan is likely to cost more rather than less. More importantly, we must follow the money; if costs are not going down, the plan is unlikely to streamline the government's efforts in counterterrorism and homeland defense. With more than 100 federal entities already involved in homeland security, more government is not better than less. With so many agencies involved, in the event of a catastrophic attack with weapons of mass destruction, we are likely to have chaos. With the president's plan, we may get fewer agencies, but probably more government. A stealthy and nimble enemy is at the gates and we do not have much time to put the government on a diet. Instead, the government may be headed to the pastry shop. More bureaucracy means more coordination problems and more opportunities for terrorists.

## The Plan Does Not Solve the Problem with Intelligence

The president's plan for a new department does not solve what at least preliminarily seems to be the primary problem—the lack of coordination within and between U.S. intelligence agencies, specifically the FBI and CIA. Those agencies are conspicuously missing from the president's plan.

Yet for enhanced homeland security, intelligence is the key ingredient. The U.S. government has infinitely more resources for use against al Qaeda and other terrorist groups than they do against it. If the U.S. government can discover plots or the location of targets and terrorists in time to take action, that overwhelming superiority in military or law enforcement resources can be brought to bear to foil the plot. Mitigating the effects of the attack after it happens is important but, in many cases, the government may only be able to marginally help reduce casualties. Yet, without good intelligence, that may be the government's only role. The United States has an unparalleled ability to collect vast amounts of raw intelligence data—the pieces of the jigsaw puzzle—but the already too numerous agencies in the U.S. intelligence community have had trouble fusing it into a complete picture.

Regrettably, in intelligence, as in his overall homeland security proposal, the president's plan will make the government even less likely to put the jigsaw puzzle together and even more ungainly and sluggish in combating terrorists. A new intelligence analysis center will be created in the new Department of Homeland Security to analyze threats to the U.S. homeland. Yet the FBI and CIA and other intelligence agencies already analyze

*"After [the September 11, 2001, terrorist attacks], everyone in Washington is racing to fix the problem before we are sure what it is."*

such threats. Apparently, the new analysis center will not be able to get raw intelligence from those agencies unless the president personally approves it. Thus, the new agency will be analyzing the analysis of other agencies. If the new analysis center is supposed to be fusing the analyses of those agencies, it would seem to be usurping the role of the intelligence community staff under the Director of Central Intelligence. Furthermore, if the FBI and CIA fail to fully cooperate or coordinate with each other because of turf jealousies, excessive secrecy, or burdensome bureaucratic rules for interagency coordination, the problem is likely to get worse as another competing bureaucracy is added. . . .

## Government Already Has the Machinery to Coordinate Homeland Security

The old maxim that a crisis leads to bigger government has never been more true than in the wake of the September 11 attacks. In Washington, the typical response to such an event is to show the public that something is being done by rearranging organizational charts and adding bureaucracies. And after this horrendous incident, everyone in Washington is racing to fix the problem before we are sure what it is. And, as noted earlier, we seem to be fixing something entirely different (not that it may not need improving) from what the intelligence hearings are preliminarily pointing to as the main problem.

> *"To reduce the chances of lapses in intelligence coordination . . . there needs to be fewer government entities in need of coordination."*

But whether or not lack of coordination among the intelligence agencies turns out to be the major or the only problem, we already have the governmental machinery to fix them. In his message, the president also mentioned that the National Security Act of 1947 also created the National Security Council (NSC), on which sit the heads of the major departments and agencies that are responsible for the nation's security. The president's powerful National Security Advisor officially only coordinates policy among the agencies but in reality is a potent independent voice in the policymaking process. It would seem logical that catastrophic terrorism against the U.S. homeland would affect the national security and thus fit under the purview of the NSC and National Security Advisor. But apparently not. . . .

## What Should Be Done

• The whole process to find a "fix" for 9/11 "failures" should be slowed down. This deceleration would allow the main problem (or problems) prior to September 11 to be discovered by Congress. It would also allow cooler heads to prevail so that we do not end up with new bureaucracies piled on top of each other . . . and on top of the old ones.

• The NSC and National Security Advisor could adequately coordinate homeland security without a new department if the intelligence and law enforcement communities were pruned (of agencies and layers of bureaucracy). Senator Richard Shelby, Vice Chairman of the Senate Select Committee on Intelligence, noted that the FBI (and CIA) are not very agile, and GAO [U.S. General Accounting Office] has recommended reducing the layers, levels, and units within the FBI. Such a recommendation should apply for all agencies that remain in the homeland security arena. But many of the more than 100 federal entities also need to be ejected from homeland security missions. To reduce the chances of lapses in intelligence coordination and chaos in domestic crisis response, there needs to be fewer government entities in need of coordination.[1]

• Although reducing the number of people and amount of bureaucracy seems to go against the tide in the present crisis atmosphere, preliminary indications are that coordination among governmental entities is the main problem, not a lack of raw information or insufficient resources.

• Fighting a new stealthy, agile enemy is not like fighting cold or hot wars against nation-states. In the rush to "do something" Congress—by enlarging an already huge and sluggish national security bureaucracy—might make the risk of another successful catastrophic terrorist [attack] more likely.

• Even with real improvements to the intelligence and homeland defense machinery (rather than adding bureaucracy), it is probably only a matter of time before the terrorists strike again. Most high-level Bush administration officials say that it will be "when and not if." Of course, in the short-term, we must decisively take down the rest of the al Qaeda terrorist network militarily and with law enforcement but, in the long-term, we might want to take steps to lower our target profile to terrorists. The United States could do this by reducing unneeded interventions, both politically and militarily, in the world—particularly in the Middle East. According to a recent Zogby poll, a majority of the populations of all Islamic states polled liked U.S. culture, including movies and television, but disliked U.S. policies toward the Middle East. Because intelligence and homeland security cannot be perfect, a change in U.S. foreign policy might lessen the chance that terrorist groups would be motivated to launch catastrophic attacks against the U.S. homeland.

1. In May 2003 the Terrorist Threat Integration Center was created in an attempt to resolve these problems. The center is charged with facilitating information-sharing between law enforcement and intelligence agencies.

# The Department of Homeland Security Is Unlikely to Prevent Another Terrorist Attack on America

## by Andrew Stephen

**About the author:** *Andrew Stephen is a contributing writer for* New States-man, *a weekly news and opinion magazine.*

I feel sorry for Tom Ridge, head of the US Department of Homeland Security. Following those decisions to ground or delay British Airways [BA] Flight 223[1]—one of the late-afternoon flights from Heathrow [in London] to Dulles [in Washington, D.C.], and one that I have taken dozens of times—he has come in for waves of the kind of sceptical disdain that Britons tend to reserve for Americans when they feel superior. I know Ridge well enough, however, to believe that he must have found the decisions not to allow the British and other international flights to head for US airspace especially agonising. Not long ago I asked him how he felt when Dubbya [U.S. President George W. Bush] first invited him to become head of a monumental new government bureaucracy [the U.S. Department of Homeland Security]—in charge of 22 hitherto independent government departments, 180,000 employees and a working budget of $38 [billion]. "Aargh," he replied immediately, showing a levity he dare not now allow to be seen in public.

Before the [September 11, 2001, terrorist attacks], he told me, he had been planning to retire as governor of Pennsylvania and go into private law practice to make some money. Then came the fateful call just days after 11 September—and he could not say no. It was (and remains) just about the most daunting job

---

1. cancelled on January 1, 2004, due to fears of a terrorist attack

Andrew Stephen, "It Is All Very Well to Criticize Decisions to Ground BA Planes, but Imagine There Was Another Atrocity and the Authorities, Despite Prior Information, Had Just Kept Their Fingers Crossed," *New Statesman*, vol. 132, January 12, 2004, p. 9. Copyright © 2004 by New Statesman, Ltd. Reproduced by permission.

in the world: one in which you are damned if you do and damned if you don't. Or, as he put it in the Washington policy-wonkese that comes naturally to him, he is continually on the receiving end of "post-incident reflection"—the reviewing of decisions in the light of what transpired following those decisions. It is possible that the department has already foiled horrible terrorist plots, but we are unlikely ever to know for certain either way. Ridge can easily be blamed if there is another security lapse, but is unlikely ever to be thanked for creating conditions that prevent more terrorist attacks than would otherwise have happened.

> *"If there is one thread running through private conversations with . . . intelligence officials, it is the inevitability of another terrorist atrocity being perpetrated."*

And if there is one thread running through private conversations with both senior American and British intelligence officials, it is the inevitability of another terrorist atrocity being perpetrated on either country. There is only so much that Ridge and his British counterparts . . . can do. Ridge told me he was working closely with both over biometrics—fingerprinting being the most simple example and iris-scanning the most sophisticated—and, indeed, compulsory fingerprinting for visitors to the US was introduced on 5 January [2004].

Or, at least, that was what the news reports said. Fingerprinting and photographing were indeed introduced at 115 airports and 14 seaports here, with Ridge saying: "It is part of a comprehensive programme to ensure that our borders remain open to visitors but closed to terrorists." But because visitors from 28, mainly European, countries are exempt, the system would not have caught Richard Reid, the British shoe bomber who all but blew up an American Airlines flight from Paris two years ago [in 2002], or David Hicks, an alleged al-Qaeda terrorist from Australia (another exempt country) currently [in 2004] held at Camp Delta in Guantanamo Bay.

## A System Riddled with Holes

Indeed, when it comes to the fingerprinting and photographing and practically every other anti-terrorist measure his department has adopted, Ridge knows full well that the system is still riddled with holes. Five hundred million people visit the US every year, and only 24 million are falling under the impressive-sounding new fingerprinting scheme. Visitors entering the US at hundreds of land crossings from Mexico or Canada, for example, are currently not included—a glaring gap for any aspiring terrorist to exploit. Then there is the problem of system overload: simply too much information coming in to be properly processed by . . . Ridge's department. Ridge told me that more than seven million shipping containers enter the United States every day; he added that the authorities were now receiving more manifests as to what the containers have inside them. However, this is hardly useful if they are not opened and yet contain explosives or WMDs [weapons of mass destruction] and have fake manifests.

Ridge meanwhile acknowledges that the fingerprinting programme is the first significant step in a series; but both this and the checking of incoming containers show that his job is virtually impossible. That is why, if a name on a flight passenger manifest matched that of one on a computer list of suspected terrorists, I would have grounded those BA223 flights myself.

"Can you imagine?" Ridge asked me rhetorically about the fallout if there was to be another aviation or shipping atrocity when prior information had been ignored, the authorities simply keeping their fingers crossed. Ridge and his department would be squarely blamed if possibly relevant information, however nebulous, was ignored and flights allowed to leave.

# The Homeland Security Advisory System Does Not Work

## by Charles V. Peña

**About the author:** *Charles V. Peña is director of defense policy studies at the Cato Institute, a public policy research foundation.*

Paradoxically, just prior to U.S. military action in Iraq, the homeland security terrorist alert threat level was raised because the U.S. war on Iraq carried with it increased risks of possible terrorist attacks from al Qaeda, Iraqi operatives, and freelance terrorists, even though the war itself was portrayed as a necessary act to reduce the terrorist threat. Now that the war in Iraq is essentially over (despite the United States not yet declaring victory), the Bush administration has lowered the national terror alert level from "orange"—meaning a high risk of terrorist attack—to "yellow" or significant risk.

For starters, can someone please explain the difference between "high" and "significant"?

And did raising the alert level prevent any terrorism? This falls into the same category as trying to prove a negative. To be sure, there were no terrorist attacks against the United States during the course of Operation Iraqi Freedom. But there is no way to know with any certainty whether this was due to Operation Liberty Shield (the code name for the alert level increase specifically tied to the war in Iraq) or because there were no attacks planned.

The nature of terrorism is to flow around obstacles and find the path of least resistance. So it makes sense that terrorists would choose not to attack if they knew that enhanced security measures were in place. The easier thing to do is wait until the United States is less alert to the possibility of an attack. Ironically, that is exactly what is communicated by lowering the alert status—by definition. Indeed, according to U.S. officials, some security measures around the country will be relaxed.

## Alert System Does Not Make Sense

Since its creation a little more than a year ago [in early 2002], the alert level system has been raised three times from yellow to orange: on the anniversary of [the] September 11 [2001, terrorist attacks]; in February 2003 in conjunction with the Muslim holiday the Hajj; and for the Iraqi war. But there have also been countless warnings about possible terrorism that didn't change the alert level. So it's hard to correlate between warnings about possible terrorist attacks and the actual alert level. And given that there haven't been any terrorist attacks regardless of the alert level, it's difficult to know if the alert level makes any difference at all.

Compounding the problem are the "don't worry, be happy" messages that accompany changes in the alert level. How can people be told to go about their normal lives and not cancel any events as if nothing has changed, when, in fact, the threat level has been changed? If the threat has increased, people need to know what they should do—beyond buying duct tape and plastic sheeting [to protect their homes from bioterrorism]. One warning cited apartment buildings as a possible terrorist target. Does that mean that people who live in apartment buildings should find another place to live for the duration of the alert? Another warning was about possible attacks against passenger trains. Incredulously, an administration spokesperson urged Americans to "continue to ride our nation's rails."

> *"Given that there haven't been any terrorist attacks regardless of the alert level, it's difficult to know if the alert level makes any difference at all."*

Equally absurd are the electronic highway signs with a toll free number for people to report terrorist activity. This is akin to being told to report "suspicious activity" (whatever that is) to the proper authorities. One can only imagine how many innocent people have been reported as a result. And exactly how do the FBI and other law enforcement agencies decide which of the myriad reports of suspicious activity to follow-up on?

The homeland security advisory system is supposed "to provide a comprehensive and effective means to disseminate information regarding the risk of terrorist acts . . . to the American people" and "to inform and facilitate decisions . . . to private citizens at home and at work." But it's really just a bouncing ball with little or no practical utility for Joe and Jane Q. Public.

Instead of needlessly raising anxiety levels or providing a false sense of security with the color-coded alert system, the Department of Homeland Security needs to focus its resources on more important tasks, such as preventing terrorists from entering the country. Indeed, all of the 19 hijackers of 9/11 entered the country through a legal point of entry, as do millions of other people each year.

# Chapter 3

# What Measures Should Be Taken to Enhance Homeland Security?

# Chapter Preface

On March 20, 2003, the United States led a preemptive attack against Iraq. Despite worldwide opposition, 250,000 U.S. troops entered the country, swiftly toppling Saddam Hussein's regime. In justification for the invasion, the U.S. government cited Iraq's suspected possession of weapons of mass destruction, and its support of terrorist organizations, both potential threats to the security of the United States. However, many people believed these threats did not warrant the attack. Both the 2003 war against Iraq and America's larger war on terrorism have fueled a debate concerning the validity of preemptive strikes.

Preemptive strikes are launched in an attempt to prevent future conflicts rather than in response to a direct attack. Many people believe that the nature of the threats facing the United States necessitates this approach. In a 2002 speech President George W. Bush outlines the rationale behind the use of preemptive strikes:

> For much of the last century, America's defense relied on the Cold War doctrines of deterrence and containment. In some cases, those strategies still apply. But new threats also require new thinking. Deterrence—the promise of massive retaliation against nations—means nothing against shadowy terrorist networks with no nation or citizens to defend. Containment is not possible when unbalanced dictators with weapons of mass destruction can deliver those weapons on missiles or secretly provide them to terrorist allies.

Policy analyst Jack Spencer believes that a failure to use preemptive strikes against nations that threaten homeland security may lead to another tragedy like the September 11, 2001, terrorist attacks in New York City, where almost three thousand Americans died when terrorists flew airliners into the World Trade Center. He argues, "No longer can the United States wait passively while hostile regimes foment terrorism, build weapons of mass destruction and propagate hatred for America." America, he concludes, "is . . . obliged—both domestically and internationally—to preemptively strike in self-defense adversaries that present imminent threat."

However, while the use of preemptive strikes has strong support, there are also many opponents to this policy. Critics argue that preemptive strikes are an act of unnecessary aggression that violates international law. According to Richard Falk, Professor Emeritus of International Law and Policy at Princeton University, "The Bush administration's . . . resolve to wage war against Iraq . . . disregard[ed] the prohibitions on the use of force that are set forth in the UN [United Nations] Charter and accepted as binding rules of international law." There are widespread fears that preemptive action may lead to abuses of power and be harmful to both the United States and other nations. Columnist Paul

Craig Roberts summarizes some of the dangers of preemptive strikes:

> A policy of pre-emptive attack creates instability by encouraging other countries to adopt the same strategy. The policy can easily be a guise for other agendas: control over oil, enhancing the safety of an ally. . . . Pre-emptive war is a recipe for Armageddon. Each time the U.S. pre-emptively attacks a future enemy, new enemies will be created.

The use of preemptive strikes is only one of a number of steps that have been taken in an attempt to make the U.S. homeland more secure. The authors in the following chapter offer various perspectives on some of the measures that have been implemented or proposed in the effort to make Americans safer.

# Airline Pilots Should Be Armed

by John R. Lott Jr.

**About the author:** *John R. Lott Jr., a resident scholar at the American Enterprise Institute, is the author of* The Bias Against Guns.

It has been almost two years since [the September 11, 2001, terrorist attacks] and yet recent news headlines warn "Al Qaeda May Be Planning More Hijack Attacks." Unfortunately, our air-travel system is still very vulnerable to hijacking, and quick measures need to be taken. Another successful attack would make it very difficult to again restore travelers' faith in security.

Last week [September 2003], pilots from around the country held rallies in Atlanta, Chicago, Dallas, Los Angeles, Miami, and Washington, D.C., to draw attention to their concerns. Consider the following:

Pilots claim that while at least one third of flights out of Washington's Reagan National are covered with air marshals, the rest of the country is being ignored. Only a small fraction of flights to Europe are being covered and then only one day a week.

The newest generation of reinforced cockpit doors was put in place in April [2003], but few experts have much faith in their effectiveness. Last summer [2002], on a bet, a cleaning crew rammed a drink cart into one of the new doors on a United Airlines plane. The door reportedly broke off its hinges.

No tests of airport screening have been made public since the government took over screening last fall, but, in private meetings that I have attended, the Transportation Security Administration acknowledges there is a wide range of undetectable lethal weapons.

For example, without full-body searches there is no way to detect ceramic or plastic knives that are taped to an inside thigh. People who have flown can readily understand that while the checks are troublesome, they are simply not patted down all over their body. Unless you are going to do full-body searches on people, determined terrorists are going to be able to get weapons on planes no matter how carefully screeners monitor x-ray machines and metal detectors.

## The Costs

Despite the gaps, these three programs have proven to be very costly. Potential cuts in airport screeners have generated a great deal of concern. Mentions of possible financial problems involving the marshals program have also been in the news.

Yet, with the ineffectiveness of screeners and so few marshals, such cuts do not pose the real threat. In terms of cost effectiveness it is hard to think of a policy that produces the ratio of benefits to costs that arming pilots has. For example, the only real financial cost to the government for pilots involves a one-week training class. Even then pilots are training on their own time. There are none of the salaries required for marshals or screeners once the training is completed.

Only $8 million of the $5 billion available to the Transportation Security Administration (TSA) for airlines security is being spent on arming pilots. A five-fold increase in expenditures on arming pilots would reduce other expenditures by only about one percent.

## Undermining the Program

Unfortunately, despite Homeland Security Secretary Tom Ridge recently voicing public support for arming pilots, the TSA has fought the program at every turn. After two years since the first attacks and two laws passed overwhelmingly by Congress to start training pilots, only about 200 out of over 100,000 commercial passenger pilots are licensed to carry guns.

Following what seemed like a successful first class of pilots this spring [2003], the TSA fired the head of the firearms training academy, Willie Ellison, for "unacceptable performance and conduct."

Ellison, who won the praise of the students, was reprimanded for holding a graduation dinner for the first graduation class and giving them baseball caps with the program logo.

The training facility was closed down and relocated immediately after the first class, prompting Oregon Representative Peter DeFazio, the ranking Democrat on the Aviation Subcommittee, to complain that the closing appeared to be "just another attempt to disrupt the program."

> *"Determined terrorists are going to be able to get weapons on planes no matter how carefully screeners monitor x-ray machines and metal detectors."*

On top of the delays, the administration has done what it can to discourage pilots from even applying for the armed-pilot program.

The intrusive application form pilots are required to fill out warns them that the information obtained by the Transportation Security Administration is "not limited to [the pilot's] academic, residential, achievement, performance, attendance, disciplinary, employment history, criminal history record information, and financial credit information."

The information can be turned over to the Federal Aviation Administration and used to revoke a pilot's commercial license. As one pilot told me, "The Transportation Security Administration is viewed as hostile to pilots, and pilots are afraid that if they are not viewed as competent for the [armed-pilots] program, they may be viewed as not competent to continue being pilots."

The screening and psychological testing required of the pilots are also much more extensive and intrusive than that required for the vast majority of air marshals who are currently on duty. Some questions even appeared designed to purposefully disqualify pilot applicants.

About half the pilots applying for the program were rejected in the initial screening process. No explanations for those rejections have been provided, making the entire system unaccountable. In the last week or so [September 2003], the TSA apparently has come to reconsider some of those rejections and called pilots to tell them that the decisions had been made too quickly. But with all the secrecy surrounding the process it is impossible to evaluate whether those who continue to be rejected deserve to be. It is hard to think of any reason why the applicant can't be told even in the most general way the basis for rejections. The initial high rates of rejection have certainly put a chill on applications.

*"The administration has done what it can to discourage pilots from even applying for the armed-pilot program."*

## Hardly Experimental

Despite all the concern about hypothetical risks, arming pilots is not some new experiment. About 70 percent of the pilots at major American airlines have military backgrounds, and military pilots flying outside the U.S. are required to carry handguns with them whenever they flew military planes.

Until the early 1960s, American commercial passenger pilots in any flights carrying U.S. mail were required to carry handguns. The requirement started at the beginning of commercial aviation to insure that pilots could defend the mail if their plane were ever to crash. In contrast to the current program, there were no training or screening requirements. Indeed, pilots were still allowed to carry guns until as recently as 1987. There are no records that any of these pilots (either military or commercial) carrying guns have ever caused any significant problems.

## Typical Objections

There are many concerns that have been raised about arming pilots or letting them carry guns, but armed pilots actually have a much easier job than air marshals. An armed marshal in a crowded cabin can be attacked from any direction; he must be able to quickly distinguish innocent civilians from terrorists. An armed pilot only needs to concern himself with the people trying to force their way into the cockpit. It is also much easier to defend a position such as the cockpit, as a pilot would, than to have to pursue the terrorist and physically subdue them, as a marshal would. The terrorists can only enter the cockpit through one narrow entrance, and armed pilots have time to prepare themselves as hijackers try to penetrate the strengthened cockpit doors.

> *"Despite all the concern about hypothetical risks, arming pilots is not some new experiment."*

Pilots must also fly the airplane, but, with two pilots, one pilot would continue flying the plane while the other defended the entrance. In any case, if terrorists are in the cockpit, concentrating on flying will not be an option.

An oft-repeated concern during the debate over arming pilots is that hijackers will take the guns from them, since "21 percent of [police] officers killed with a handgun were shot by their own service weapon." (Similar concerns are frequently raised when discussing civilians using guns for their personal protection.) But the FBI's Uniform Crime Report paints a quite different picture. In 2000, 47 police officers were killed with a gun, out of which 33 cases involved a handgun, and only one of these firearm deaths involved the police officer's gun. It is really not that easy to grab an officer's gun and shoot him. Assaults on police are not that rare, but only in a miniscule fraction of assaults on officers do officers end up losing control and being shot with their own gun. Statistics from 1996 to 2000 show that only eight thousandths of one percent of assaults on police resulted in them being killed with their own weapon.

The risk to pilots would probably be even smaller. Unlike police who have to come into physical contact with criminals while arresting them, pilots will use guns to keep attackers as far away as possible.

Unable to accept pilots carrying guns, the administration continues to float suggestions for Tasers (stun guns) instead of guns, ignoring their limitations. Not only are there well-known cases such as Rodney King [beaten by the Los Angeles police in 1991] who "fought off Tasers" twice, but thick clothing can also foil their effectiveness. The New York City police department reports that: "Even Taser guns—which the department uses to administer electric shocks to people—fail about a third of the time." Because of these problems, even the Taser manufacturer recommends lethal weapons as a backup. Use against terrorists would be even less reliable since terrorists would prepare in advance to wear clothing or take other precautions to protect themselves from stun guns.

The fears of having guns on planes are exaggerated. As Ron Hinderberger, director of aviation safety at Boeing, noted in testimony before the U.S. House of Representatives:

Boeing commercial service history contains cases where guns were fired on board in service airplanes, all of which landed safely. Commercial airplane structure is designed with sufficient strength, redundancy, and damage tolerance that a single or even multiple handgun holes would not result in loss of an aircraft. A bullet hole in the fuselage skin would have little effect on cabin pressurization. Aircraft are designed to withstand much larger impacts whether intentional or unintentional. For instance, on 14 occasions Boeing commercial airplanes have survived, and landed, after an in flight bomb blast.

## Need to Protect People

The Bush administration can hardly claim confidence that its screening, reinforced doors and air marshals are enough. A successful attack will make it very difficult for the government to restore travelers' confidence for years. The damage to the airline industry would be even greater than after the first attack.

Protecting people should be as important as protecting the mail once was.

# Airline Pilots Should Not Be Armed

**by George F. Will**

**About the author:** *Columnist, television personality, and author George F. Will won the Pulitzer Prize for commentary in 1977.*

Three pilots of a major airline recently [in 2002] gathered here at George Bush Intercontinental Airport [in Houston] to discuss whether, as an anti-terrorism measure, pilots should be armed. The Transportation Department says guns will not be permitted in cockpits. Some in Congress will try to overturn this ban. The Air Line Pilots Association (ALPA), which represents 62,000 pilots working for 42 airlines, adamantly favors arming them.

These three pilots—two trained in the military, one in civilian life—are ALPA members. They have a cumulative 75 years of experience flying for commercial airlines. None has an aversion to guns. Says one, "I was raised around guns all my life." Says another, "I've not got any affinity for gun control." Says the third, "I love guns. Been a hunter all my life. I'm adamantly against gun control."

All three oppose arming pilots. Here is why.

## Arguments Against Arming Pilots

They note that [the Sept. 11, 2001, terrorist attacks] triggered a reversal of assumptions. The policy for pilots regarding a hijacking had been: *Don't deal with it.* Before suicidal hijackers took over four planes, the procedure was for pilots to fly their aircraft to the destination the hijacker demanded.

Now, these three pilots say, the overriding priority must be to guarantee that cockpits are sealed behind bulletproof doors, protecting the flight deck from intrusion while pilots get the plane on the ground as quickly as possible. Which can be 10 minutes—as pilots know from training to deal with the problem of sudden decompression of an aircraft.

Prior to Sept. 11, if a passenger became unruly, the pilot might come back into the cabin to assert authority. No more. Says one of these three, "The flight attendants know they are on their own."

"You cannot fly an airplane and look over your shoulder, firing down the cabin," says one of these pilots. What you could do, he says, is look down the cabin by means of a closed-circuit television camera that would warn the flight deck of cabin disturbances requiring quick action to take the plane to the ground. Flight plans should show the nearest alternative airport at every stage of every flight.

Another potential problem with arming America's 120,000 commercial airline pilots is what one of the three pilots here calls, with no demurral from the other two, "cowboys or renegade pilots." Many commercial pilots began their flying careers as fighter pilots. Two of the three speaking here this day did. One of them says: There is some truth to the profile of fighter pilots as, well, live wires and risk-takers. Arming them might incite them to imprudent bravery. Armed pilots would be more inclined to go out into the cabin, whereas the primary goal should be getting the plane to the ground.

## Lack of Support from Pilots

"The popularity of an idea does not make it a good idea," says one of these pilots, and all three, although members of ALPA, question whether the idea of arming pilots is as popular with pilots as ALPA suggests. One of these pilots was polled by phone by ALPA and considered the questions written so as to produce an expression of support for arming pilots.

There is in the airline industry the suspicion that the drive to arm pilots, to equip them for potential action back in the cabin, is for ALPA a new front in the organization's long-standing campaign to revive the requirement for a third pilot in the cockpit. The three pilots gathered here would prefer that ALPA concentrate on protecting existing jobs rather than creating new ones.

Many thoughtful pilots do favor guns as an additional layer of deterrence, and a last resort to restoring control over an aircraft before F-16s [jet fighter aircraft] are scrambled to shoot it from the sky. Had armed pilots been flying the four planes hijacked on Sept. 11, box cutters would not have sufficed. And you do not want to know how many dangerous implements escape the detection of airport screeners while they are X-raying your shoes and frisking grandmothers to demonstrate innocence of racial or ethnic profiling.

However, the pilots of El Al, Israel's airline, are not armed, and the airline has not had a hijacking in 34 years. The three pilots consider this evidence for the argument that the deterrence effect of armed pilots is not essential. Furthermore, gunfire in the cockpit could easily shatter the windshield. In which case, says one of these pilots, "someone is going to be sucked out—the terrorist, if he's not strapped in."

"There are," says one of the three, "a lot of what-ifs and don't knows" when you decide to arm pilots. These pilots know they are against that.

# National ID Cards Would Make Americans Safer

**by David Bursky**

**About the author:** *David Bursky is editor-at-large for* Electronic Design, *a bimonthly magazine that provides information about technological advances and trends.*

[As of September 2002] a year has now passed since the tragedy that took place at the World Trade Center and other locations on the east coast. The [terrorist attacks] on September 11, 2001, did a lot more than end thousands of lives and make an impact on countless millions of others. They shook the country out of its complacency and confidence that terrorists couldn't do major damage within our borders. But now that a year has gone by in which the justice system has slowly turned its great wheels to make those who masterminded and participated in the events pay for their acts of terror, we must look forward. We must determine how to prevent another terrorist act.

Many new security measures are in place, especially at airports and other major public facilities. However, the electronics industry has fallen behind, with demand for the security scanners and X-ray systems outstripping the supply. This will change as production ramps up. But many airports may not be able to meet government mandates to have the systems in place by year's end.

These systems also are very expensive, making it even harder to justify their purchase, especially because travel is down and several airlines are on the brink of bankruptcy. So lower-cost solutions are needed to meet the requirements of the travel industry and allow screening systems to be placed in venues such as sports arenas, government buildings, and schools.

At this point we should ask ourselves if we're becoming too paranoid and going overboard in the amount of screening that we're doing. Perhaps we are, but it will take time to find the right balance of quick once-overs versus full screening. Part of the paranoia comes from the libertarians who feel total anonymity is an essential part of the freedoms granted by the U.S. Constitution. They shy away from any standardized approach like a national ID card that can be used to identify individuals. Their stated concern is that the government could use the information on the card or in the main database to track, trap, or otherwise limit the freedom of individuals.

## A National ID Card

My view is more benign. I think some type of uniform ID card would be appropriate provided that certain restrictions on use and access are in place. Most of us already carry several identification cards, including a driver's license and a Social Security card, so why not something that's a little more robust?

Such a card could contain some biometric information—a fingerprint, picture, or voiceprint—perhaps some user passwords, and possibly even some emergency medical information about allergies or other special conditions. The card could also double as a passport, driver's license, Social Security card, credit card or debit card, and much more.

> *"Most of us already carry several identification cards, including a driver's license and a Social Security card, so why not something that's a little more robust?"*

I also see a national ID card as an additional deterrent to yet another escalating problem plaguing our country—identity theft. A card that really proves you are you would simplify transactions and prevent future applications from being hindered by suspicion. It could also streamline the current procedures and reduce the backups at entry points. No longer will double or triple proofs of identity be requested for simple things like check cashing or serious tasks such as global travel.

Of course the success of this entire scenario will depend heavily on cryptography and the ability to keep the data secure to prevent copying and alterations. Will current encryption schemes be up to the task, or will new algorithms and schemes be needed? I think the latter. Already hackers have found ways to "break" some of the algorithms that use 32- and even 48-bit encryption keys. Before long, due to increases in CPU [central processing unit] performance, large keys (64- and 128-bit) will be cracked as well.

Only when the data on the ID card is secure and can't be duplicated will people feel assured that the data won't be misused. This will go a long way toward the goal of creating a nationwide ID card to provide secure storage for personal information and allay fears that Big Brother is always watching.

# National ID Cards Would Not Make Americans Safer

**by Timothy Lynch and Charlotte Twight**

**About the authors:** *Timothy Lynch is director of the Cato Institute's Project on Criminal Justice. Charlotte Twight is an economist and attorney, and author of* Dependent on D.C.: The Rise of Federal Control over the Lives of Ordinary Americans.

*Timothy Lynch:* After [the terrorist attacks of September 11, 2001], it makes perfect sense for policymakers to review various laws and procedures with an eye to changes that would better protect us from similar attacks in the future. But we should not throw out our freedom and our privacy for any proposal that somebody claims will make us safer. We should not rush into anything.

The national ID card proposal would be a very bad deal for our society, because it would require some 250 million people to surrender some of their freedom, some of their privacy, for something that is not going to make us safe from terrorist attack. The national ID card proposal has been put forward in Washington many times before; in the wake of the September 11 attacks, it is now being packaged as a "security" measure.

Let me begin by dispelling the idea that the card will be a great security device that will make us safe from terrorists. There are several ways that terrorists will be able to get around a national ID card system. Terrorists are evil, but they are not stupid.

It does not take much imagination to see the weak spots in the national ID card system. If terrorists are determined to attack America, they can bribe the people who issue the cards or the people who check the cards. Terrorists will also be able to recruit people who have valid cards—U.S. citizens or lawful permanent residents.

We are told that we should look at countries in Europe, such as France, that already have national ID card systems. OK, let's look. The people in those

Timothy Lynch and Charlotte Twight, "Security and Freedom in a Free Society," *Cato Policy Report*, vol. XXIV, September/October 2002. Copyright © 2002 by the Cato Institute. All rights reserved. Reproduced by permission.

countries have surrendered their privacy and their liberty and yet they continue to experience terrorist attacks.

## ID Cards and Civil Liberties

I also want to draw your attention to how a national ID card system will affect the Bill of Rights. The Fourth Amendment to our Constitution protects all of us against unreasonable searches and seizures. The quintessential "seizure" under the Fourth Amendment is to be arrested or detained by the police.

The police can seize or arrest a person when they have an arrest warrant or when they have probable cause to believe that the person has just committed a crime in their presence. But the police cannot stop us on the street and demand an ID, at least not under current law. They can *request* an ID. They can *request* that we answer their questions. But the key point is that we can decide whether or not we want to cooperate. The legal presumption right now [in 2002] is on the side of the individual citizen. We do not have to justify ourselves to the police or to the government. The government has to justify its interference with our liberty.

A national ID card system will turn that important legal principle upside down. After enactment of the system, pressure will begin to build to enact laws that will require citizens to produce an ID whenever a government official demands it. I know that is going to happen for two reasons. First, in the countries that already have national ID card systems, the police have acquired such powers.

Second, in this country there already are cases in which the police have arrested Americans for failure to produce IDs. Thus far our courts have rejected such arrests. But if Congress passes a law that says people must produce IDs, the courts may well yield on that point.

Op-eds about a national ID card by [professor] Alan Dershowitz at Harvard Law School or [corporate chief executive officer] Larry Ellison from Oracle present the idea in the best possible light. They tell us that it will be a "voluntary" card and that you will have to present it only at airports. They say there will be no legal duty to produce an ID card.

## Inevitable Expansion of Surveillance

But, over time, the amount of information on the card will expand. The number of places where you will have to present your ID card will expand, and it will eventually become compulsory. And sooner or later a legal duty to produce an ID whenever a government official demands it will be created. I strongly recommend Charlotte Twight's book, *Dependent on D.C.*, in which she details the ways government power creeps into our lives.

Secretary of Defense Donald Rumsfeld has already warned us to expect more terrorist attacks, so we will see more anti-terrorism proposals in Congress. Perhaps there will be an attack a year from now, and a limited national ID card will be proposed and enacted.

Maybe five years later we will be attacked again, people will die, and law enforcement will go to Congress and say, look, we have a national ID card, but the problem is that it is voluntary. Thus, by increments, we will get the full-blown national ID card system that we see in other countries. If somebody just proposed the same national ID card system that they have in Singapore or France, and we could have an up-or-down debate on that one proposal, then everybody would fully understand what we were going to give up in return for the card. But instead, time after time, we see the government expand in small, incremental steps.

It is very important that we not lose sight of what we are fighting for in the war on terrorism. Our goal should be to fight the terrorists within the framework of a free society. We should be taking the battle to the terrorists, to their base camps, and killing the terrorist leadership. We should not be transforming our society into a surveillance state.

*Charlotte Twight:* As part of the current push for new measures to increase our national security, some members of Congress are calling for computer chips to be put into our driver's licenses or for other forms of a national ID card. With current technology, a key component of any national ID card will be a microchip containing biometric information and other data as well as links to a variety of databases.

As Simon Davies, an expert in privacy security and data protection, stated recently [in 2002]: "The modern ID card is no simple piece of plastic. It is the visible component of a web of interactive technology that fuses the most intimate characteristics of the individual with the machinery of the state," creating a "national surveillance infrastructure."

As Tim [Lynch] mentioned, legislators and others are likely to push incrementally for such an ID in order to minimize opposition at the outset. Consider what Rep. Jane Harman said in May [2002]: "We don't automatically have to call it a national ID card. That's a radioactive term. But we can certainly think about smart cards for essential functions, and we need the database to support that." As Steven Levy of *Newsweek* put it, "Translation: Show us your papers."

## A Threat to Privacy

A national ID card system unquestionably poses a threat to our privacy. The card would permit vast amounts of personal information about us to be linked. Many Americans do not realize the virtual treasure trove of detailed data that the federal government requires banks, schools, employers, and now even doctors, in addition to many federal agencies, to collect about law-abiding individuals in our country.

Think about something like the Bank Secrecy Act that sailed through Congress in 1970. It required, and still requires, our banks to make copies of our checks and deposit slips, as well as records of other financial transactions. So there are all kinds of government-mandated databases out there, and they can be either embedded in or linked to a national ID card and the computer chip in it.

Moreover, government agencies already have contracted with private firms to purchase additional information about law-abiding American citizens. For example, the *Washington Post* recently [in 2002] reported that the Internal Revenue Service had purchased access to some 10 billion public records of housing, financial, and other personal information about individuals in our country. The same private company, ChoicePoint, Inc., also provides information to other government agencies, including the Federal Bureau of Investigation [FBI].

This sort of power inevitably grows. Recall the experience with Social Security numbers. In 1935 the public was promised by government officials that those numbers would never be used for anything other than identifying specific Social Security accounts.

But, of course, within just a few years, the government itself began mandating increased usage of Social Security numbers. As described in my book, *Dependent on D.C.*, year by year the government expanded the number of agencies and entities that were required to use Social Security numbers to identify us. And we have reached the point today, I think, where everybody takes it as a given that our Social Security numbers serve as de facto national ID numbers.

## Possibilities for Abuse

Another concern is that, with the new technology, adding additional information or linking additional information to a national ID card will be virtually invisible. How will a person know what's on that card or what it's linked to?

Past abuses of federal data collection power should give us pause about further expanding that authority. Just think about the FBI files in the [former president Bill] Clinton White House, about the [former president Richard] Nixon administration's abuses of IRS [Internal Revenue Service] and FBI files, and all the rest of that long history of abuse.

A national ID system would alter our nation at its very core. As a thought experiment, reread the U.S. Constitution and the Declaration of Independence and then imagine trying to explain a national ID system to the Founders, to James Madison and his fellows.

People will learn to tolerate national IDs if they are required, and that too jeopardizes liberty. Because future generations won't have any other experience, they will think it is the normal course of things to add more and more information to a national ID card.

Finally, I would urge, in considering a national ID card system, that we consider the emerging pattern and not focus our attention on just one piece at a time. In the past we built financial databases, education databases, labor databases, all the rest of it, and we looked at each little slice instead of at the whole picture. I would urge that we look at that whole emerging pattern and ask ourselves: What are we building? What are we becoming?

# A Home Guard Should Be Created to Increase Homeland Security

## by Robert Cottrol

**About the author:** *Robert Cottrol is a professor of law and history at George Washington University in Washington, D.C., and a retired lieutenant in the U.S. Air Force Reserve.*

The September 11 [2001] terrorist attacks did more than bring a tragic end to over 3,000 American lives. They also helped shatter two long-cherished illusions. The first, that we live in a secure homeland, was shared by most Americans. Blessed by geography, twentieth-century Americans came to think of wars as unpleasant events that happened "over there." With the exception of those who witnessed Pearl Harbor, no living American can remember a time when civilians were under enemy attack on American soil. No more. September 11 was a searing indicator that warfare in the twenty-first century will be brutal, indiscriminate, and over here.

The second shattered illusion, that we can avoid violence by being passive, has gained widespread currency among our academic and professional elites. This illusion and its corollary, that the average citizen is too feckless to defend himself, much less participate in the defense of his community, must be shed quickly if American civil society is to survive this new and terrifying century. This will involve rediscovering, and re-defining, the venerable but badly eroded tradition of the citizen soldier. It also means revitalizing the role of the Reserve Officers Training Corps on the nation's campuses.

On the heels of the 9/11 attacks came a new concern for homeland security. As a nation, we present a virtually limitless number of targets for terrorists. We don't have the manpower to guard those targets and also secure our borders, coastlines, harbors, airports, and railway stations while allowing the nation's police forces to do their routine jobs of protecting public safety *and* allowing

Robert Cottrol, "Homeland Security: Restoring Civil Virtue," *The American Enterprise*, January/February 2003. Copyright © 2003 by the American Enterprise Institute for Public Policy Research. Reproduced by permission of *The American Enterprise*, a magazine of Politics, Business, and Culture. On the Web at www.TAEmag.com.

the armed forces to fulfill their traditional missions of guarding the nation and its allies against conventional or nuclear attack.

Presuming the National Guard will always be available to augment police and military forces as it did immediately after 9/11 is also an illusion. Today's National Guard is so thoroughly integrated into Defense Department contingency planning that it would be impossible for the President to send significant forces into an overseas conflict without substantial deployment of the Guard. Under those circumstances, state and local police, whose ranks would also be depleted because many of their members are military reservists, would find that in addition to their already difficult mission of maintaining public safety, they would be charged with guarding large numbers of potential terrorist targets.

## A Home Guard

That's why we need a home guard, a group of citizens trained and organized to assist police and military forces in times of crisis, especially when the National Guard has been deployed overseas. This force, unlike the National Guard, should not be subject to long-term service in the armed forces. It should exist exclusively for domestic contingencies, and be used primarily at the local level. There are police auxiliary programs in many communities and some states have State Defense Forces designed to back up the National Guard, but they don't quite meet the need. Training for these forces varies widely. Even worse, there has been little effort to recruit large numbers of young people into these programs and to make participation in them an expected and respected act of civic engagement. Existing auxiliary and defense forces are also problematic because they are purely under state control. While the primary employment of a home guard force would be local, such a force should have dual state and federal control enabling federal authorities to deploy units outside their home states if necessary.

> *"We need to revive the traditional notion of a broad-based citizens' militia, organized and trained to help defend their communities."*

In short, we need to revive the traditional notion of a broad-based citizens' militia, organized and trained to help defend their communities.

## Cultural Constraints

So why isn't this idea part of the public debate about terrorism and homeland defense? Part of the answer is bureaucratic inertia. But something more is at work. Strong cultural constraints prevent us from even considering this option. These constraints are evident in the gun control debate, which, boiled down to its essentials, is about whether ordinary people can be trusted to defend themselves and their communities. Ordinary citizens, conventional wisdom goes, should not train to defend themselves, particularly not with guns, not only because resistance might be dangerous, but also because resistance or training for self-defense contributes to a culture of violence.

This view isn't confined to a small group of liberals in the media or the academy. Consider the . . . controversy over arming airline pilots. For months Congress and the administration resisted this eminently sensible idea. We don't have, and never will have, enough air marshals for every flight. Almost all airline pilots are college graduates and military veterans. They hold the lives of tens of thousands of passengers and millions of dollars of equipment in their hands every year. Do

> *"We simply cannot sustain a secure society without widespread participation in the common defense."*

we really believe that a person who can fly a 747 [airplane] can't be trained to handle a .38 [gun]?

One reason for the firm entrenchment of the myth of the feckless citizen is the great gulf that has developed between our university-educated leaders and the armed forces. The end of the draft in 1973 brought with it the end of a long-standing tradition of widespread participation in national and community defense. From 1940 to the late 1960s military experience was common among men of every social class. Not every man was a combat veteran, far from it, but most men learned important lessons even in basic training: that you have unrealized strengths, that you can do more than you thought you could, that you must be dependable and be able to depend on the people in your unit, and, most important of all, that supermen are rare and that the people who are important are ordinary folks who put aside their fears and get the job done. Add to these lessons a few basic skills, safe handling of firearms and rudimentary first aid, and you have a person who has learned how to be an asset instead of a liability in a crisis. Increasingly, military service and these important lessons are unknown among those who teach our college classes, write in the nation's newsrooms, draft memos in law firms, serve in the nation's legislatures, or produce or perform on TV. One consequence is that we readily accept the myth that ordinary citizens do not have a role in protecting society.

## Reviving the ROTC

What might bridge this chasm? The Reserve Officers Training Corps. ROTC has its origins in the 1862 Morrill Act establishing land grant universities. The idea was to provide a basic military familiarization for all men attending state universities, not just for future officers. This was considered training for citizenship as well as preparation for possible military action. Until the 1960s, all men at land grant universities were required to take the first two years of ROTC. That requirement became a casualty of the anti-military sentiment that swept many campuses in the '60s.

A revival of the notion that ROTC training is an integral part of an education for citizenship and vital for the common defense would be a healthy development. It would help close the dangerous gap between the academic and military cultures, a gap that often leads our soldiers and our scholars to wildly inaccurate misperceptions of each other. A renewed emphasis on ROTC training could also be a way of teaching the critical lessons of military service to an important segment of the young adult population.

Most of all, such a program could provide the basic training for a broad-based citizen militia. Here is how it might work: The state universities, in cooperation with the armed forces, would open the first two years of ROTC to all students on a volunteer basis. Those who sign up for the program would have to agree to serve an additional six years in a home guard program. In return for volunteering, students would receive tuition reduction and a degree of admissions preference. The latter could provide a real incentive for some of our future best and brightest. Voluntary ROTC participation might be the tiebreaker between going to a state's flagship campus or a less-well-regarded school. Of course, state universities should offer similar or greater benefits to veterans.

After completing two years of ROTC, students would serve in the home guard. A revamped Civil Air Patrol, trained and organized to provide back-up security as well as perform its traditional search and rescue mission, would serve admirably in this capacity. Members would spend about two weeks a year to get refresher training in first aid, marksmanship, and other essential skills. Cadre would come from the ranks of military and police retirees. Special efforts would be made to get prominent people in their 20s and 30s to volunteer. Who knows, perhaps the enlistment of [actor] Ben Affleck or [actress] Halle Berry might have the effect on today's twenty-somethings that the enlistments of [actors] Jimmy Stewart and Clark Gable had on a previous generation.

September 11, 2001, should cause us to re-think some long-cherished, wrong, and dangerous assumptions. We simply cannot sustain a secure society without widespread participation in the common defense. And academia can no longer remain aloof from and often hostile to those charged with defending the nation. Reconsidering ROTC could be one way of fighting the threats of this new era.

# A New Intelligence System Must Be Created for Effective Homeland Security

by James B. Steinberg, Mary Graham, and Andrew Eggers

**About the authors:** *James B. Steinberg is the vice president and director of Foreign Policy Studies at the Brookings Institution, Mary Graham is a visiting fellow in Governance Studies at the institution, and Andrew Eggers is a senior research analyst in Governance Studies there.*

Cold war intelligence policies aimed to protect sources and methods and keep adversaries from gaining access to military secrets. To achieve these goals, defense and intelligence agencies compartmentalized acquisition, analysis, and dissemination of information, an approach that worked reasonably well as long as policymakers knew who the enemy was, what information to look for, where to look for it, and who needed to have it. Analysts became specialists and information was shared among carefully defined groups of federal officials and contractors who were specified in advance and who held appropriate security clearances based on lengthy, costly background investigations.

These policies are ill-suited to the challenge of counterterrorism. Their dual requirements of appropriate security clearance and "need to know" designation inhibit the free flow of information to and from today's diverse community of relevant federal, state, local, and private sector actors.

It is impossible to anticipate "need to know" in a world where enemies are little understood, means of attack are unpredictable, and potential targets are many, diverse, and changing. The need to cast a broad net—to gather information about threats and vulnerabilities from state and local governments and the private sector and return needed information to them—creates a heightened government responsibility to protect core values of openness and privacy.

Since [the terrorist attacks on] September 11, 2001, the administration and Congress have adopted a number of incremental changes designed to improve the quality and integration of intelligence information. They have broadened government screening of airline passengers, foreign visitors, and imported goods, and added federal resources to state and local public health and emergency communication systems. Incremental changes are not enough. Policymakers must build a new intelligence system to fight terrorism. The formal, hierarchical, and compartmentalized information strategies of the past need to be replaced with a new architecture featuring flexible, decentralized networks of public and private information providers, analysts, and users. Policymakers should establish procedures to assure access to critical information needed to address national security priorities while taking into account openness and privacy concerns. Public guidelines will ensure that new information strategies are consistent with these goals.

## Antiterrorism Information Strategies

Policymakers recognize that the intelligence system in place before September 11 failed to get the right information to the right people at the right time. As the joint House-Senate committee that investigated the 9/11 attacks observed: "Serious problems in information sharing . . . persisted, prior to September 11, between the Intelligence Community and relevant non-Intelligence Community agencies. This included other federal agencies as well as state and local authorities. This lack of communication and collaboration deprived those other entities, as well as the Intelligence Community, of access to potentially valuable information in the 'war' against [terrorist leader Osama] Bin Ladin."

To date, administration and congressional efforts to reorganize national security intelligence have focused mainly on reducing barriers to sharing information among federal agencies, improving federal information technology capabilities, coordinating analysis of federal and local law enforcement and intelligence data, and supporting state and local emergency communication. At the borders, customs officials have enhanced cargo screening using radiation detectors and x-ray scanners and immigration authorities have upgraded checks on foreign visitors using improved databases. Around the country, newly expanded joint terrorism task forces bring together federal and local law enforcement officials. Terrorism investigators more easily combine law enforcement and intelligence data as permitted by the USA PATRIOT Act, which Congress passed one month after the terrorist attacks. Federal airport security officers conduct more rigorous screening of passengers under the terms of the Aviation and Transportation Se-

> *"[Cold war intelligence] policies are ill-suited to the challenge of counterterrorism."*

curity Act, enacted two months after the attacks. The new Department of Homeland Security, charged with coordinating domestic intelligence gathering and information sharing, has begun collecting data about vulnerabilities in the nation's critical infrastructure. A new Terrorist Threat Integration Center, under the supervision of the director of central intelligence, is charged with synthesizing counterterrorism intelligence from all sources.

Some of the changes have created serious concerns about potential conflicts between national security measures and principles of personal privacy and government openness. The Defense Advanced Projects Administration (DARPA), which sponsored research into data mining and pattern recognition technologies under its Terrorist Information Awareness (formally Total Information Awareness) program, was temporarily halted by Congress because the sponsors failed to address potential privacy concerns. Civil liberties advocates have challenged administration efforts to harness new information technology to screen airline passengers (the CAPPS II program) and proposals to share personal information about individuals gathered from a variety of sources authorized by the USA PATRIOT Act.

Similar concerns have arisen about conflicts with government openness, especially when secrecy has been expanded without public debate. Soon after September 11, federal agencies removed thousands of pages of public documents about the nation's infrastructure from their websites, including maps of pipeline and water supply locations and data about ship-

> *"The intelligence system in place before September 11 failed to get the right information to the right people at the right time."*

ments of hazardous materials and security breaches at airports. In October 2001, Attorney General [John] Ashcroft reversed a long-standing policy under the Freedom of Information Act (FOIA) that required agencies to disclose information unless disclosure would cause "foreseeable harm" and replaced it with one that allows agencies to keep government information secret if there is a "sound legal basis" for doing so. In March 2002, White House Chief of Staff Andrew Card ordered all agencies to adopt guidelines to prevent inappropriate disclosure of "sensitive but unclassified" information. Rejecting a bipartisan compromise, the administration supported a broad new exemption to FOIA in the Homeland Security Act for information voluntarily provided by businesses to the government about infrastructure vulnerabilities that might cause massive casualties or disruptions in a terrorist attack.

Many of these actions were couched as emergency measures—extraordinary steps to counter extraordinary threats. However, [in September 2003] nearly two years after September 11, it is clear that they represent important building blocks for a new generation of intelligence policy. The president [George W. Bush] emphasized in his 2002 national homeland security strategy that "protecting the homeland from terrorist attack is a permanent mission."

More security issues that affect openness and privacy will be decided in the coming months [2003–2004]. The administration will determine if additional rules are needed to shield "sensitive but unclassified" information from public view, which might include scientific research, law enforcement records, or infrastructure vulnerability reports. Policymakers have to define policies and procedures for the Terrorist Threat Integration Center as well as determine the future of the

> *"Defending against terrorism threats will require policymakers to replace the formal, hierarchical intelligence structure with a . . . fluid architecture."*

Terrorist Information Awareness and CAPPS II programs. Congress has promised to revisit the broad and controversial requirement in the Homeland Security Act that allows the government to withhold information about infrastructure vulnerabilities, and key components of the PATRIOT Act expire in 2005.

## A New Intelligence Architecture

Defending against terrorism threats will require policymakers to replace the formal, hierarchical intelligence structure with a horizontal, cooperative, and fluid architecture that gets information from those who have it to those who need it through the development of virtual communities of information sources, analysts, and users. "Hard-wiring" intelligence relationships when actors, methods, and targets are uncertain impairs our ability to adapt to changing threats and vulnerabilities.

Advances in information technology can facilitate this transformation. Internet and teleconferencing technologies allow virtual communities to gather and share information in real time. Instead of focusing on central control, federal officials should spend more time setting priorities, coordinating communication, supplying technical assistance, and assuring data quality. Collecting more information from more sources will require more federal analytical capability to prevent information overload.

## Assessing Information Needs

The first step in designing an intelligence system to fight terrorism while protecting openness and privacy is to understand what information is needed to support each homeland security challenge. For example, to protect America's borders, we need more complete information about people and goods entering the country. To detect potential terrorist threats within the United States, we need to enhance traditional investigative techniques by cross-referencing databases such as airline reservation records, phone logs, and credit histories with government law enforcement, immigration, and intelligence information. To protect critical infrastructure in areas such as agriculture, food, water, public health, emergency services, telecommunications, energy, transportation, banking, and finance, we need to map vulnerabilities against capabilities of potential terrorists, people who have access to those infrastructures, and the means available to carry out effective attacks. To respond to emergencies, we need two-way communication in real time between first responders and other officials about the extent and nature of the attack, the resources available to respond, and the risk of further terrorist action.

## Guidelines for Protecting Openness and Privacy

The long-term acceptance by the American people of an enhanced intelligence effort will depend heavily on the adoption of clear, public guidelines governing the collection, retention, and dissemination of information, and the development of strong procedures for oversight and accountability. Modern information technology can play an important role in helping to implement and enforce these policies.

In principle, no one disputes that anti-terrorism measures should protect the values that anchor democratic processes and personal security in the United States. Introducing his homeland security strategy, President Bush called for protecting national security in ways that keep our fundamental values intact and

> *"To respond to emergencies, we need two-way communication in real time between first responders and other officials."*

cautioned that "we should guard scrupulously against incursions on our freedoms, recognizing that liberty cannot exist in the absence of government restraint." He acknowledged that protecting such values might mean accepting a higher level of risk: "Because we must not permit the threat of terrorism to alter the American way of life, we have to accept some level of terrorist risk as a permanent condition."

In practice, however, policymakers must make difficult choices. Guidelines to promote security while furthering openness and privacy should be a matter of public debate and will need mid-course corrections as policymakers and analysts gain experience with new information practices and technologies. The recommendations that follow provide a framework for beginning such a deliberative process.

*Emphasize information sharing.* Openness can further security. Quickly identifying terrorist threats and infrastructure vulnerabilities calls for cooperative, fluid information networks. Reducing barriers to information-sharing rather than compartmentalizing secrets represents the greatest challenge in fostering such networks. State and local governments, the private sector, and the public have a central role to play in identifying suspicious activities and individuals and in finding and correcting security vulnerabilities. Sharing information about threats and infrastructure vulnerabilities enhances security by multiplying sources of information, empowering Americans to make their own choices about what risks they are prepared to accept, and creating market incentives and political pressures to reduce vulnerabilities.

On the other hand, security or commercial interests will sometimes override a presumption of openness. There may be little public benefit and considerable security risk in revealing floor plans of nuclear power plants or exact locations of military weapons or vaccine stockpiles, for example. In addition, trade secrets, which provide an underpinning for competitive enterprise, should continue to receive careful protection under federal laws.

An analogous situation occurs in the field of computer security, where software companies grapple with the question of whether to alert customers about vulnerabilities that hackers can exploit. Proponents of secrecy argue that revealing security weaknesses invites exploitation of those weaknesses. Proponents of openness argue that public knowledge helps spur solutions and provides users with information to guard against breaches. There is growing support for the idea of making programming code more accessible as a way to enhance overall security.

*Maintain high hurdles for sharing personally identifiable information.* Sharing personally identifiable information among commercial and government databases raises serious privacy concerns. In many cases the value of intelligence information does not depend on links to identified individuals. Sharing data about imported goods, suspected means of attack, likely targets, critical vulnerabilities, and emergency response plans raises few privacy issues. However, combining databases to screen individuals at border crossings, sharing law enforcement and intelligence information to identify suspects, "data-mining" to determine suspicious patterns of behavior, and employing commercial databases to screen airline passengers alters the patchwork of privacy protections that has been constructed over many years by private companies, Congress, and the courts. Requests to acquire and share such information should meet threshold tests:

• Intelligence architecture should be designed to minimize privacy intrusions and construct consistent technological barriers that limit users of personally identified information, restrict time periods for information-sharing, or remove personal identifiers altogether until a specified level of evidence is reached.

• Authorizations to access personal data should be subjected to rigorous substantive standards that balance the importance of national security needs against the seriousness of privacy intrusions.

• Access to data should require third party review. Depending on the seriousness of the privacy intrusion, approval could range from a signature by a high-ranking federal official to a court order.

• Data collection, analysis, and feedback should document how authorizations are used in practice, providing a basis for periodic adjustments based on experience.

*Protect important secrets.* While the emphasis of the new intelligence architecture needs to be on information sharing, important secrets must still be protected. In the cold war context, classifying data as top secret, secret, or confidential protected sources and methods of obtaining information and guarded military plans and capabilities. In the homeland security context, such priorities remain important. But new areas of sensitive information—such as protecting the gene sequence of a lethal pathogen developed in a private lab—call for new approaches to limiting information access.

> *"While the emphasis of the new intelligence architecture needs to be on information sharing, important secrets must still be protected."*

The traditional system of classification should be strengthened by congressional action to rationalize and update the system to reflect the new threat environment. Important as it is, the nation's protection of national security secrets remains a legal patchwork of mandates created by executive orders and presidential directives. Over time, the classification system has also suffered from overuse. More than two million individuals—mostly Defense Department officials and federal contractors—hold federal security clearances. According to the Information Security Oversight Office, an arm of the National Archives and Records Administration that oversees the classification system, federal agencies still create more than 260,000 official secrets each year and that number is increasing. It is too early to predict the character and extent of new secrets that will be created by four agencies recently granted classification authority by President Bush (the Department of Health and Human Services, the Department of Homeland Security, the Environmental Protection Agency, and the Department of Agriculture).

Increasingly sophisticated tools can help protect sensitive information while assuring appropriate information sharing, such as "tear sheets" (unclassified versions of classified reports) and "metadata" (which can point individuals without security clearances to potentially relevant sources of information without revealing the sensitive information itself).

Even if policymakers are careful in defining a new structure for gathering, analyzing, and disseminating national security information, they cannot avoid difficult questions about how to improve security while furthering openness and protecting personal privacy. Vigorous public debate is essential to answering these questions. Clear guidelines, formulated in a deliberative process, can assure public confidence in new policies. Information technology can provide tools to minimize these conflicts, foster collaboration, and help assure that the right information gets to the right people at the right time. Nonetheless, missteps are inevitable. Procedures that provide accountability and oversight can assure that lessons from early experiences strengthen the nation's information strategies to fight terrorism.

# Chapter 4

# Do Efforts to Enhance Homeland Security Threaten Civil Liberties?

CURRENT CONTROVERSIES

# Chapter Preface

Racial profiling occurs when law enforcement officers question, search, or arrest someone based on their race, ethnicity, or national origin rather than on evidence that they have actually engaged in criminal activity. Before September 11, 2001, polls reported that 80 percent of Americans believed this practice was racist and should not be used. However, following September 11—a day when Arab-Muslim terrorists flew planes into the World Trade Center and the Pentagon, causing the loss of more than three thousand lives—many attitudes changed as people feared for their safety. Large numbers of Americans suddenly wondered whether preventing racism might be less important than granting law enforcement the power to do whatever was needed to catch terrorists. Recent polls show that 60 percent of Americans now favor ethnic profiling, as long as it is directed at Arabs and Muslims.

Many people believe that because the September 11 terrorists were Arab men, it is only common sense to pay closer attention to Arab-looking men boarding planes. Columnist Michael Kinsley explains why this practice should not be considered racist:

> An Arab-looking man heading toward a plane is statistically more likely to be a terrorist. That likelihood is infinitesimal, but the whole airport rigmarole is based on infinitesimal chances. . . . Logic says you should pay more attention to people who look like Arabs than to people who don't. This is true even if you are free of all ethnic prejudices. It's not racism.

In Kinsley's opinion, because the stakes are so high, racial profiling must be used. "We're at war with a terrorist network that . . . has anonymous agents in our country planning more slaughter," he argues. "Are we really supposed to ignore the one identifiable fact we know about them?"

However, critics believe that racial profiling is a serious threat to civil liberties in the United States. According to authors David Cole and James X. Dempsey, a ban on racial profiling is an important part of protecting the freedom of all Americans, "precisely because of the history of racial discrimination in this country." Cole and Dempsey argue that while protecting citizens from terrorism is a compelling interest, it is not more important than protecting their civil liberties. Activist Penn Jillette echoes this belief, asserting that, "There's no such thing as an acceptable loss of innocent life. But, isn't the same true for freedom? Isn't any loss of freedom unacceptable?"

Following the September 11, 2001, terrorist attacks, the U.S. government has taken a number of controversial actions, such as the use of racial profiling, in an attempt to ensure homeland security. In the following chapter the authors debate whether or not these efforts have threatened civil liberties.

# The USA PATRIOT Act Has Decimated Many Civil Liberties

## by Barbara Dority

*About the author: Barbara Dority is the executive director of the Washington Coalition Against Censorship and the cochair of the Northwest Feminist Anti-Censorship Task Force.*

On November 11, 2003, former President Jimmy Carter condemned U.S. leaders' attacks on American civil liberties, particularly the Uniting and Strengthening America by Providing Appropriate Tools Required to Intercept and Obstruct Terrorism Act (USA PATRIOT Act). Speaking at a gathering of Human Rights Defenders on the Front Lines of Freedom at the Carter Center in Washington, D.C., Carter said that post-9/11 policies "work against the spirit of human rights" and are "very serious mistakes." Egyptian human rights activist and sociology professor Saad Eddin Ibrahim added, "Every dictator is using what the United States has done under the Patriot Act to justify human rights abuses in the past, as well as a license to continue human rights abuses."

Since its passage in October 2001, the Patriot Act has decimated many basic American civil liberties. The law gives broad new powers to domestic law enforcement and international intelligence agencies. Perhaps worse still, it eliminates the system of checks and balances that gave courts the responsibility of ensuring that these powers weren't abused. The Electronic Frontier Foundation (EFF), an electronic privacy watchdog group, believes that the opportunities for abuse of these broad new powers are immense.

A particularly egregious part of the Patriot Act gives the government access to "any tangible things." This section grants the Federal Bureau of Investigation (FBI) the authority to request an order "requiring the production of any tangible things (including books, records, papers, documents, and other items)" relevant to an investigation of terrorism or clandestine intelligence activities. Although the section is entitled "Access to Certain Business Records," the scope of its authority is far broader and applies to any records pertaining to an individual. This section, which overrides state library confidentiality laws, permits the FBI to compel production of business records, medical records, educational records, and library records without showing probable cause.

## Unfair Treatment of Immigrants

Many aspects of the Patriot Act unfairly target immigrants. The attorney general has the ability to "certify" that the government has "reasonable grounds to believe that an alien is a terrorist or is engaged in other activity that endangers the national security of the United States." Once that certification is made and someone is labeled a potential threat, the government may detain him or her indefinitely—based on secret evidence it isn't required to share with anyone.

Currently [in 2004] over thirteen thousand Arab and Muslim immigrants are being held in deportation proceedings. Not one of them has been charged with terrorism. Most are being deported for routine immigration violations that normally

*"Since its passage in October 2001, the Patriot Act has decimated many basic American civil liberties."*

could be rectified in hearings before immigration judges. Families are being separated and lives ruined because of selective enforcement of immigration laws that have been on the books for many years and are now being used to intimidate and deport law-abiding Arab and Muslim Americans. Fear and confusion are pervasive in the Arab-American community today. Many people are too afraid to step forward when they are harassed on the job or fired, when they are denied housing because of their last name, or when a family member is picked up by immigration authorities and detained in another state on evidence that remains undisclosed to both detainees and lawyers alike. According to [Arab American rights advocate] Karen Rignal's article "Beyond Patriotic" on Alternet.org, some of these people have been detained for as long as eight months, mistreated, and confined twenty-three hours a day. Some Arab immigrants have opted to return to the Middle East because they no longer feel welcome in the United States.

## Looking for "Un-American" Material

Nearly seven hundred men are being held at "Camp X-Ray" in Guantanamo Bay, Cuba. But it isn't just "foreigners" who are being deemed dangerous and un-American. For example, there is Tom Treece, a teacher who taught a class on "public issues" at a Vermont high school. A uniformed police officer entered Treece's classroom in the middle of the night because a student art project on the wall showed a picture of Bush with duct tape over his mouth and the words, "Put your duct tape to good use. Shut your mouth." Residents refused to pass the school budget if Treece wasn't fired, resulting in his removal.

The American Civil Liberties Union (ACLU) went to court to help a fifteen-year-old who faced suspension from school when he refused to take off a T-shirt with the words "International Terrorist" written beneath a picture of [President George W.] Bush. And there was the college student from North Carolina who was visited at home by secret service agents who told her, "Ma'am, we've gotten a report that you have anti-American material." She refused to let them in but eventually showed them what she thought they were after, an anti-death-penalty poster showing Bush and a group of lynched bodies over the epithet "We hang on your every word." The agents then asked her if she had any "pro-Taliban stuff."

Then there's art dealer Doug Stuber, who ran the 2000 North Carolina presidential campaign for Green Party candidate Ralph Nader. Stuber was told he couldn't board a plane to Prague, Czech Republic, because no Greens were allowed to fly that day. He was questioned by police, photographed by two secret service agents, and asked about his family and what the Greens were up to. Stuber reports that he was shown a Justice Department document suggesting that Greens were likely terrorists.

Michael Franti, lead singer of the progressive hip hop band Spearhead, reports that the mother of one of his colleagues, who has a sibling in the Persian Gulf, was visited by "two plain-clothes men from the military" in March 2003. They came in and said, "You have a child who's in the Gulf and you have a child who's in this band Spearhead who's part of the resistance." They had pictures of the band at peace rallies, their flight records for several months, their banking records, and the names of backstage staff.

> *"The Patriot Act allows U.S. foreign intelligence agencies to more easily spy on U.S. citizens."*

A report by the ACLU called "Freedom Under Fire" states, "There is a pall over our country. The response to dissent by many government officials so clearly violates the letter and the spirit of the supreme law of the land that they threaten the very underpinnings of democracy itself."

## Surveillance Under the Patriot Act

In the face of these cases and many more, Justice Department spokespeople have repeatedly claimed that the Patriot Act doesn't apply to Americans. But this is false. First of all, under the Patriot Act the four tools of surveillance—wiretaps, search warrants, pen/trap orders, and subpoenas—are increased. Second, their counterparts under the Foreign Intelligence Surveillance Act (FISA), which allows spying in the United States by foreign intelligence agencies, are concurrently expanded. New definitions of terrorism also increase the amount of government surveillance permitted. And three expansions of previous terms increase the scope of spying allowed. The Patriot Act provides a FISA detour around limitations on federal domestic surveillance and a domestic detour around FISA limitations. The attorney general can nullify domestic surveillance limits on the Central Intelligence Agency, for example, by obtaining an FISA wiretap where probable cause cannot be shown but the person is a suspected foreign government agent. All this information can be shared with the FBI and vice versa.

> *"The Patriot Act specifically gives the government and the FBI authority to monitor people not engaged in criminal activity or espionage and to do so in complete secrecy."*

In sum, the Patriot Act allows U.S. foreign intelligence agencies to more easily spy on U.S. citizens and FISA now provides for increased information sharing between domestic law enforcement and foreign intelligence officials. This partially repeals the protections implemented in the 1970s after the revelation that the FBI and CIA were conducting investigations on thousands of U.S. citizens during and after the McCarthy era [of intense anti-communism in the mid-1950s]. The Patriot Act allows sharing wiretap results and grand jury information when that constitutes "foreign intelligence information."

In response to other criticisms, Justice Department spokespeople have also claimed that the Patriot Act applies only to "terrorists and spies" and that the FBI can't obtain a person's records without probable cause. As one might expect, all of this is false as well.

The Patriot Act specifically gives the government and the FBI authority to monitor people not engaged in criminal activity or espionage and to do so in complete secrecy. It also imposes a gag order that prohibits an organization that has been forced to turn over records from disclosing the fact of the search to its clients, customers, or anyone else.

## Expanding Federal Powers

Furthermore, in other statements, federal officials contradict themselves by saying that the government is using its expanded authority under the far-reaching law to investigate suspected blackmailers, drug traffickers, money launderers, pornographers, and white-collar criminals. Dan Dodson, speaking to the Associated Press this past September [2003] on behalf of the National Association of Criminal Defense Attorneys, reported, "Within six months of passing the Patriot Act, the Justice Department was conducting seminars on how to stretch the new wiretapping provisions to extend them beyond terror cases."

A guidebook used in a 2002 Justice Department employee seminar on financial crimes says: "We all know that the USA Patriot Act provided weapons for the war on terrorism. But do you know how it affects the war on crime as well?"

Eric Lichtblau, writing in the September 28, 2003, *New York Times*, reveals that a September report to Congress from the Justice Department "cites more than a dozen cases that are not directly related to terrorism. In them, federal authorities have used their expanded power to investigate individuals, initiate wiretaps and other surveillance or seize millions in tainted assets." In one case, e-mail and other electronic evidence made possible "the tracking of an unidentified fugitive and an investigation into a computer hacker who stole a company's trade secrets." In other instances, expanded federal authority was used "to investigate a major drug distributor, a four-time killer, an identity thief and a fugitive who fled on the eve of trial by using a fake passport." The Bureau of Immigration and Customs Enforcement has benefited as well. Lichtblau provides information from a senior official that "investigators in the past two years had seized about $35 million at U.S. borders in undeclared cash, checks and currency being smuggled out of the country," much of which "involved drug smuggling, corporate fraud and other nonterrorism crimes." Furthermore, officials in the Justice Department have indicated that the examples cited in the report to Congress are among hundreds of such non-terrorism cases pursued by federal authorities.

Publicly, of course, Attorney General John Ashcroft continues to speak almost exclusively of how Patriot Act powers are helping fight terrorism. In his nationwide tour this past fall [2003] to bolster support for the act (which has engendered growing discontent), Ashcroft lauded its "success" stories. However, his department also officially labels many cases as terrorism which aren't. A January 2003 study by the General Accounting Office concluded that, of those convictions classified as "international terrorism," fully 75 percent actually dealt with more common nonterrorist crimes. . . .

## The Death Penalty for Terrorist Acts

Bush also wants to expand the reach of the federal death penalty by making it applicable to "domestic terrorism." Under the act, domestic terrorism is broadly defined as any criminal act intended to influence the government through "intimidation or coercion" involving "dangerous acts." Aggressive protestors of all stripes—from Greenpeace activists to abortion foes—could easily fall within this definition, opening the door for politically motivated executions. Bush also wants passage of the "Antiterrorism Tools Enhancement Act of 2003" (H.R. 3037) and the Anti-Terrorism Intelligence Tools Improvement Act of 2003 (H.R. 3179). Both were proposed in the fall [2003] and are now [in 2004] in committee. They would give the FBI "administrative subpoena" authority to confiscate any records and compel any testimony on its authorization alone, thus eliminating court oversight entirely—or as Bush would call it, "interference."

> *"Perhaps the most frightening thing about the Patriot Act . . . is how similar the act is to legislation enacted in the eighteenth century."*

Civil rights and liberties of ordinary U.S. citizens won't be respected. Indeed, should a certain chain of events occur, all one would have to do is donate some money to a group or organization to possibly be linked to terrorism. Consider the following scenario: you send a contribution to Greenpeace. The following week, Greenpeace activists non-violently blockade an oil tanker coming into New York harbor to protest the company's safety record; however, in the ensuing face-off, a tanker crewmember drowns trying to break the blockade. Under the proposed act's definition of domestic terrorism, a prosecutor could charge the Greenpeace protestors with terrorism—and they could face the death penalty. When the prosecutor subpoenas a list of Greenpeace donors, any one of them can be indicted for "material support" of "terrorism" and face a prison term if convicted. This could mean you. This isn't as farfetched as it sounds. Derived from an ACLU analysis, this is just one of many nightmare scenarios possible—and there are worse—if a recently revealed Justice Department draft of new anti-terrorism legislation becomes law.

Interestingly, according to the October 27, 2003, Long Island, New York, *Newsday*, the top White House aides who identified an American undercover agent[1] may have committed an act of domestic terrorism as defined in the Patriot Act. Section 802 defines, in part, domestic terrorism as "acts dangerous to human life that are a violation of the criminal laws of the U.S. of any state that appear to be intended to intimidate or coerce a civilian population." Clearly, disclosing the identity of a CIA undercover agent is an act dangerous to life—the lives of the agent and her contacts abroad whom terrorist groups can now trace—and a violation of the criminal laws of the United States. The obvious intent of the White House in disclosing this classified information was to intimidate the agent's husband, former Ambassador Joseph Wilson, who had become a strong critic of Bush's Iraq policies. And by showing their willingness to make such a dangerous disclosure, officials sent a clear message to all critics that they, too, could be destroyed if they persist. The apparent intention "to intimidate or coerce a civilian population" also meets the act's definition of domestic terrorism. This places the Justice Department investigators in a dilemma: will they treat this investigation differently from others? Under the act, they have acquired expanded powers to wiretap and search—but will they place sweeping and roving wiretaps on White House aides? Will they engage in secret searches of their offices, computers, and homes? Will they arrest and detain White House aides incommunicado and without access to counsel?

> *"Apparently, many Americans were initially so traumatized by 9/11 that they were ready to surrender their most treasured liberties."*

---

1. In July 2003, a White House aide leaked the name of a CIA operative to the press.

## Violating Civil Liberties

Perhaps the most frightening thing about the Patriot Act—even putting aside these other impending restrictions on civil liberties—is how similar the act is to legislation enacted in the eighteenth century. The Alien and Sedition Acts are notorious in history for their abuse of basic civil liberties. For example, in 1798, the Alien Friends Act made it lawful for the president of the United States "to order all such aliens, as he shall judge dangerous to the peace and safety of the United States, or shall have reasonable grounds to suspect are concerned in any treasonable or secret machinations against the government thereof, to depart out of the territory of the United States." For years Americans have pointed to legislation like this as a travesty never to be repeated. Yet now it is back!

It seems unimaginable that any presidential administration would impose such brazen attacks as these on the civil liberties of a supposedly free people. Apparently, many Americans were initially so traumatized by 9/11 that they were ready to surrender their most treasured liberties. But pockets of resistance are developing and organizations forming. Three states and more than two hundred cities, counties, and towns around the country have passed resolutions opposing the Patriot Act. Many others are in progress. The language of these resolutions includes statements affirming a commitment to the rights guaranteed in the Constitution and directives to local law enforcement not to cooperate with federal agents involved in investigations deemed unconstitutional. . . .

Some leading organizations, such as the ACLU and EFF [Electronic Frontier Foundation] continue to keep the pressure on and are always worthy of support. American citizens who treasure their heritage of freedom should find at least one group to join and support—keeping in mind that the government may one day know the organizations they have checked out.

# New Surveillance Technologies Threaten Civil Liberties

**by Clyde Wayne Crews Jr.**

**About the author:** *Clyde Wayne Crews Jr. is director of technology studies at the Cato Institute, a public policy research foundation.*

The convergence of privacy-invading technologies and Washington's appetite for surveillance have put civil liberties on the run. This is especially true in the war against terrorism.

Controversial initiatives have included biometric face cameras, wiretap enhancements, invasive computer-assisted airline passenger screening, escalated e-mail monitoring fostered by the USA Patriot Act and the Pentagon's Total Information Awareness data-mining project (now renamed the "Terrorism" Information Awareness, or TIA).[1] Even a national ID card was proposed.

In the right circumstances, data-mining technologies and "biometrics"—such as voice prints, retina, iris and face scanners, digitized fingerprints, and even implantable chips—can benefit us. That's because data-mining and biometrics, at least in principle, are about enhancing convenience, service, authentication and individual security more than they are about invading privacy.

Biometrics, for example, promises increased privacy and security by guarding against identity theft in our myriad marketplace transactions. We'll see their use in cell phones, laptop computers, car doors, doorknobs and office keys—basically everywhere. They can increase security in online commerce, help locate a lost youngster, relay medical information to doctors and much more.

But inherently invasive technologies like these can threaten fundamental values of privacy and liberty if misused. No one wants to be treated like a human bar code by the authorities or monitored around the clock by the Homeland Se-

---

1. This program was temporarily suspended in 2003.

curity Department. Thus, we need a framework by which to distinguish appropriate and inappropriate uses or surveillance-enabling technologies.

## Compulsory Databases

The most pressing threat to liberty is a compulsory database encompassing everyone. Examples are a mandatory national ID with biometric identifiers or involuntary data-mining like the TIA that would permit real-time monitoring of our whereabouts, movements and transactions. This is a Big Brother[2] scenario, one of constant surveillance or harassment of citizens unrelated to addressing terrorist threats. You can't opt out.

Compulsory databases would undermine the many potential benefits of authentication technologies. If government is hell-bent on assembling and mining massive databases of our credit card purchases, car rentals, library books, airline ticket

> *"The convergence of privacy-invading technologies and Washington's appetite for surveillance have put civil liberties on the run."*

purchases and so on, then banks, airlines, hotels, Internet service providers and other private businesses we deal with have no choice but to routinely transfer our private information to the government against our wishes. They cannot promise to safeguard our privacy as they otherwise could.

Another threat, but less sweeping, is a partial governmental database containing details on criminals and suspects, not the general population. An example would be biometric face recognition camera systems deployed in public places. Individuals are observed as they pass, which is creepy, but presumably only to see if they match a face already in the underlying database.

Allegedly, the substantive information collection—that pertaining to the criminals—has already taken place under appropriate Fourth Amendment procedures, and no data are ever collected on passersbys not already in the database. However, many doubt governments can be trusted to discard incidental data collected on innocents. Indeed, the needed safeguards against abuse of such systems do not yet exist.

## Safeguarding Civil Liberties

To safeguard civil liberties in the new surveillance state enabled by digital technologies, there are basically three requirements:

• Avoid mandatory databases or any form of national ID, because they violate the Fourth Amendment, and because government's dominance of the evolution of these technologies would effectively destroy the privacy sector's ability to offer any privacy guarantees to us.

---

2. Big Brother is a totalitarian dictator in *1984*, a novel by George Orwell that describes a state where everybody is under complete government surveillance.

- Ensure Fourth Amendment protections even for surveillance in open, public places.
- Avoid the mixing of public (compulsory) and private (voluntary) databases as new technologies emerge and proliferate.

While people have alternatives to dealing with private parties that snoop too much, they have little protection against an overly suspicious government. Thus, government must not have access to our private information without going through the appropriate legal hurdles.

On the other side of the coin, instead of piggybacking on government-mandated information, private industry should be forced to generate its own databases for purposes limited by the market's twin engines of consumer choice—and consumer rejection.

Countless private uses of biometrics offer the opportunity for extraordinary security by preventing others from posing as us. This is where the new contingent of "privacy-invading" technologies can shine. But if private applications of biometrics and data-mining merely piggyback on data gleaned by government coercion, they will give the entire industry a black eye and make it impossible to defend the industry from regulation.

In the new "surveillance" state, or whatever we call the rise of government-run biometrics, cameras, compulsory IDs and data-mining, keeping public and private data separate is critical for the health of our civil liberties, our personal privacy and even the health of industries specializing in authentication technologies and techniques. New technologies always bring risks. But even the risks of a "database nation" are controllable if we adhere to constitutional principle. Orwell's Big Brother need not win.

# Efforts to Increase Homeland Security Have Resulted in the Mistreatment of Immigrants

by Mark Engler

**About the author:** *Mark Engler is a writer and activist based in New York City. He has previously worked with the Arias Foundation for Peace and Human Progress in San José, Costa Rica, as well as the Public Intellectuals Program at Florida Atlantic University.*

In late May [2003], an internal Department of Justice review confirmed what critics had long charged were frightening violations of civil liberties and due process in the wake of [the September 11, 2001, terrorist attacks on America]. The report showed that the 762 non-citizens who were rounded up after the attacks were put in cells where the lights were never turned off and kept in solitary confinement for 23 hours a day. They were cuffed and shackled in leg irons before they were moved. Guards slammed them against walls in advance of videotaping their statements.

The report showed that, when detainees went to contact their lawyers, guards gave them wrong numbers to dial or interfered with their calls and that authorities lied to those outside as well. When family members asked after a loved one at the Metropolitan Detention Center in Brooklyn, New York, they were repeatedly told that the person was not being held at that facility.

In the end, none of those Muslim men who were held in the post-9/11 sweep was charged with crimes relating to terrorism. (Zacarias Moussaoui, the only individual with relevant charges pending, was in custody before the attacks.) Many were never even suspected of such crimes. Although they did not learn of their charges for weeks on end, they were held only for minor immigration violations. The common denominators among them were race and religion.

# A Trend of Mistreatment

Accusations of mistreatment at the hands of federal authorities are not new. Family members and community organizations have been working to publicize the plight of detainees since their initial arrests. Yet the internal report not only confirms the claims of these activists, it points to a wider trend. In the age of "homeland security" immigrant rights have come under an intensified assault. Government abuses are only feeding the atmosphere of intolerance.

Since most of the detainees have been deported or released, commentators overwhelmingly spoke about the contents of the inspector general's report in past tense. Many, while critical, appeared to agree with Joseph Billy Jr., the FBI's overseer of counter-terrorism in New York City, who pointed to special circumstances and cited "the tenor of the times after 9/11."

But a flood of news items since the report's release in late May [2003] show that the government's actions do not reflect an anomalous period of abusiveness. They mark instead an official attitude that increasingly views immigrants as criminals, rather than a key source of strength and diversity for our country.

For its part, the Justice Department's attitude of indignation mutes its vows to implement reforms based on the inspector general's recommendations. As other observers have noted, the [Bush] Administration has taken an unbalanced stance: [U.S. attorney general John] Ashcroft's lieutenants swear they have done nothing wrong—and that it will never happen again.

Meanwhile, the Department's attorneys continue fighting in court to defend their practices. They have been distressingly successful in legitimating tactics that strike at core protections afforded by our legal system. On May 27 [2003], the Supreme Court rejected a challenge to secret deportation proceedings, which are closed to family members, the press, and the public.

Three weeks later, on June 17, the DC [District of Columbia] Circuit Court of Appeals upheld the Justice Department practice of secret arrests—holding suspects in secret and refusing to release the names and locations of detainees. Dissenting Judge David S. Tatel called the decision an "uncritical deference to the government's vague, poorly explained arguments" for withholding basic information about suspects' conditions, an act that prevents watchdogs from determining whether the Bush administration is violating the constitutional rights of those in custody.

> *"In the age of 'homeland security' immigrant rights have come under an intensified assault. Government abuses are ... feeding the atmosphere of intolerance."*

## Discrimination Against Immigrants

The president [George W. Bush] assures us that he is not waging a war on Islam and that he wants to work with local neighborhoods to locate the real terrorists. Yet he has treated huge numbers of Arab and South Asian non-citizens as suspects, fueling discrimination against immigrant communities. Since last November [2002], the government has mandated that non-citizen men from 25 nations report for mass "special registrations." Except North Korea, all are predominately Muslim countries. Among the 82,000 people who waited in long lines to voluntarily comply with the order to register—a contingent unlikely to include a lot of terrorists—hundreds were shackled and jailed for problems as trivial as falling a few credits short of the course-load requirements on a student visa.

Some 13,000 who registered were given orders to appear for court proceedings that could possibly result in expulsion from the country. Deportations and fear of discrimination has sparked an exodus of residents from neighborhoods like New York's "Little Pakistan" on Coney Island Avenue, where storefronts and restaurants are emptied.

> *"It would be nice to have a president who is above suspicion of supporting vigilantism. But we are not so fortunate today."*

On June 17 [2003], the Bush administration announced with great fanfare prohibitions on the discriminatory policing practices of racial profiling that have attracted so much attention in the past decade. But, as the ACLU [American Civil Liberties Union] pointed out, the guidelines were released by the Justice Department's civil rights division, the same office that "has come under increasing fire over the past year for dropping a number of ongoing cases against municipalities accused of police brutality and racially prejudicial law enforcement." Moreover, the "ban" perpetuates selective persecution committed in the name of national security. Top officials point to exceptions in the new rules for investigations involving "terrorists," and assure us that programs like Special Registration[1] will continue.

Muslims, Arabs, and South Asians are not the only ones under attack. In the third week of June [2003], [human rights organizations] Amnesty International and Physicians for Human Rights each released reports decrying the treatment of asylum-seekers—those who come to our country to escape torture and oppression abroad. These investigations shown that already poor conditions have only worsened in the past year. About one-third of all children in the custody of U.S. immigration authorities, although accused of no crime, are reportedly subjected to shackling, verbal abuse, solitary confinement, or exposure to the adult prisoner population.

## Wave of Vigilantism

On Arizona's border with Mexico, a new wave of vigilantism has risen since 9/11. Increasingly large groups patrol the desert suited in camouflage, vowing

---

1. This program, begun in 2002, requires immigrants from selected countries, including many countries with substantial Muslim populations, to attend an interview with immigration authorities.

to take homeland security into their own hands. Organizations like the Civil Homeland Defense militia have ties to white supremacists and are suspected by immigrant rights advocates of involvement in the murders of undocumented Mexicans, but have thus far escaped serious scrutiny from local authorities.

In response to these gangs, the White House has taken a frighteningly ambiguous position. [Former U.S. press secretary] Ari Fleisher responded to questions about the militias by saying, "The president believes that the laws of the land need to be observed and the laws need to be enforced." As [writer] Max Blumenthal reported in Salon.com, this "might mean one of two things. Perhaps it was a warning that militia groups should stay within the law. Or perhaps it was an acknowledgment that federal agencies have failed at the border—and a careful way of cheering on the vigilantes."

It would be nice to have a president who is above suspicion of supporting vigilantism. But we are not so fortunate today. In early March [2003], when he was working to pressure Mexico to side with the U.S. in UN deliberations about the Iraq War, President Bush publicly worried—or threatened—that a "No" vote could lead to reprisals against some of the 28 million Mexicans living in the United States.

"I don't expect there to be significant retribution from the government," he noted in an interview with Copley News Service. But then he called attention to the "backlash against the French, not stirred up by anybody except the people," and said that if Mexico opposed the U.S. "there will be a certain sense of discipline."

As *New York Times* columnist Paul Krugman commented at the time, "These remarks went virtually unreported by the ever-protective U.S. media, but they created a political firestorm in Mexico. The White House has been frantically backpedaling, claiming that when Mr. Bush talked of 'discipline' he wasn't making a threat. But in the context of the rest of the interview, it's clear that he was."

White House spin doctors may claim that the president's posturing falls short of a threat, but George W. Bush's apparent disregard for the safety of immigrants goes hand-in-hand with the abuses perpetuated by his Justice Department. Ultimately, it's hard to tell which is worse for the future of the country: that the climate of fear and discrimination nurtured in the age of homeland security is making life less safe for millions of people living in this country or that the Bush administration makes no apologies.

# Using the U.S. Military to Aid Domestic Security Efforts Would Lead to Violations of Civil Liberties

## by Gene Healy

**About the author:** *Gene Healy is senior editor at the Cato Institute, a public policy research foundation.*

As its overwhelming victories in Afghanistan and Iraq have demonstrated, the U.S. military is the most powerful fighting force in human history. In fact, the military has been so brilliantly effective abroad that it is not altogether surprising that many people think it can be equally effective fighting the war on terrorism here at home. Since the September 11, 2001, terrorist attacks, there has been a rising chorus of calls for deploying military personnel on the home front to fight terrorism. In the immediate aftermath of the attacks, troops were stationed in airports, and fighter jets patrolled the skies over New York and Washington. Later, in early 2002, the Pentagon deployed troops on the borders with Canada and Mexico. Even though that border deployment was temporary, it was a blatant violation of federal law—and a disturbing indication that the Bush administration is willing to disregard the law when it gets in the way. Meanwhile, the Department of Defense has shown an unhealthy interest in domestic surveillance, exploring technologies that could open the door to surveillance of American citizens on an unprecedented scale.

High-level officials in Congress and the Bush administration have proposed revising or rescinding the Posse Comitatus Act, the 125-year-old law that restricts the government's ability to use the U.S. military as a police force. Sen. John Warner (R-VA), chairman of the Senate Armed Services Committee, has said that the legal doctrine of *posse comitatus* (force of the county) may have had its day. That view was echoed by Gen. Ralph E. Eberhart, who as head of the new Northern Command oversees all military forces within the United States. Eberhart has declared, "We should always be reviewing things like Posse Comitatus . . . if we think it ties our hands in protecting the American people."

The notion that the military is the appropriate institution for fighting terrorism at home, as well as abroad, is ill-conceived. On the home front, there are many tasks for which the military is ill suited and situations in which its deployment would be hazardous to both civilian life and civil liberties.

Americans have long distrusted the idea of soldiers as domestic police officers—a distrust that is reflected in both the Constitution and federal statutory law. Col. Patrick Finnegan, who heads the Department of Law for the U.S. Military Academy, has observed, "The military is designed

> *"The notion that the military is the appropriate institution for fighting terrorism at home, as well as abroad, is ill-conceived."*

and trained to defend our country by fighting and killing the enemy, usually faceless, with no individual rights. . . . The training, mission, and role of the military and police are so dissimilar that it is not surprising that we do not, and should not, want the military to act as a police force." Experience has shown that when America departs from that principle, the results can be disastrous.

It is unfortunate that the call to have soldiers assume a more active police role domestically has not generated more media and scholarly attention. Such a dramatic move away from the American tradition must be carefully studied. As this paper argues, Americans have good reason to distrust proposals to militarize the home front. . . .

## Historical and Legal Background

A strong preference for civilian law enforcement is deeply rooted in the American tradition. Historian Bernard Bailyn notes that the generation that fought the American Revolution considered the use of soldiers to maintain law and order a grave threat to freedom: "[The colonists'] fear was not simply of armies, but of *standing armies*, a phrase that had distinctive connotations . . . the colonists universally agreed that 'unhappy nations have lost that precious jewel *liberty* . . . [because] their necessities or indiscretion have permitted a standing army to be kept amongst them.' There was, they knew, no 'worse state of thralldom than a military power in any government, unchecked and uncontrolled by the civil power.'"

That fear was reinforced by one of the epochal events of the Revolutionary period: the Boston Massacre. In March 1770 a civilian mob started to taunt British soldiers who had been sent to Boston to reinforce the local colonial government. Under threat from the crowd, the troops opened fire, wounding eight and killing five, including Crispus Attucks, a runaway slave who had been working as a seaman and day laborer. Later, Boston was placed under military rule, and the Intolerable Acts passed in 1774 in the wake of the Boston Tea Party provided for quartering of troops in private houses.

American hostility toward militarized law enforcement, born in republican political theory and stoked by the experiences of the Revolutionary period, found expression in the Declaration of Independence's bill of particulars against King George III [of England]: "He has kept among us, in times of peace, Standing Armies, without the consent of our legislatures. He has affected to render the Military independent of and superior to the Civil power."

Seven years after the Revolutionary War [in 1740], America adopted a Constitution that authorized Congress to raise an army. So great was the fear that a standing army might be used to oppress the people, however, that the movement for a Bill of Rights included calls for safeguarding the right to keep and bear arms so as to ensure that an armed populace would be able to resist abuses of power. The Constitution authorizes the federal government to suppress insurrections and restore order but identifies the militia, not the regular army, as the force to be used for such tasks. In fact, there is no explicit constitutional authority for use of the Army to suppress domestic violence.

Later, following the struggles of the Reconstruction period, Congress passed the Posse Comitatus Act, which made it a criminal offense to use the Army to "execute the laws." As one federal judge has written, the

> *"Americans have good reason to distrust proposals to militarize the home front."*

act expresses "the inherited antipathy of the American to the use of troops for civil purposes."

However, along with the American tradition of hostility toward domestic militarization has come a series of bloody departures from that tradition, both before and after the passage of the Posse Comitatus Act. Throughout American history, presidents have deployed troops against civilians, often with tragic results. Here are just a few of the abuses that have occurred when presidents have disregarded the bedrock principle that the military should not intervene in civilian affairs:

• In the years leading up to the Civil War, efforts to enforce the odious Fugitive Slave Laws often met with forceful resistance in the North. In response, the federal government repeatedly used federal troops to disperse abolitionist protestors and forcibly return escaped slaves to bondage. In 1851, for example, 300 armed federal deputies and soldiers led a 17-year-old escaped slave named Thomas Sims from a Boston courthouse to the Navy yard, where 250 more Army regulars waited to put him on a ship heading South.

• In the late 19th century, the federal government repeatedly and illegally used troops to intervene in labor disputes. Particularly egregious was the Army's suppression of the 1899 miners' strike in Coeur d'Alene, Idaho. Army regulars engaged in house-to-house searches and assisted in more than a thousand arrests. Troops arrested every adult male in the area and jailed the men without charges for weeks, imposing martial law. After two years of military occupation, the union was destroyed.

• During World War I, the War Department quashed strikes and destroyed the International Workers of the World union. Military intelligence agents harassed and arrested union leaders. The Army suppressed strikes in Gary, Indiana; Butte, Montana; and Seattle, Washington, as well as occupying the copper mining regions of Arizona and Montana for three years. Historian Jerry Cooper notes that "unrestrained federal military intervention . . . substantially slowed unionization for more than a decade."

• Concerns about German saboteurs during World War I led to unrestrained domestic spying by U.S. Army intelligence operatives. Civilian spies for the Army were given free rein to gather information on potential subversives and were often empowered to make arrests as special police officers. The War Department relied heavily on a quasi-private volunteer organization called the American Protective League. The APL was composed of self-styled "patriots" who agreed to inform on their fellow citizens. At the War Department's request, APL volunteers harassed and arrested opponents of the draft.

• During the Vietnam War, National Guardsmen shot four student protesters to death at Kent State University. After four days of protests following President Richard Nixon's announcement that American troops were being sent to Cambodia, the governor of Ohio called in National Guard units to restore order. The troops arrived on campus and ordered the crowd to disperse, advancing on the unarmed students with fixed bayonets. Some of the protesters responded by throwing rocks at the soldiers. Without firing a warning shot, 28 Guardsmen began firing into the crowd of demonstrators—at least 61 shots in 13 seconds—killing students Allison Krause, Jeffrey Miller, Sandra Scheuer, and William Schroeder and wounding nine others, paralyzing one.

• Military involvement in the 1993 standoff between federal police agencies and the Branch Davidian community in Waco, Texas, contributed to the worst disaster in law enforcement history—military-style attacks that left more than 80 civilians dead, including 27 children. First, U.S. Army Special Forces helped the Bureau of

*"Throughout American history, presidents have deployed troops against civilians, often with tragic results."*

Alcohol, Tobacco and Firearms to rehearse its aggressive initial raid on the Davidian residence. Federal law enforcement officials used false allegations of drug trafficking by the Branch Davidians to obtain military training and National Guard helicopters. Second, U.S. Army Delta Force commanders advised Attorney General Janet Reno to end the 51-day standoff by launching a tank and chemical gas assault against the Branch Davidians' residence.

As those appalling incidents demonstrate, colonial fears about military law enforcement were well-grounded. The abuses of power and risks to civilians that come with using soldiers as cops caution against legal changes that encourage further military involvement in domestic security.

## Posse Comitatus and the September 11 Attacks

The phrase *posse comitatus* refers to the sheriff's common law power to call upon the male population of a county for assistance in enforcing the laws. Enacted by Congress in 1878, the Posse Comitatus Act forbids law enforcement officials to employ the U.S. military for that purpose. The act consists of a single sentence:

> Whoever, except in cases and under circumstances expressly authorized by the Constitution or Act of Congress, willfully uses any part of the Army as a posse comitatus or otherwise to execute the laws shall be fined under this title or imprisoned not more than two years, or both.

Supporters of the act believed it merely affirmed principles that were already embodied in the Constitution. During the congressional debate in 1877, for example, Rep. Richard Townsend of Illinois said that "it was the real design of those who framed our Constitution that the Federal Army should never be used for any purpose but to repel invasion and to suppress insurrection when it became too formidable for the State to suppress it.". . .

*"In July 2002 the White House indicated its openness to a new role for the military in providing domestic security."*

Yet [Deputy Secretary of Defense Paul] Wolfowitz and other administration officials have called for rethinking the Posse Comitatus Act. In July 2002 the White House indicated its openness to a new role for the military in providing domestic security; its *National Strategy for Homeland Security* called for a "thorough review of the laws permitting the military to act within the United States." The views expressed by Gen. Eberhart, the newly appointed commander of all U.S. armed forces within North America, are particularly troubling. In October 2002 Eberhart became head of the new Northern Command, responsible for homeland defense—the first time since America's founding that the command of all military personnel in North America has been centralized under a single officer. So long as the military confines itself to its traditional role, the new homeland command is, in itself, no cause for concern. But Gen. Eberhart has repeatedly contemplated a broader role for the military. In September 2002, for example, Eberhart said, "My view has been that Posse Comitatus will constantly be under review as we mature this command." He did not elaborate on what that "maturation" process will entail. . . .

Before policymakers embrace proposals that will radically restructure the role of the American military, the dangerous implications of such a move must be carefully considered. Those dangers are not limited to collateral damage to civilians from combat-trained soldiers; they include threats to our open, partici-patory, republican institutions.

*Will There Be Accountability for Accidents, Misconduct, Brutality?*

"The blue wall of silence" is the popular term for a pattern of collusion and coverup that can often be found among police officers seeking to shield lawless violence and corruption in the ranks. It denotes "an unwritten rule and custom that police will not testify against a fellow officer and that police are expected

> *"The prospect of lawless and unaccountable military units patrolling America should concern people across the political spectrum."*

to help in any cover-up of illegal ac-tion." The blue wall of silence frus-trates citizens and elected officials who are investigating possible abuses of power. Civilian authorities have developed institutions, such as inter-nal affairs boards, that are designed to overcome that wall, but those insti-tutions work only imperfectly, and cover-ups persist.

However much the code of silence obstructs the search for truth in cases of po-lice abuse or negligence, the problem is likely to be far worse if policymakers expand and normalize the use of military policing. People trying to ascertain ex-actly what happened when citizens are killed or seriously injured by soldiers en-gaged in police actions on the home front are likely to run into a "green wall of silence" that will be even more impenetrable than the culture of secrecy in do-mestic police agencies. The prospect of lawless and unaccountable military units patrolling America should concern people across the political spectrum.

Consider, for example, the military's response to the . . . Esequiel Hernandez incident, in which an American high school student was killed by a Marine Corps anti-drug patrol. The Pentagon and other federal agencies repeatedly stonewalled the local civilian investigators, according to Rep. Lamar Smith (R-TX), who conducted a congressional oversight inquiry into the circumstances surrounding the slaying. Two days after the incident, the soldiers involved in the shooting were abruptly transferred from the Texas border to Camp Pendle-ton, California, which obviously hampered the investigation of the incident. Rep. Smith's report notes that "the Marines were treated much differently from most potential suspects in homicide cases, and as a result they benefited from ample opportunities to coordinate and memorize their stories before being sub-jected to professional law enforcement interrogation." Moreover,

> During their criminal investigation, the Texas Rangers and District Attorney Valadez found it difficult to obtain necessary information, documents and testi-mony from the Marines, JTF-6 [Joint Task Force Six, the multiservice military command responsible for counterdrug operations within the United States] and the Border Patrol. The federal agencies failed to provide evidence in response to simple requests, so the District Attorney served subpoenas. The Defense De-partment responded to those subpoenas by asserting federal immunity.

Rep. Smith's investigation concluded that the Defense Department, along with the Justice Department, operated so as to "obstruct and impede state criminal law enforcement in the Hernandez case."

The Pentagon and federal agencies also evaded scrutiny when wrongful death lawsuits were filed in the aftermath of the Waco incident. Lawyers for the victims' families, seeking to determine what role Delta Force soldiers played at Waco, were repeatedly rebuffed with assertions of "national security." For example, when the lawyers sought the names of the soldiers so that they could be interviewed, the government's reply was that only written questions could be submitted and the lawyers would eventually receive anonymous answers from military personnel involved in the incident. Although three Delta operatives were eventually questioned face to face, the Pentagon refused to declassify 5,000 pages of documents the plaintiffs' lawyers believed were instrumental to resolving whether military personnel acted illegally during the standoff. "Public interest demands the public be informed of the military activities undertaken against U.S. citizens on U.S. soil," attorney Jim Brannon wrote to then-secretary of defense William Cohen in protest.

Should use of soldiers to fight the domestic war on terror be expanded, the compelling public interest in government transparency will run up against a powerful legal barrier preventing disclosure of the facts when citizens are killed or injured. That barrier is the so-called state secrets privilege, which allows federal agencies to shield information from civil or criminal courts when "compulsion of the evidence will expose military matters which, in the interest of national security, should not be divulged." Courts accord "utmost deference" to executive assertions of privilege on national security grounds. The judge will generally not examine the documents sought, to ensure that they in fact contain military secrets, lest too much judicial inquiry into the claim of privilege "force disclosure of the thing the privilege was meant to protect." If through a narrow review, a court satisfies itself that military secrets are at issue, "even the most compelling necessity [on the part of the litigant] cannot overcome the claim of privilege."

> *"During the Cold War . . . military leaders occasionally showed appalling judgment about the kinds of clandestine activities that should be carried out domestically."*

There is no parallel claim of "public safety privilege" or the like protecting police methods and tactics from disclosure in cases involving civilian police personnel. That helps to keep the police accountable to the people. In contrast, the more policymakers turn to, and rely on, military personnel to fight crime domestically, the harder it will be for innocent injured parties to attain redress in the courts. Judicial review of the state secrets privilege is so deferential that courts may uphold it even where it is invoked, not to protect genuine national security interests, but to shield wrongdoers from civil or criminal liability. . . .

If broadscale, hands-on policing by the military is adopted and citizens are injured or killed, there is no guarantee that the state secrets privilege will not be abused. . . . Those who seek to bring the military into domestic law enforcement will increase the danger to civilians while at the same time making it difficult or impossible for the public to find out the truth about incidents of "collateral damage."

*Covert Operations on the Home Front?*

Americans have traditionally been uneasy about greater involvement of the military in domestic affairs because military culture mixes uneasily with open, participatory, republican institutions. During the Cold War, for example, military leaders occasionally showed appalling judgment about the kinds of clandestine activities that should be carried out domestically in the name of national security. . . .

Between 1949 and 1969 the military conducted open-air tests of biological agents 80 times, often using American civilians as guinea pigs. The Army used biological agents that were thought to be harmless, dispersing *Serratia* bacteria on Key West and Panama City, Florida, and other areas during the 1950s. In at least one case, however, the experiment appears not to have been harmless. In 1950 the Navy staged a mock biological attack on San Francisco, spraying *Serratia* and *Bacillus* microbes from hoses on an offshore vessel. Soon, 11 men and women checked into Stanford hospital with a rare form of pneumonia caused by exposure to *Serratia marcescens*. One of the men, a retired pipefitter named Edward J. Nevin, died three weeks later. Three decades later, when information about the experiments was revealed, Nevin's surviving family members sued the federal government. A federal appellate court rebuffed the claimants with the following words: "Our review would likely impair the effective administration of government programs believed to be vital to the defense of the United States at the time that they are conducted."

One of the witnesses at the Nevin trial was retired general William Creasy, former commander of the testing program. Creasy was unapologetic about his actions, noting that biological agents are "designed to work against people. You have to test them in the kind of place where people live and work." And in such cases, he argued, it would be "completely impossible to conduct such a test trying to obtain informed consent. I could only conduct such a test without informing the citizens it was being conducted.". . .

> *"The real problem is not that the Posse Comitatus Act is too restrictive but that it is not restrictive enough."*

[This] episode [is] not revived to impugn the integrity of the men and women who serve in America's armed forces or the integrity of their leaders in general. The point is to recall that, on occasion, U.S. military leaders' zeal for victory has inspired actions that are profoundly dangerous to free, democratic institutions. That sort of zeal is a serious danger—and never more so than when the military is engaged, as it is now, in a justified struggle against an evil foe.

## Necessary Reforms

There is ample reason, then, to be cautious about proposals for further domestic military involvement. The burden ought to lie on those who seek to cast aside the time-honored principle that day-to-day protection of civilians on the home front is a civilian responsibility. Thus far, the proponents of such a move have not come close to discharging that burden. The Posse Comitatus Act does not hamstring the government in fighting the war on [terrorist group] Al Qaeda. The act leaves ample room for any appropriate use of the military to aid civilian authorities in protecting Americans from violence. The real problem is not that the Posse Comitatus Act is too restrictive but that it is not restrictive enough. The current law allows far too much military involvement in law enforcement, in areas where it is neither necessary nor appropriate. Congress should close those loopholes.

*Demilitarize the War on Drugs*

For more than 20 years the federal government has steadily ramped up the militarization of the war on drugs. In 1986 [former U.S.] President [Ronald] Reagan signed a National Security Decision Directive that declared the drug trade a "national security threat." Congress, in a series of statutory revisions passed in the 1980s, made the war on drugs a bona fide war, with the Pentagon a central player in the struggle. Though those statutory provisions are commonly referred to as the "drug war exceptions" to the Posse Comitatus Act, they do not grant soldiers arrest authority. However, the provisions do encourage the Pentagon's involvement in surveillance and drug interdiction near the national borders.

> "The militarization of the drug war has led to abuses of power at home and abroad."

In some cases, the loopholes also promote direct involvement by soldiers in law enforcement. In 1990 Congress authorized the secretary of defense to fund National Guard involvement in state-level drug war operations. That funding has encouraged the use of uniformed National Guardsmen in state drug interdiction operations, which range from leveling crack houses to lecturing high school students about the dangers of drug abuse. One state-level anti-drug program, California's Campaign against Marijuana Planting [CAMP] has long been a source of friction between rural residents and law enforcement. Under CAMP, National Guard helicopters buzz California farms and Guardsmen and police officers invade private property looking for marijuana plants during growing season. As one irate Californian described CAMP: "It's like a Boy Scout outing for law enforcement. It is a kick. . . . They get up here, and everyone in the countryside is a criminal."

The Department of Defense spent about a billion dollars fighting the drug war during fiscal year 2002. But that may be about to change. With the shift in priorities after September 11, the Pentagon is prepared to scale back its role in drug interdiction. "The top priorities are now to defend the homeland and to win the war on terrorism," said Andre Hollis, head of the Pentagon's drug war efforts. That is good news. Secretary of Defense Donald Rumsfeld has referred to military efforts to stop drug trafficking as "nonsense." In his

> *"On the home front, there are many tasks for which the military is ill suited, and for which its deployment would be profoundly unwise."*

confirmation hearing in January 2001, Rumsfeld noted that "the drug problem in the United States is overwhelmingly a demand problem and to the extent that demand is there and it is powerful, it is going to find ways to get drugs in this country." Former defense secretary Caspar Weinberger has been equally blunt, arguing that military involvement in the war on drugs has been "detrimental to military readiness and an inappropriate use of the democratic system."

Weinberger's assessment is accurate. The militarization of the drug war has led to abuses of power at home and abroad. Abroad, U.S. Army involvement in the fight against drugs has destabilized Latin American governments and cost scores of innocent lives, including those of Americans. In April 2001 in Peru, for example, a U.S. surveillance plane identified a small Cessna airplane as a possible drug-trafficking vehicle. The Peruvian air force sent up an A-37B Dragonfly attack plane, which fired on the Cessna, killing an innocent American missionary, Roni Bowers, and her infant daughter.

Incredibly, in the midst of drug war hysteria, some legislators have even considered adopting the Peruvian shoot-to-kill policy for drug interdiction inside the continental United States. In 1990 Sen. Mitch McConnell (R-KY) introduced an amendment to the FY90 Pentagon budget that would have allowed the military to shoot down planes suspected of carrying drugs. Though the amendment passed the Senate, it did not become law.

But the loopholes for military participation in the drug war have done damage enough. By putting heavily armed and inappropriately trained Marines on the U.S.-Mexican border, the "drug war" exceptions to the Posse Comitatus Act led inexorably to the death of Esequiel Hernandez. And by encouraging the transfer of military ordnance to civilian peace officers, the drug war exceptions have encouraged a dangerous culture of paramilitarism in police departments.

Given this record, the Pentagon's move to divert resources from drug interdiction is a step in the right direction. But that policy change is not nearly enough. Instead of a sub rosa effort to limit Pentagon involvement in the war on drugs, Congress should repeal the "drug war exceptions" to the Posse Comitatus Act. American military personnel should be focusing on Al Qaeda operatives who are plotting mass murder, not marijuana smugglers.

*Weapons of Mass Destruction*

Military involvement in the drug war has been a tragic mistake. But that does not mean that every use of military resources domestically ought to be reflexively opposed. There are limited areas in which military expertise, equipment, and even personnel can help to secure Americans from terrorist threats—and where such assistance does not present the kind of dangers the Posse Comitatus Act is designed to prevent.

For example, there are 32 Civil Support Teams currently operational in the United States, tasked with responding to suspected chemical, biological, or radiological attacks. The teams are not combat units; rather, they consist of full-time National Guardsmen specially trained in analyzing and responding to threats involving weapons of mass destruction (WMD). The Civil Support Teams operate under the command of their respective state governors, but they can be placed under federal command, if necessary. They bring special expertise and capabilities not normally available to civilian first responders—such as high-tech mobile laboratories that can allow the teams' WMD experts to analyze suspected chemical or biological agents on-site to determine whether the suspected threat is genuine. If it is, the teams advise civilian authorities on the likely consequences and preferred courses of action. Congress has authorized the creation of 23 additional teams.

> *"The disturbing history of Army involvement in domestic affairs strongly cautions against giving the military a freer hand at home."*

The Civil Support Teams are a good example of how military resources can be deployed effectively and appropriately to improve homeland security. Regrettably, most other proposed domestic uses of American military post-9/11 have not met that standard. Public officials, most of them outside the uniformed services, have uncritically accepted the notion that because the military has been so spectacularly effective at its appointed task of waging war, it can be equally effective providing security on the home front. That notion is as simplistic as it is dangerous.

## Conclusion

The U.S. military is the most effective fighting force in human history; it is so effective, in fact, that some federal officials have come to see it as a panacea for domestic security problems posed by the terrorist threat. But on the home front, there are many tasks for which the military is ill suited, and for which its deployment would be profoundly unwise.

The soldier's mission, as soldiers often phrase it, is "killing people and breaking things." In contrast, police officers, ideally, are trained to operate in an environment where constitutional rights apply and to use force only as a last resort. Accordingly, Americans going back at least to the Boston Massacre of 1770 have understood the importance of keeping the military out of domestic law enforcement. That understanding is reflected in the Posse Comitatus Act of 1878, which makes it a criminal offense to use U.S. military personnel as a police force.

In the more than two years since the terror attacks of September 11, 2001, however, there has been a slowly building chorus of calls to amend or weaken the Posse Comitatus Act and give the U.S. military a hands-on role in homeland security. Prominent figures in Congress and the Bush administration have complained that legal barriers to domestic militarization tie their hands in protecting the American people. Of course, where appropriate, we *want* constitutional and statutory constraints to "tie the hands" of the authorities in their pursuit of domestic security. Safety and security are not the only ends of government—liberty is our highest political end. The Posse Comitatus Act is, unfortunately, a weak and porous barrier to military involvement in domestic law enforcement, but it is designed to protect both our liberty and our safety.

Changed circumstances after September 11 provide no compelling reason to weaken the statute further. Moreover, the disturbing history of Army involvement in domestic affairs strongly cautions against giving the military a freer hand at home.

# The USA PATRIOT Act Provides the Security That Protects Americans' Liberty

**by John Ashcroft**

**About the author:** *John Ashcroft is the attorney general of the United States.*

[Since the September 11, 2001, terrorist attacks, there has been] debate about how best to preserve and protect our liberty in the face of a very real terrorist threat.

America has an honored tradition of debate and dissent under the First Amendment. It is an essential piece of our constitutional and cultural fabric. As a former politician, I have heard a few dissents in my time, and even expressed a couple of my own.

The Founders believed debate should enlighten, not just enliven. It should reveal truth, not obscure it. The future of freedom demands that our discourse be based on a solid foundation of facts and a sincere desire for truth. As we consider the direction and destiny of our nation, the friends of freedom must practice for themselves . . . and demand from others . . . a debate informed by fact and directed toward truth.

Take away all the bells and whistles . . . the rhetorical flourishes and occasional vitriol . . . and the current debate about liberty is about the rule of law and the role of law.

## Law Enhances Freedom

The notion that the law can enhance, not diminish, freedom is an old one. [Philosopher] John Locke said the end of law is, quote, ". . . not to abolish or restrain but to preserve and enlarge freedom." [Former U.S. president] George Washington called this, "ordered liberty."

There are some voices in this discussion of how best to preserve freedom that

John Ashcroft, "Prepared Remarks of Attorney General John Ashcroft," Federalist Society National Convention, November 15, 2003.

reject the idea that law can enhance freedom. They think that passage and enforcement of any law is necessarily an infringement of liberty.

Ordered liberty is the reason that we are the most open and the most secure society in the world. Ordered liberty is a guiding principle, not a stumbling block to security.

When the first societies passed and enforced the first laws against murder, theft and rape, the men and women of those societies unquestionably were made more free.

A test of a law, then, is this: does it honor or degrade liberty? Does it enhance or diminish freedom?

> *"The [Patriot] Act uses court-tested safeguards and time-honored ideas to aid the war against terrorism, while protecting the rights and lives of citizens."*

The Founders provided the mechanism to protect our liberties and preserve the safety and security of the Republic: the Constitution. It is a document that safeguards security, but not at the expense of freedom. It celebrates freedom, but not at the expense of security. It protects us *and* our way of life.

Since September 11, 2001, the Department of Justice has fought for, Congress has created, and the judiciary has upheld, legal tools that honor the Constitution . . . legal tools that are making America safer while enhancing American freedom.

It is a compliment to all who worked on the Patriot Act to say that it is not constitutionally innovative. The Act uses court-tested safeguards and time-honored ideas to aid the war against terrorism, while protecting the rights and lives of citizens.

[Former U.S. president James] Madison noted in 1792 that the greatest threat to our liberty was centralized power. Such focused power, he wrote, is liable to abuse. That is why he concluded a distribution of power into separate departments is a first principle of free governments.

The Patriot Act honors Madison's "first principles" . . . giving each branch of government a role in ensuring both the lives and liberties of our citizens are protected. The Patriot Act grants the executive branch critical tools in the war on terrorism. It provides the legislative branch extensive oversight. It honors the judicial branch with court supervision over the Act's most important powers.

## Critical Tools in the War on Terrorism

First, the executive branch.

At the Department of Justice, we are dedicated to detecting, disrupting, and dismantling the networks of terror before they can strike at our nation. In the past two years [since 2001] no major terrorist attack has been perpetrated on our soil.

Consider the bloodshed by terrorism elsewhere in that time:

• Women and children slaughtered in Jerusalem;

- Innocent, young lives snuffed out in Indonesia;
- Saudi citizens savaged in Riyadh;
- Churchgoers in Pakistan murdered by the hands of hate.

We are using the tough tools provided in the USA Patriot Act to defend American lives and liberty from those who have shed blood and decimated lives in other parts of the world.

The Patriot Act does three things:

*First*, it closes the gaping holes in law enforcement's ability to collect vital intelligence information on terrorist enterprises. It allows law enforcement to use proven tactics long used in the fight against organized crime and drug dealers.

*Second*, the Patriot Act updates our anti-terrorism laws to meet the challenges of new technology and new threats.

*Third*, with these critical new investigative tools provided by the Patriot Act, law enforcement can share information and cooperate better with each other. From prosecutors to intelligence agents, the Act allows law enforcement to "connect the dots" and uncover terrorist plots before they are launched.

## How the Act Has Been Used

Here is an example of how we use the Act. Some of you are familiar with the Iyman Faris case. He is a naturalized American citizen who worked as a truck driver out of Columbus, Ohio. Using information sharing allowed under the Patriot Act, law enforcement pieced together Faris's activities:

- How Faris met senior Al Qaeda operatives in a training camp in Afghanistan.
- How he was asked to procure equipment that might cause train derailments and sever suspension system of bridges.
- How he traveled to New York to scout a potential terrorist target.

Faris pleaded guilty on May 1, 2003, and on October 28, he was sentenced under the Patriot Act's tough sentences. He will serve 20 years in prison for providing material support to Al Qaeda and conspiracy for providing the terrorist organization with information about possible U.S. targets for attack.

The Faris case illustrates what the Patriot Act does. One thing the Patriot Act does not do is allow the investigation of individuals, quote, ". . . solely upon the basis of activities protected by the first amendment to the Constitution of the United States."

> *"The Patriot Act provides for close judicial supervision of the executive branch's use of Patriot Act authorities."*

Even if the law did not prohibit it, the Justice Department has neither the time nor the inclination to delve into the reading habits or other First Amendment activities of our citizens.

Despite all the hoopla to the contrary, for example, the Patriot Act . . . which allows for court-approved requests for business records, including library records . . . has never been used to obtain records from a library. Not once.

Senator Dianne Feinstein recently said, quote, "I have never had a single abuse of the Patriot Act reported to me. My staff e-mailed the ACLU [American Civil Liberties Union] and asked them for instances of actual abuses. They e-mailed back and said they had none."

> *"We are protecting the American people while honoring the Constitution and preserving the liberties we hold dear."*

The Patriot Act has enabled us to make quiet, steady progress in the war on terror.

Since September 11, we have dismantled terrorist cells in Detroit, Seattle, Portland, Tampa, Northern Virginia, and Buffalo.

We have disrupted weapons procurement plots in Miami, San Diego, Newark, and Houston.

We have shut down terrorist-affiliated charities in Chicago, Dallas, and Syracuse.

We have brought criminal charges against 286 individuals. We have secured convictions or guilty pleas from 155 people.

Terrorists who are incarcerated, deported or otherwise neutralized threaten fewer American lives. For two years, our citizens have been safe. There have been no major terrorist attacks on our soil. American freedom has been enhanced, not diminished. The Constitution has been honored, not degraded.

## Strict Oversight of the Executive Branch

Second, the role Congress plays.

In six weeks of debate in September and October of 2001, both the House of Representatives and the Senate examined studiously and debated vigorously the merits of the Patriot Act. In the end, both houses supported overwhelmingly its passage.

Congress built into the Patriot Act strict and structured oversight of the Executive Branch. Every six months, the Justice Department provides Congress with reports of its activities under the Patriot Act.

Since September 24, 2001, Justice Department officials, myself included, have testified on the Patriot Act and other homeland security issues more than 115 times. We have responded to hundreds of written and oral questions and provided reams of written responses.

To date [2003], no congressional committee has found any evidence that law enforcement has abused the powers provided by the Patriot Act.

Legislative oversight of the executive branch is critical to "ordered liberty." It ensures that laws and those who administer them respect the rights and liberties of the citizens.

There has not been a major terrorist attack within our borders [since September 11, 2001]. Time and again, Congress has found the Patriot Act to be effective against terrorist threats, and respectful and protective of citizens' liberties. The Constitution has been honored, not degraded.

## Judicial Supervision

Finally, the judiciary.

The Patriot Act provides for close judicial supervision of the executive branch's use of Patriot Act authorities.

The Act allows the government to utilize many long-standing, well-accepted law enforcement tools in the fight against terror. These tools include delayed notification, judicially-supervised searches, and so-called roving wiretaps, which have long been used in combating organized crime and in the war on drugs.

In using these tactics to fight terrorism, the Patriot Act includes an *additional* layer of protection for individual liberty. A federal judge supervises the use of each of these tactics.

Were we to seek an order to request business records, that order would need the approval of a federal judge. Grand jury subpoenas issued for similar requests by police in standard criminal investigations are issued without judicial oversight.

Throughout the Patriot Act, tools provided to fight terrorism require that the same predication be established before a federal judge as with similar tools provided to fight other crime.

In addition, the Patriot Act includes yet another layer of judicial scrutiny by providing a civil remedy in the event of abuse. Section 223 of the Patriot Act allows citizens to seek monetary damages for willful violations of the Patriot Act. This civil remedy serves as a further deterrent against infringement upon individual liberties.

Given our overly litigious society, you are probably wondering how many such civil cases have been filed to date. It is a figure as astronomical as the library searches. Zero.

There is a simple reason for this . . . the Patriot Act has *not* been used to infringe upon individual liberty.

> *"Again and again, Congress has determined and the courts have determined that our citizens' rights have been respected."*

Many of you have heard the hue and cry from critics of the Patriot Act who allege that liberty has been eroded. But more telling is what you have not heard. You have not heard of one single case in which a judge has found an abuse of the Patriot Act because, again, *there have been no abuses.*

It is also important to consider what we have not *seen* . . . no major terrorist attacks on our soil over the past two years.

The Patriot Act's record demonstrates that we are protecting the American people while honoring the Constitution and preserving the liberties we hold dear.

While we are discussing the judiciary, allow me to add one more point. To be at its best, the judiciary requires a full bench. This is not like football or basketball, where the bench consists of reserves who might not see action. The judicial bench, to operate best for the people, must be at full strength.

Let me say this . . . President [George W.] Bush has performed his duties admirably in selecting and nominating highly qualified jurists to serve.

The language in a judge's commission reads, and I quote, "George W. Bush, President of the United States of America . . . to all who shall see this, presents greeting: Know ye that reposing special confidence and trust in the wisdom, uprightness and learning, I have nominated . . . ", you can fill in the blank, with the name Janice Rogers Brown, or Bill Pryor, or Priscilla Owen, or Carolyn Kuhl.

The commission's language may seem anachronistic. The ideals the men and women of the bench must uphold are not: Wisdom. Uprightness. Learning.

The president's nominees personify those noble ideals. They are proven defenders of the rule of law. They should be treated fairly. They deserve to be treated with the dignity that befits the position to which they seek to serve our country and its citizens.

## Preserving Liberty in America

You may think that some of the best of the president's nominees are being treated unfairly. In that case, *you* may want to exercise your right to dissent. The future of freedom and the rule of law depend on citizens informed by fact and directed toward truth.

To be sure, the law depends on the integrity of those who make it, enforce it, and apply it. It depends on the moral courage of lawyers . . . and our citizens . . . to insist on being heard, whether in town hall meetings, county council meetings, or the Senate.

There is nothing more noble than fighting to preserve our God-given rights. Our proven tactics against the terrorist threat are helping to do just that.

For more than two years, we have protected the lives of our citizens here at home. Again and again, Congress has determined and the courts have determined that our citizens' rights have been respected.

Twenty-six months ago, terrorists attacked our nation thinking our liberties were our weakness.

They were wrong. The American people have fulfilled the destiny shaped by our forefathers and founders, and revealed the power of freedom.

Time and again, the spirit of our nation has been renewed and our greatness as a people has been strengthened by our dedication to the cause of liberty, the rule of law, and the primacy and dignity of the individual.

I know we will keep alive these noble aspirations that lie in the hearts of all our fellow citizens, and for which our young men and women are at this moment fighting and making the ultimate sacrifice.

What we are defending is what generations before us fought for and defended: a nation that is a standard, a beacon, to all who desire a land that promises to uphold the best hopes of all mankind. A land of justice. A land of liberty.

# New Surveillance Technologies Can Be Used Without Endangering Civil Liberties

## by Tony Tether

*About the author: Tony Tether is the director of the Defense Advanced Research Projects Agency (DARPA), the central research and development organization for the Department of Defense.*

Some of you might be unfamiliar with DARPA [Defense Advanced Research Project Agency]. We are, essentially, tool makers, sponsoring high-payoff research for the Department of Defense (DoD). This research includes several new software tools that DARPA is developing to assist the DoD in its counterterrorism mission. We are developing new data search and pattern recognition technologies, which have little in common with existing data mining technology, and represent just one element of DARPA's counterterrorism research. Other critical areas of our research include secure collaborative problem solving, structured knowledge discovery, data visualization, and decision making with corporate memory.

It is important to remember that the technologies I will be discussing do not yet exist in their final form, and, no doubt, they will change. Some will succeed and some will fail, and we will learn as we go along. That is the nature of research.

Moreover . . . DARPA is not an agency that will actually use these tools, if they work. Other agencies in the DoD, Federal government, or Congress will decide *if* they want to use the tools we create and *how* they will use them.

When most people talk about "data mining," they are referring to the use of clever statistical techniques to comb through large amounts of data to discover

Tony Tether, testimony before the House Subcommittee on Technology, Information Policy, Intergovernmental Relations and the Census Committee on Government Reform, Washington, DC, May 6, 2003.

162

previously unknown, but useful patterns for building predictive models. This is typically done in the commercial world to better predict customer purchases, understand supply chains, or find fraud—or address any number of other issues where a better understanding of behavior patterns would be helpful. The basic approach is to find statistical correlations as a means of discovering unknown behavior patterns, and then build a predictive model.

At first, one might think that data mining would be very helpful for the most general attempts to find terrorists. It would appear ideal to have software that could automatically discover suspicious, but previously unnoticed patterns in large amounts of data, and which could be used to create models for "connecting-the-dots" and predicting attacks beforehand. However, there are fundamental limitations to expanding today's data mining approaches to the challenge of generally finding and interdicting complex and meticulously well-planned terrorist plots that involve various individuals.

Skeptics believe that such techniques are not feasible because it is simply too difficult to program software to answer the general question, "Is that activity suspicious?" when terrorist plans are so variable and evidence of them is so rare. The results, skeptics say, will contain unmanageable numbers of "false positives"—activities flagged as suspicious that turn out to be innocent.

Beyond the skeptics, critics claim that such an approach must inevitably lead to "fishing expeditions" through massive amounts of personal data and a wholesale invasion of Americans' privacy that yields, basically, nothing in terms of finding terrorists. . . . This approach has been referred to as "mass dataveillance."

In fact, these objections are among the reasons why DARPA is *not* pursuing these techniques, but is developing a different approach in our research.

DARPA is *not* trying to bring about "mass dataveillance," regardless of what you have read or heard. We believe that the existing data mining approach of discovering previously unknown patterns is ill-suited to ferreting out terrorist plans.

The purpose of data mining is, typically, to find previously unknown but useful patterns of behavior in large amounts of data on activities that are narrowly defined and identified, such as credit card usage or book purchases. These behavior patterns relate to individual transactions or classes of transactions (but not to individuals, themselves), again in narrowly defined and identified areas of activity.

> *"DARPA is **not** trying to bring about 'mass dataveillance,' regardless of what you have read or heard."*

The counter-terrorism problem is much more difficult than this. To detect and prevent complex terrorist plots, one must find *extremely rare* instances of patterns across an *extremely wide* variety of activities—and *hidden* relationships among individuals. Data mining is ill-suited to this task because the domains of potentially interesting activity are so much more numerous and complex than purchasing behavior.

Accordingly, we believe that better tools and a different approach are needed for the most general efforts to detect and prevent complicated, well-planned terrorist plots, particularly if we are to prevent them well before they can occur and long before they can reach U.S. shores. Consequently, our research goal to create better counterterrorism tools will not be realized by surveilling huge piles of data representing a collection of broad or ill-defined activities in the hope of discovering previously unknown, unspecified patterns. Instead, we are pursuing an approach of searching for *evidence* of specified patterns.

## Detecting Data That Fits Specified Patterns

Our approach starts with developing attack scenarios, which are used to find specific patterns that could indicate terrorist plans or planning. These scenarios would be based on expert knowledge from previous terrorist attacks, intelligence analysis, new information about terrorist techniques, and/or from wargames in which clever people imagine ways to attack the United States and its deployed forces. The basic approach does not rely on statistical analysis to discover unknown patterns for creating predictive models. Instead, we start with expert knowledge to create scenarios in support of intelligence analysis versus a data mining approach that scans databases for previously unknown correlations.

> *"We believe that better tools and a different approach are needed for the most general efforts to detect and prevent complicated, well-planned terrorist plots."*

The scenarios would then be reduced to a series of questions about which data would provide evidence that such attacks were being planned. We call these scenarios "models," and they are, essentially, hypotheses about terrorist plans. Our goal is to detect data that supports the hypotheses.

Contrast this approach with trying to discover a suspicious pattern without having a model as a starting point—when the pattern is not known in advance. Consider a truck bomb attack, involving a rental truck filled with fertilizer and other materials. Trying to get software to discover such an attack in its planning stages by combing through piles of data—not knowing what it was looking for, but trying to flag "suspicious" activities suggestive of terrorist planning—is unlikely to work. Terrorist activity is far too rare, and spotting it across many different activities by broadly surveilling all available data requires enormous knowledge about the world in order to identify an activity or individual as being "suspicious."

DARPA's approach, instead, focuses a search on detecting evidence for the scenario model or hypothesis, "Are there foreign visitors to the United States who are staying in urban areas, buying large amounts of fertilizer and renting trucks?" Again, the model or hypothesis is not created by meandering through vast amounts of data to discover unknown patterns.

Finding the evidence of a suspicious pattern is, of course, not as simple as I have made it sound. DARPA's counterterrorism research in the areas of data search and pattern recognition is based on two basic types of queries that, as a practical matter, would probably be used in combination.

> *"The focus is* investigative *as opposed to broad surveillance."*

The first type of query is subject-based and begins with an entity, such as people *known* to be suspects. Analysts would start with actual suspects' names and see if there is evidence of links with other suspects or suspicious activities. Current technology and policy pertaining to subject-based queries are fairly well developed and understood. One method of subject-based query with enormous potential is link analysis, which seeks to discover knowledge based on the relationships in data about people, places, things, and events. Link analysis makes it possible to understand the relationships between entities. Properly assembled, these links can provide a picture of higher-level terrorist networks and activities, which, in turn, forms a basis for early indications and warning of a terror attack. Data mining offers little as a tool for investigating such relationships—it creates models by finding statistical correlations within databases without using a starting point, and then applies these models indiscriminately over entire data sets. Link analysis differs because it detects connectedness within rare patterns using known starting points, reducing the search space at the outset.

The second type of query is strictly pattern-based. Analysts would look for evidence of a specified pattern of activity that might be a threat.

It is crucial to note that both types of queries start with either known, identified suspects or known, identified patterns. The focus is *investigative* as opposed to broad surveillance. In both cases, the data that one is looking for is likely to be distributed over a large number of very different databases. Querying distributed, heterogeneous databases is not easy, particularly if we are trying to detect patterns, and we do not know how to do it right now. Pattern query technology is a critical element of our counter-terrorism research; it is rather immature, as are the policies governing its application.

The data that analysts get back in response to a query might not tell them everything. The response may depend on who is doing the analysis and their levels of authorization. This brings me to the second aspect of our approach, detecting in stages.

## Detecting in Stages

We envision that analysts will search for evidence of specified patterns in stages. They will ask questions, get some results, and then refine their results by asking more questions. This is really just common sense, but it is worth highlighting that detecting in stages offers a number of advantages: it uses information more efficiently; it helps limit false positives; it can conform to legal investigative procedures; and it allows privacy protection to be built-in.

Detecting in stages helps deal with the crucial challenge of false positives—that is, mistakenly flagging activities and people as suspicious that are, in fact, innocuous. False positives waste investigative resources and, in the worst cases, can lead to false accusations. Unfortunately, much of the discussion of false positives and counter-terrorism has tended to emphasize technology as the key issue by implicitly assuming a caricature of an investigative process in which a computer program fishes through massive piles of data, officials press the "print" button, and out pop a bunch of arrest warrants. Of course, such an approach is unworkable.

We recognize that false positives must be considered as a product of the whole system. They result from how the data, the technology, the personnel, *and* the investigative procedures interact with each other—they are not solely the result of the application of less-than-perfect technology. DARPA's research seeks to provide analysts with powerful tools, not replace the analysts themselves. Moreover, how we react to positives and what we plan to do with the result is what matters enormously to this issue.

It is also important to remember that all investigations—whether they use databases or not—will yield false positives. Therefore, the relevant question is, "Can we improve our overall ability to detect and prevent terrorist attacks without having an unacceptable false positive rate at the system level?" That is the key challenge to be answered by our research.

No doubt many of the "positives" found during the first queries that analysts make will be false ones. The positives must be further examined to start weeding out the false ones and confirming the real ones, if there are any. This will require analysis in several stages to find independent, additional evidence that either refutes or continues to support the hypothesis represented by the model. Moreover, the level of proof depends, in part, on the nature of the planned response to a positive.

> *"Detecting in stages helps deal with the crucial challenge of false positives—that is, mistakenly flagging activities and people as suspicious that are, in fact, innocuous."*

We do not, for example, arrest everyone who sets off the metal detector when entering this building [the Capitol].

An analogy we sometimes use to illustrate this is submarine detection. In submarine warfare, we do not simply attack something based on first indications that a single sensor has detected an object. We refine the object's identification in stages—from "possible" enemy submarine, to "probable" enemy submarine, to "certainly" an enemy submarine. To be sure of our actions, we confirm the identification over time, using different, independent sensors and sources of information. Our approach to data searching and pattern recognition would proceed in a similar fashion.

Proceeding in stages also means that the entire process can conform to required, legal procedures or steps. In fact, many of these steps exist *precisely* to protect people's rights and weed out false positives. We envision hard-wiring many of the required procedures, permissions, or business rules into the software to ensure that they are actually being followed at each stage of the process.

Let us go back to the truck bomb example. One might incorporate a process called "selective revelation" into data queries. In selective revelation, the amount of information revealed to the analyst depends on who the analyst is, the status of the investigation, and the specific authorization the analyst has received. The analyst's credentials would be automatically included with the query, and the level of information returned would vary accordingly.

Perhaps the result of the truck bomb query I talked about earlier is that 17 people fit the truck bomber pattern, but no personal information about those 17 is revealed. To retrieve additional personal information, a higher level of authorization might be required, based on an independent evaluation (by a court, for example) of the evidence that the analyst is actually "on to" something suspicious.

> *"The American public and their elected officials must have confidence that their liberties will not be violated."*

This suggests that there is a special class of business rules and procedures that could be put into the technology to strengthen privacy protection, so let me turn to that now.

## Built-in Privacy Protection

From the very start of our research, we began looking for ways to build privacy protection into DARPA's approach to detecting terrorists.

We had two motivations. First, we knew that the American public and their elected officials must have confidence that their liberties will not be violated before they would accept this kind of technology.

Second, much of what Federal agencies need to share is *intelligence* data. Historically, agencies have been reluctant to share intelligence data for fear of exposing their sources and methods. Accordingly, protecting privacy and intelligence sources and methods are integral to our approach.

We are putting policies into place that will highlight protecting privacy. As I previously alluded, DARPA does not own or collect any intelligence or law enforcement databases. Our policies will address the development and transition of new tools to the agencies authorized by law to use those databases, reinforcing to everyone the importance of privacy. Moreover, we are fully aware of and intend for the tools to be only used in a manner that complies with the requirements of the Privacy Act, as well as the privacy provisions of the E-Government

Act regarding a Privacy Impact Assessment where such an assessment is required. And we recognize that under Office of Management and Budget policy, major agency information systems employing the technology will have to be justified by a business case that addresses how privacy and security are built into the technology.

To further assist agencies that have collected the data for analysis, we are developing other tools that will help them protect the integrity of the information—even during searches. I previously mentioned "selective revelation" as one way to protect privacy, and we are looking at other related techniques as well, such as separating identity information from transaction information. These separate pieces of information could only be reassembled after the analyst has received the proper authorizations.

Until then, an analyst might only know the basic facts but not the identity of who was involved. We are also looking at ways to anonymize data before it is analyzed. We are evaluating methods for filtering out irrelevant information from the analysis, such as the use of "software agents" that utilize experience-based rules. These software agents would automatically remove data that appears to be irrelevant before the analyst even sees it.

Going beyond privacy protection, we are also looking into building-in indelible audit technology that makes it exceedingly difficult to abuse the data search and pattern recognition technology without the abuse being detected. This audit technology would answer the question, "Who used the system to retrieve what data?". . .

We take privacy issues very seriously. DARPA is, in fact, one of the few Federal agencies sponsoring significant research in the area of privacy protection technologies.

You will often hear talk in this debate about how there are trade-offs—for instance, that we may need to trade less privacy for more security. People may disagree about the proper balance, but DARPA's efforts in developing privacy protection technology are designed, in fact, to improve prospects for providing both improved privacy protection and improved security by the legally relevant agencies

In closing, I would like to emphasize two points:

First, remember that what I have been describing here today is research, and exactly how the technology will work—indeed, *if* it works—will only be shown over time.

Second, because of the high profile of DARPA's research in this area, in February 2003 the Department of Defense announced the establishment of two boards to provide oversight of our Information Awareness programs, including our data search and pattern recognition technologies. These two boards, an internal oversight board and an outside advisory committee, will work with DARPA as we proceed with our research to ensure full compliance with U.S. constitutional law, U.S. statutory law, and American values related to privacy.

# Immigrants Have Been Treated Fairly in Efforts to Increase Homeland Security

## by Michael Chertoff

**About the author:** *Michael Chertoff is the U.S. assistant attorney general in charge of the Justice Department's Criminal Division.*

The country faces a truly extraordinary threat to our national security and the physical safety of the American people, one that has necessitated an extraordinary redefinition of our mission. The President [George W. Bush] and the Attorney General [John Ashcroft] have directed the Justice Department to make prevention of future terrorist attacks our top and overriding priority. We are pursuing that priority aggressively and systematically with a national and international investigation of unprecedented scope, but we are carefully doing so within established constitutional and legal limits.

Since [the September 11, 2001, terrorist attacks], hundreds of federal prosecutors from the Department's Criminal Division and from U.S. Attorney's Offices across the country, along with thousands of federal, state, and local law-enforcement personnel, have been working tirelessly, above and beyond the call of duty, to carry out the investigation. We should all be grateful for their extraordinary efforts. At the same time, we owe a debt of gratitude to Congress for passing the USA PATRIOT Act which makes their work more efficient. In conducting the investigation, we are already taking advantage of the new tools and authorities provided by the USA PATRIOT Act to enhance our investigation. For example, we have, on a number of occasions made use of the new authorities relating to nationwide search warrants, and amendments to . . . that allow us to more efficiently obtain e-mail and other information from internet

Michael Chertoff, testimony before the Senate Committee on the Judiciary, Washington, DC, November 28, 2001.

service providers. Furthermore, we have also relied on the Act to begin expanding our sharing of information with the Intelligence Community.

I know from recent correspondence that the Department has received from members of this Committee that a number of you have raised important questions about some of the investigatory steps we have taken apart from the new legislation. I look forward during the course of this hearing to learning more about your specific concerns and to explaining—to the extent I can without compromising the on-going investigation—the reasons for the investigative approaches we have taken.

In my opening remarks, I would like to briefly outline the nature of the threat we are facing and explain why we believe the threat necessitates the type of investigative response we have been pursuing.

## An Enemy Committed to Killing Americans

The images of September 11th—the planes crashing into the twin towers; the grieving and devastated faces of survivors, the heroism of the police, the fire-fighters and those passengers who were forced into the role of combatants against terrorists—these images and many others have been permanently seared into our collective national consciousness. Each of us has personal recollections of that day where we were when we first heard, what our first thoughts were, what we did to see if our loved ones were safe. It is a day that each of us will always remember in his or her own way.

But as a nation, the overwhelming, brute fact of September 11th is this: This country was wantonly and deceitfully assaulted by an enemy intent on destroying as many innocent lives as possible. Before September 11th, [terrorist leader] Usama Bin Laden and his henchmen wanted to kill thousands of innocent American civilians. On September 11th, they succeeded. Since September 11th, Bin Laden and his co-conspirators have brazenly announced that they will kill more of us. He and his followers actually believe they have a duty to kill Americans. And those are not my words; those are his words.

In a February 1998 directive, Bin Laden ordered his followers "to kill Americans and plunder their money whenever and wherever they find it." Just last month [October 2001], Bin Laden made a video declaring to his supporters in the Al Qaida network: "Bush and [British Prime Minister Tony] Blair . . . don't understand any language but the language of force. Every time they kill us, we will kill them, so the balance of terror can be

> *"This country was wantonly and deceitfully assaulted by an enemy intent on destroying as many innocent lives as possible."*

achieved." He went on: "The battle has been moved inside America, and we shall continue until we win this battle, or die in the cause and meet our maker."

So we have a terrorist organization with thousands of members and followers

# Chapter 4

worldwide, which is fanatically committed to killing Americans on our own soil, through suicide attacks if necessary. And unlike the enemies we have faced in past wars, this is an enemy that comes not openly, but cravenly, in disguise. We know from what we have learned about the 19 hijackers from September 11th and what we know about those responsible for earlier attacks against America that the terrorists in the [terrorist group] Al Qaida network plan their terror years in advance. They are sophisticated, meticulous, and very patient.

## Use of Sleepers

Of particular concern is their use of so-called "sleepers." A sleeper is a committed terrorist sent sometimes years in advance into a possible target location, where he may assume a new identity and lead an outwardly normal lifestyle, while waiting to spring into action to conduct or assist in a terrorist attack. Although it would be inappropriate for me to get into details of the pending investigations, I can give you an illustrative example of a sleeper from one of the 1998 embassy bombing cases.

Mohamed Sadeek Odeh was convicted early this year [2001] for participating in the August 1998 bombing of the U.S. embassy in Nairobi, Kenya. He was sentenced to life imprisonment in October. The evidence at trial established that Odeh was the technical advisor to those who carried out the bombing, having received explosives training at some of Al Qaida's terrorist camps in Afghanistan. One of the

> *"Unlike the enemies we have faced in past wars, this is an enemy that comes not openly, but cravenly, in disguise."*

key pieces of evidence against Odeh was a memo book that had sketches of the vicinity of the embassy and what appeared to be a suggested location for the bomb truck.

The evidence in the case revealed that Odeh became a sworn member of Al Qaida in 1992 in Afghanistan and was subsequently sent to Somalia to train Islamic militants. In 1994, Odeh moved to Mombasa, a coastal town in southeast Kenya. Once in Mombasa, Odeh set up a fishing business with the help of Muhammad Atef, the apparently late military commander of Al Qaida. As part of this business, Odeh was given a large boat, which was to be used to transport fish along the Kenyan coast. According to at least one of the co-defendants, this boat was used to transport Al Qaida members from Kenya to Somalia in 1997 and was otherwise used for jihad [holy war].

Odeh got married in Mombasa in November 1994. Several individuals who later carried out the bombings of our embassies in Nairobi and Dar es Salaam attended the wedding. Between 1994 and 1997, Odeh maintained regular contact with various Al Qaida leaders, including Wadih el Hage and Mustafa Fadhil, two of the leaders of the East African cell of Al Qaida. In 1997, he was sent to Somalia once again to train Islamic militants.

After living in Mombasa for a few years, Odeh moved to Malindi, another coastal town in Kenya, and then later to a small village known as Witu, where he lived until August 1998. At all times, Odeh lived modestly and quietly. For example, in Witu, Odeh lived in a hut, where he had no telephone or other means of communication.

But when the time came to participate in plotting the embassy bombings, Odeh sprang into action. In the Spring and Summer of 1998, he met other Al Qaida members in Kenya and discussed ways to attack the United States. In the days immediately preceding the August 7, 1998, embassy bombings, Odeh met repeatedly with Al Qaida members who participated in the bombing in Mombasa and Nairobi. Hours before the bombing, Odeh suddenly left Kenya, flying to Pakistan during the night of August 6 and through to the early morning of August 7. Odeh was detained at the Karachi airport (due to a bad false passport), and eventually returned to Kenya.

> *"Are we being aggressive and hard-nosed? You bet. In the aftermath of September 11th, how could we not be?"*

Odeh is just one example of how an Al Qaida member was able over time to integrate himself into the local environment in a way that made his terrorist activities much more difficult to detect. Examples of other sleepers can be found in the Millennium bombing case, which involved planned attacks against various U.S. facilities during the millennium, and in the 1993 World Trade Center bombing.

## Necessity of an Aggressive Approach

How can we combat the terrorists' use of sleepers? In many ways it is more difficult than trying to find a needle in a haystack because here the needle is masquerading as a stalk of hay. We could continue as before, and hope we get lucky as we did in the Ressam case.[1] Or, as we are currently doing, we can pursue a comprehensive and systematic investigative approach, informed by all-source intelligence, that aggressively uses every available legally permissible investigative technique to try to identify, disrupt and, if possible incarcerate or deport sleepers and other persons who pose possible threats to our national security.

Without understanding the challenge we face, one cannot understand the need for the measures we have employed. Are we being aggressive and hard-nosed? You bet. In the aftermath of September 11th, how could we not be? Our fundamental duty to protect America and its people requires no less.

Yet it is equally important to emphasize that the detentions, the targeted interviews, and the other aggressive investigative techniques we are currently employing are all legal under the Constitution and applicable federal law as it ex-

---

1. Ahmed Ressam, an Algerian, was convicted in a plot to bomb the Los Angeles International Airport after he was caught crossing the U.S.-Canada border with illegal explosives in 1999.

isted both before and after September 10th. Nobody is being held incommunicado; nobody is being denied the right to an attorney; nobody is being denied due process. As federal prosecutors, we have great discretion under the Constitution and well-established federal law to decide how aggressively to investigate and charge cases. In light of the extraordinary threat facing our country, we have made a decision to exercise our lawful prosecutorial discretion in a way that we believe maximizes our chances of preventing future attacks against America. . . .

Let me now turn briefly to four areas that I know are of particular interest. . . .

## Status of Detainees

First, the number of persons who have been arrested or detained arising out of the investigation into the events of September 11th and the conditions of their detention. . . . [In November 2001] 548 individuals . . . are in custody on INS [former Immigration and Naturalization Service] charges and 55 individuals in custody on federal criminal charges. The Department has charged 104 individuals on federal criminal charges (which includes the 55 in custody), but some of the indictments or complaints are under seal by order of court. Every detention is fully consistent with established constitutional and statutory authority. Every person detained has been charged with a violation of either immigration law or criminal law, or is being lawfully detained on a material witness warrant.

Every one of these individuals has a right to access to counsel. In the criminal cases, and the case of material witnesses, the person is provided a lawyer at government expense if the person cannot afford one. While persons detained on immigration charges do not have a right to lawyers at public expense, INS policy is to provide each person with information about available pro bono representation. Every one of the persons detained, whether on criminal or immigration charges or as a material witness, has the right to make phone calls to family and attorneys. None is being held incommunicado.

The identity of every person who has been arrested on a criminal charge is public. We have not released the names of persons being held on material witness warrants because they are issued under seal as related to grand jury proceedings in different districts. Finally, although the identity of INS detainees is not a secret, we have not compiled a public list of the persons detained on immigration charges, both to protect the privacy of those detained and for legitimate law-enforcement purposes. I emphasize, however, that there is nothing preventing any of these individuals from identifying themselves.

> *"Every one of the persons detained . . . has the right to make phone calls to family and attorneys. None is being held incommunicado."*

Second, law enforcement is seeking to interview just over 5,000 persons voluntarily. These are people who we believe may have information that is helpful to the investigation or to disrupting ongoing terrorist activity. The list of persons we wish to interview was developed as an effort to identify those who might have some information that could be helpful to the investigation. The list was assembled by using common-sense criteria that take into account the manner in which Al Qaida has traditionally operated. So, for example, persons have been identified for interview because they entered the United States with a passport from one of about two dozen countries, where Al Qaida typically recruits. Or people are identified for interviews because they entered the country on particular types of visas that terrorists appear to favor. Importantly, these persons are not suspects, but simply people with whom we want to talk because they may have helpful information.

## Attorney-Client Communications

Third, I would like to discuss the monitoring of attorney-client communications under a Bureau of Prisons regulation promulgated on October 31 [2001]. The Justice Department has amended a 1996 regulation that permits the monitoring of certain communications of inmates who are subject to special administrative measures. This regulation currently applies to only 16 of the 158,000 inmates in the federal system. Under this pre-existing regulation, a very small group of the most dangerous inmates are subject to special administrative measures if the attorney general determines that unrestricted communication with these inmates could result in death or serious bodily harm to others. When that determination has been made, restrictions are put on

*"Military commissions are a traditional way of bringing justice to persons charged with offenses under the laws of armed conflict."*

those inmates' ability to communicate with and contact others. The amendment promulgated on October 31 extends the regulation to permit the monitoring of attorney-client communications for this very small and discrete group of inmates only if the Attorney General makes an additional finding that reasonable suspicion exists that a particular detainee may use communications with attorneys to further or facilitate acts of terrorism.

The regulation provides for important safeguards to protect the attorney-client privilege. First, the attorney and his client will be notified if their communication will be monitored. Second, the team monitoring the communications will have no connection with any ongoing prosecution that involves the client. Third, no privileged information will be retained by the persons monitoring the conversations; the only information retained will be unprivileged threat information. Fourth, absent an imminent emergency, the government will have to seek court approval before any information is used for any purpose from those conversations. And fifth, no information that is protected by the attorney-client privilege may be used for prosecution. This regulation accords with established constitutional and legal authority. Courts have long recognized that a client's communications are not privileged if they are in furtherance of criminal activity. And the Supreme Court has expressly recognized that the government may, consistent with the right to counsel, monitor attorney-client communications if there is a legitimate law-enforcement reason for doing so and if privileged communications are not used against the defendant. Both those conditions are met here.

## Military Commissions

Finally, I'd like to briefly mention military commissions. We are at war: Our homeland was suddenly and deliberately attacked from abroad on September 11, resulting in the intentional murder of thousands of unarmed civilians. Usama Bin Laden has candidly said he intends to continue his attacks as long as he and his organization are able. In view of such circumstances, military commissions are a traditional way of bringing justice to persons charged with offenses under the laws of armed conflict. The Supreme Court has repeatedly upheld the use of such commissions.

The use of such commissions is not only legally proper; there may be sound policy reasons to employ it in individual cases. Proceedings before military commissions may be needed to safeguard classified information at the trial of particular members of Al Qaida. Also, military commissions are equipped to deal with the significant security concerns that can arise from a trial of the terrorists. We are all aware that trying terrorists in our cities could place judges and juries—and, indeed, the cities themselves—at risk. Finally, bear in mind that the attacks of September 11 were launched by a foreign power and killed thousands of innocent people. These were war crimes, in addition to domestic crimes. There is nothing inappropriate or unfair in trying war crimes as they often have been tried—before military commissions.

The President's order represents just the first step in invoking this traditional power to prosecute those who violate the well-settled law of war. The order assigns the Department of Defense primary responsibility for developing the specific procedures to be used. Because that process is still ongoing, it is simply too early to discuss the specific details of how any such commissions would operate. However, certain protections are already built into the order, which can be expanded upon by regulations promulgated by the Defense Department. The order specifies that all persons will have the right to an attorney. The order specifies that the proceedings must allow a full and fair trial of the charges. In addition, the order requires humane conditions of pretrial detention, including the right to free exercise of religion during detention. And notably, the President will himself make the determination whether trial by commission will be appropriate in an individual case.

# Chronology

## 1993

**February 26:** A truck bomb at the World Trade Center in New York City kills six people and wounds one thousand.

## 1995

**April 19:** A truck bomb at the federal building in Oklahoma City, Oklahoma, kills 168 people.

## 2001

**September 11:** Arab terrorists hijack four U.S. airliners, crashing two into the World Trade Center, one into the Pentagon, and one into a field in western Pennsylvania, killing about three thousand people.

**September 13:** Osama bin Laden, leader of the terrorist group al Qaeda, is named as the prime suspect in the September 11 attacks.

**October–November:** Letters containing anthrax are sent to offices in several U.S. cities, killing five and sickening seventeen.

**October 7:** The United States launches Operation Enduring Freedom to remove the Taliban regime in Afghanistan, which is believed to be harboring al Qaeda.

**October 8:** Pennsylvania governor Tom Ridge is appointed as homeland security adviser.

**October 26:** The Uniting and Strengthening America by Providing Appropriate Tools Required to Intercept and Obstruct Terrorism Act (USA PATRIOT Act) is passed. This law provides for indefinite imprisonment without trial of non-U.S. citizens determined to be a threat to national security; it allows a wiretap to be issued against an individual instead of against a specific telephone number; it permits law enforcement agencies to obtain a warrant and search a residence without immediately informing the occupants; it also allows intelligence gathering at religious events.

**November:** President George W. Bush signs an executive order on allowing military tribunals against any foreigners suspected of having connections to terrorist acts or planned acts on the United States.

**November 19:** The president signs the Aviation and Transportation Security Act, creating the Transportation Security Administration (TSA).

## 2002

**February:** The Total Information Awarness (TIA) project is announced. The project is designed to collect, index, and consolidate all available information on Americans in a central repository for perusal by the U.S. government. Due to widespread protest, the program is suspended in late 2003.

**June:** President Bush proposes consolidating twenty-two government agencies into a new Department of Homeland Security.

**September:** The Justice Department launches a special registration procedure for certain male noncitizens in the United States, requiring them to register in person at immigration service offices; Ramzi Binalshibh, believed to be one of the planners of the September 11 attacks, is captured in Pakistan.

**October 4:** Six suspected members of the al Qaeda terrorist network operating near Buffalo, New York, are indicted.

**November:** President Bush signs the Homeland Security Act of 2002, establishing the Department of Homeland Security.

## 2003

**March 1:** Khalid Sheikh Mohammed, the alleged architect of the September 11 attacks, is captured in Pakistan.

**March 17:** The Homeland Security Department commences Operation Liberty Shield, an increase in protective measures to defend the homeland.

**March 19:** The United States launches Operation Iraqi Freedom to end the regime of Iraqi president Saddam Hussein and its support of terrorism.

**April 2:** The U.S. House of Representatives passes the $79 billion Wartime Supplemental Appropriations bill to provide crucial funding for Operation Iraqi Freedom.

**April 15:** President Bush declares an end to major combat operations in Iraq.

**May 1:** The Terrorist Threat Integration Center, created to integrate intelligence on terrorism collected at home and abroad, begins operations.

**June 24:** The first ever Homeland Security Appropriations bill is approved, providing $29.4 billion to bolster homeland security.

**November 26:** Mohammed Hamdi al Ahdal, a top al Qaeda leader in Yemen, is captured.

**December 13:** Saddam Hussein is captured by U.S. forces in Iraq.

## 2004

**March 1:** The Department of Homeland Security celebrates its one-year anniversary.

# Organizations to Contact

The editors have compiled the following list of organizations concerned with the issues debated in this book. The descriptions are derived from materials provided by the organizations. All have publications or information available for interested readers. The list was compiled on the date of publication of the present volume; the information provided here may change. Be aware that many organizations take several weeks or longer to respond to inquiries, so allow as much time as possible.

**American Civil Liberties Union (ACLU)**
125 Broad St., 18th Floor, New York, NY 10004
(212) 549-2500
e-mail: aclu@aclu.org • Web site: www.aclu.org

The American Civil Liberties Union is a national organization that works to defend Americans' civil rights guaranteed by the U.S. Constitution, arguing that measures to protect national security should not compromise fundamental civil liberties. It publishes and distributes policy statements, pamphlets, and press releases, including *Civil Liberties After 9-11: The ACLU Defends Freedom* and *Bigger Monster, Weaker Chains: The Growth of an American Surveillance Society.*

**American Enterprise Institute (AEI)**
1150 Seventeenth St. NW, Washington, DC 20036
(202) 862-5800 • fax: (202) 862-7177
Web site: www.aei.org

The American Enterprise Institute is a scholarly research institute that is dedicated to preserving limited government, private enterprise, and a strong foreign policy and national defense. It publishes books, including *Study of Revenge: The First World Trade Center Attack* and *Saddam Hussein's War Against America.* Articles about terrorism and homeland security can be found in its magazine, *American Enterprise*, and on its Web site.

**ANSER Institute for Homeland Security**
e-mail: homelandsecurity@anser.org • Web site: www.homelandsecurity.org

The institute is a nonprofit, nonpartisan think tank that works to educate the public about homeland security issues. The institute's Web site contains fact sheets, reports, legislation, and government documents and statistics on homeland security issues. It also publishes the *Journal of Homeland Security* and a weekly newsletter.

**Arab American Institute (AAI)**
1600 K St. NW, Suite 601, Washington, DC 20006
(202) 429-9210
Web site: www.aaiusa.org

AAI is a nonprofit organization committed to the civic and political empowerment of Americans of Arab descent. The institute opposes ethnic profiling and the restriction of immigrants' civil liberties in the name of homeland security. It provides policy, research, and public affairs services to support a broad range of community activities. It publishes a quarterly newsletter called *Issues*, a weekly bulletin called *Countdown*, and the report *Healing the Nation: The Arab American Experience After September 11*.

## Brookings Institution
1775 Massachusetts Ave. NW, Washington, DC 20036
(202) 797-6000 • fax: (202) 797-6004
e-mail: brookinfo@brook.edu • Web site: www.brookings.org

The institution, founded in 1927, is a think tank that conducts research and education in foreign policy, economics, government, and the social sciences. In 2001 it began America's Response to Terrorism, a project that provides briefings and analysis to the public and which is featured on the center's Web site. Other publications include the quarterly *Brookings Review*, periodic *Policy Briefs*, and books including *Protecting the American Homeland: One Year On*.

## Cato Institute
1000 Massachusetts Ave. NW, Washington, DC 2001-5403
(202) 842-0200 • fax: (202) 842-3490
e-mail: cato@cato.org • Web site: www.cato.org

The Cato Institute is a nonpartisan public policy research foundation dedicated to limiting the role of government and protecting individual liberties. It publishes the quarterly magazine *Regulation*, the bimonthly *Cato Policy Report*, and numerous policy papers and articles. Works on homeland security include "Breaking the Vicious Cycle: Preserving Our Liberties While Fighting Terrorism" and "How Should the U.S. Respond to Terrorism?"

## Center for Constitutional Rights (CCR)
666 Broadway, 7th Floor, New York 10012
(212) 614-6464 • fax: (212) 614-6499
Web site: www.ccr-ny.org

CCR is a nonprofit legal and educational organization dedicated to protecting and advancing the rights guaranteed by the U.S. Constitution and the Universal Declaration of Human Rights. The organization uses litigation to empower minority and poor communities and to strengthen the broader movement for constitutional and human rights. It opposes the government's curtailment of civil liberties since the September 11, 2001, terrorist attacks. CCR publishes books, pamphlets, fact sheets, and reports, such as *The State of Civil Liberties: One Year Later*.

## Center for Defense Information
1779 Massachusetts Ave. NW, Suite 615, Washington, DC 20036
(202) 332-0600 • fax: (202) 462-4559
e-mail: info@cdi.org • Web site: www.cdi.org

The Center for Defense Information is a nonpartisan, nonprofit organization that researches all aspects of global security. It seeks to educate the public and policymakers about issues such as weapons systems, security policy, and defense budgeting. It publishes the monthly publication *Defense Monitor* and the studies "Homeland Security: A Competitive Strategies Approach" and "Reforging the Sword."

## Center for Democracy and Technology (CDT)
1634 Eye St. NW, Suite 1100, Washington, DC 20006
(202) 637-9800
Web site: www.cdt.org

CDT's mission is to develop public policy solutions that advance constitutional civil liberties and democratic values in the new computer and communications media. With regard to homeland security, CDT maintains that surrendering freedom will not purchase security and that open communications networks are a positive force in the fight against violence and intolerance. It opposes measures to increase government surveillance, such as in some of the provisions of the USA PATRIOT Act. The CDT Web site provides numerous fact sheets and news updates on government electronic surveillance, wiretapping, and cybersecurity.

### Center for Immigration Studies
1522 K St. NW, Suite 820, Washington, DC 20005
(202) 466-8185 • fax: (202) 466-8076
e-mail: center@cis.org • Web site: www.cis.org

The Center for Immigration Studies is the nation's only think tank dedicated to research and analysis of the economic, social, and demographic impacts of immigration on the United States. An independent, nonpartisan, nonprofit research organization founded in 1985, the center aims to expand public support for an immigration policy that is both pro-immigrant and low-immigration. It believes that restricting immigration should be a top priority in the government's homeland security strategy. Among its publications are the papers "Visas for Terrorists: What Went Wrong?" "The Open Door: How Militant Islamic Terrorists Entered and Remained in the United States," and "The USA PATRIOT Act of 2001: A Summary of the Anti-Terrorism Law's Immigration-Related Provisions."

### Central Intelligence Agency (CIA)
Office of Public Affairs, Washington, DC 20505
(703) 482-0623 • fax: (703) 482-1739
Web site: www.cia.gov

The CIA was created in 1947 with the signing of the National Security Act (NSA) by President Harry S. Truman. The NSA charged the Director of Central Intelligence (DCI) with coordinating the nation's intelligence activities and correlating, evaluating, and disseminating intelligence that affects national security. The CIA is an independent agency, responsible to the president through the DCI, and accountable to the American people through the Intelligence Oversight Committee of the U.S. Congress. Publications, including *National Strategy for Combating Terrorism* and *Factbook on Intelligence*, are available on its Web site.

### Chemical and Biological Arms Control Institute (CBACI)
1747 Pennsylvania Ave. NW, 7th Floor, Washington, DC 20006
(202) 296-3550 • fax: (202) 296-3574
e-mail: cbaci@cbaci.org • Web site: www.cbaci.org

CBACI is a nonprofit corporation that promotes arms control and nonproliferation, with particular focus on the elimination of chemical and biological weapons. It fosters this goal by drawing on an extensive international network to provide an innovative program of research, analysis, technical support, and education. Among the institute's publications is the bimonthly report *Dispatch* and the reports "Bioterrorism in the United States: Threat, Preparedness, and Response" and "Contagion and Conflict: Health as a Global Security Challenge."

### Department of Homeland Security (DHS)
Washington, DC 20528
Web site: www.dhs.gov

The DHS, created in March 2003, merges twenty-two previously disparate domestic agencies into one department to protect the nation against threats to the homeland.

DHS's priority is to protect the nation against terrorist attacks. Component agencies analyze threats and intelligence, guard America's borders and airports, protect critical infrastructure, and coordinate the U.S. response to future emergencies. The DHS Web site offers a wide variety of information on homeland security, including press releases, speeches and testimony, and reports on topics such as airport security, weapons of mass destruction, planning for and responding to emergencies, and border control.

### Electronic Privacy Information Center (EPIC)
1718 Connecticut Ave. NW, Suite 200, Washington, DC 20009
(202) 483-1140
Web site: www.epic.org

EPIC is a public interest research center that works to focus public attention on emerging civil liberties issues and to protect privacy, the First Amendment, and constitutional values. It supports privacy-protection legislation and provides the *EPIC Alert* newsletter and the Privacy Law Sourcebook as well as the report "Your Papers, Please: From State Drivers License to a National Identification System."

### Federal Aviation Administration (FAA)
800 Independence Ave. SW, Washington, DC 20591
(800) 322-7873 • fax: (202) 267-3484
Web site: www.faa.gov

The Federal Aviation Administration is the component of the U.S. Department of Transportation whose primary responsibility is the safety of civil aviation. The FAA's major functions include regulating civil aviation to promote safety and fulfill the requirements of national defense. Among its publications are *Technology Against Terrorism; Air Piracy, Airport Security, and International Terrorism: Winning the War Against Hijackers*; and *Security Tips for Air Travelers.*

### Federal Bureau of Investigation (FBI)
935 Pennsylvania Ave. NW, Room 7972, Washington, DC 20535
(202) 324-3000
Web site: www.fbi.gov

The FBI, the principle investigative arm of the U.S. Department of Justice, evolved from an unnamed force of special agents formed on July 26, 1909. It has the authority and responsibility to investigate specific crimes assigned to it. The FBI is also authorized to provide other law enforcement agencies with cooperative services, such as fingerprint identification, laboratory examinations, and police training. The mission of the FBI is to uphold the law through the investigation of violations of federal criminal law; to protect the United States from foreign intelligence and terrorist activities; to provide leadership and law enforcement assistance to federal, state, local, and international agencies; and to perform these responsibilities in a manner that is responsive to the needs of the public and is faithful to the Constitution of the United States. Press releases, congressional statements, and major speeches on issues concerning homeland security are available on the agency's Web site.

### Heritage Foundation
214 Massachusetts Ave. NE, Washington, DC 20002
(202) 546-4400 • fax: (202) 546-8328
e-mail: info@heritage.org • Web site: www.heritage.org

The Heritage Foundation is a conservative public-policy research institute. Its mission is to formulate and promote conservative public policies based on the principles of free enterprise, limited government, individual freedom, and a strong national defense. Heritage research and analysis on homeland security issues includes the papers "Principles for Safeguarding Civil Liberties in an Age of Terrorism" and "Improving Efficiency and Reducing Costs in the Department of Homeland Security."

**Independence Institute**
14142 Denver West Pkwy., Suite 185, Golden, CO 80401
(303) 279-6536
Web site: www.i2i.org

The institute is established upon the eternal truths of the Declaration of Independence. It is a nonpartisan, nonprofit public policy research organization dedicated to providing timely information to concerned citizens, government officials, and public opinion leaders. It emphasizes private sector and community-based solutions to social issues. Institute papers on homeland security include "The Expanding Surveillance States: Facial Recognition" and "Just Say No to National ID Cards."

**National Immigration Forum (NIF)**
220 I St. NE, Washington, DC 20002
(202) 544-0004
Web site: www.immigrationforum.org

The purpose of the NIF is to embrace and uphold America's tradition as a nation of immigrants. The forum advocates and builds public support for public policies that welcome immigrants and refugees and that are fair and supportive to newcomers to the United States. The NIF Web site offers a special section on immigration in the wake of the September 11, 2001, terrorist attacks, which includes the reports "Immigrants in the Crosshairs: Diverse Voices Speak Out Against the Backlash" and "The Way Forward on Immigration Policy."

**National Security Agency**
9800 Savage Rd., Ft. Meade, MD 20755
(301) 688-6524
Web site: www.nsa.gov

The National Security Agency coordinates, directs, and performs activities such as designing cipher systems, which protect American information systems and produce foreign intelligence information. It is the largest employer of mathematicians in the United States and also hires the nation's best code makers and code breakers. Speeches, briefings, and reports are available on its Web site.

**United States Department of State, Counterterrorism Office**
Office of Public Affairs, Room 2507
2201 C St. NW, Washington, DC 20520
(202) 647-4000
e-mail: secretary@state.gov • Web site: www.state.gov/s/ct

The Office of Public Affairs works to develop and implement American counterterrorism strategy and to improve cooperation with foreign governments. Articles and speeches by government officials are available at its Web site.

# Bibliography

**Books**

Peter Andreas and
Thomas J. Biersteker,
eds.
*The Rebordering of North America: Integration and Exclusion in a New Security Context.* New York: Routledge, 2003.

Lee C. Bollinger and
Geoffrey R. Stone, eds.
*Eternally Vigilant: Free Speech in the Modern Era.* Chicago: University of Chicago Press, 2002.

Kurt M. Campbell and
Michelle A. Flourney
*To Prevail: An American Strategy for the Campaign Against Terrorism.* Washington, DC: Center for Strategic and International Studies, 2001.

Nancy Chang et al.
*Silencing Political Dissent: How Post–September 11 Anti-Terrorism Measures Threaten Our Civil Liberties.* New York: Seven Stories Press, 2002.

Eric Cody et al.
*Chemical and Biological Warfare: A Comprehensive Guide for the Concerned Citizen.* New York: Copernicus, 2002.

David Cole and
James X. Dempsey
*Terrorism and the Constitution: Sacrificing Civil Liberties in the Name of National Security.* New York: New Press, 2002.

Anthony H.
Cordesman
*Terrorism, Asymmetric Warfare, and Weapons of Mass Destruction: Defending the U.S. Homeland.* Westport, CT: Praeger, 2002.

Lynn E. Davis
*Organizing for Homeland Security.* Santa Monica, CA: Rand, 2002.

Alan M. Dershowitz
*Shouting Fire: Civil Liberties in a Turbulent Age.* Boston: Little, Brown, 2002.

Steven Emerson
*American Jihad: The Terrorists Living Among Us.* New York: Free Press, 2002.

William H. Frist
*When Every Moment Counts: What You Need to Know About Bioterrorism from the Senate's Only Doctor.* Lanham, MD: Rowman & Littlefield, 2002.

Simson Garfinkel
*Database Nation: The Death of Privacy in the 21st Century.* Cambridge, MA: O'Reilly, 2001.

| Kathlyn Gay | *Silent Death: The Threat of Chemical and Biological Terrorism.* Brookfield, CT: Twenty-First Century Books, 2001. |
| --- | --- |
| Ted Gottfried | *Homeland Security vs. Constitution Rights.* Brookfield, CT: Twenty-First Century Books, 2003. |
| Stanley Hauerwas and Frank Lentricchia, eds. | *Dissent from the Homeland: Essays After September 11.* Durham, NC: Duke University Press, 2002. |
| Katrina vanden Heuvel, ed. | *A Just Response: The Nation on Terrorism, Democracy, and September 11.* New York: Thunder's Mouth, 2002. |
| Jessica Kornbluth and Jessica Papin, eds. | *Because We Are Americans: What We Discovered on September 11, 2001.* New York: Warner, 2001. |
| Michael A. Ledeen | *The War Against the Terror Masters.* New York: St. Martin's, 2002. |
| Michael E. O'Hanlon et al. | *Protecting the American Homeland: A Preliminary Analysis.* Washington, DC: Brookings Institution, 2002. |
| John V. Parachini, Lynn E. Davis, and Timothy Liston | *Homeland Security: A Compendium of Public and Private Organizations' Policy Recommendations.* Santa Monica, CA: Rand, 2003. |
| Daniel Pipes | *Militant Islam Reaches America.* New York: W.W. Norton, 2002. |
| Marcus J. Ranum | *The Myth of Homeland Security.* Indianapolis, IN: John Wiley, 2003. |
| Phil Scranton, ed. | *Beyond September 11: An Anthology of Dissent.* London: Pluto, 2002. |
| Paul Wilkinson | *Terrorism Versus Democracy: The Liberal State Response.* London: Frank Cass, 2001. |

**Periodicals**

| William J. Bicknell and Kenneth D. Bloem | "Smallpox and Bioterrorism: Why the Plan to Protect the Nation Is Stalled and What to Do," *Cato Briefing Paper*, September 5, 2003. |
| --- | --- |
| Robert Block and Gary Fields | "Is Military Creeping into Domestic Law Enforcement?" *Wall Street Journal*, March 9, 2004. |
| Steven Brill | "The Biggest Hole in the Net: One Day Soon, America May Be Rocked by a Suicide Bomber. We Have No System to Deal With That Eventuality. Why the Debate over a National ID Card Is Long Overdue," *Newsweek*, December 30, 2002. |
| Allan C. Brownfield | "Ramblings," *St. Croix Review*, February 2003. |
| Charlotte Bunch | "Whose Security?" *Nation*, September 23, 2002. |

# *Bibliography*

| Sheila R. Cherry | "Reorganization Brings Tsunami of Change: Critics Wonder Whether All the State and Federal Money Being Spent on Homeland Security Will Make the Nation Any Safer than Enforcing the Laws Already on the Books," *Insight on the News*, March 18, 2003. |
| --- | --- |
| Mary H. Cooper | "Weapons of Mass Destruction," *CQ Researcher*, March 2, 2002. |
| Robert Cottrol | "Homeland Security: Restoring Civic Virtue," *American Enterprise*, January/February 2003. |
| Ivo H. Daalder and I.M. Destler | "Behind America's Front Lines: Organizing to Protect the Homeland," *Brookings Review*, Summer 2002. |
| *Economist* | "A Hole in the Middle: Homeland Security," September 7, 2002. |
| *Economist* | "America the Unready: Homeland Security," December 22, 2001. |
| Nick Gillespie | "Freedom for Safety: An Old Trade—and a Useless One," *Reason*, October 2002. |
| Scott Gottlieb | "Wake Up and Smell the Bio Threat," *American Enterprise*, January/February 2003. |
| Jesse Helms | "Emerging Threats to United States National Security," *Imprimis*, January 2002. |
| Nat Hentoff | "Bush-Ashcroft vs. Homeland Security," *Village Voice*, April 23–29, 2003. |
| Edward S. Herman | "George Bush Versus U.S. National Security," *Z Magazine*, October 2003. |
| Michael Hirsh | "How Much Safer Are We? Despite Progress, America Remains Vulnerable Around the Edges," *Newsweek*, September 15, 2003. |
| Daniel Kanstroom | "'Unlawful Combatants' in the United States: Drawing the Fine Line Between Law and War," *Human Rights*, Winter 2003. |
| Donald Kerwin | "The Catholic Tradition on Migrants Amid Heightened Security Concerns," *Origins*, August 28, 2003. |
| James Andrew Lewis | "Three Reforms to Make America More Secure—Intelligence, Government Organization, Law, and Technology Must Change to Build U.S. Security," *World & I*, October 2002. |
| John R. Lott Jr. | "Arming of Pilots Is Way Overdue," *Los Angeles Times*, April 14, 2003. |
| Timothy Lynch | "Breaking the Vicious Cycle: Preserving Our Liberties While Fighting Terrorism," *Policy Analysis*, June 26, 2002. |
| Timothy Lynch | "More Surveillance Equals Less Liberty: Patriot Act Reduces Privacy, Undercuts Judicial Review," *The Hill*, September 10, 2003. |

| Kate Martin | "Intelligence, Terrorism, and Civil Liberties," *Human Rights*, Winter 2002. |
| Elisa Massimino | "Alien Justice: What's Wrong with Military Trials of Terrorist Suspects?" *Human Rights*, Winter 2003. |
| Bill McIntyre | "Crush the Terrorists . . . Not the Bill of Rights," *Shield*, Spring 2002. |
| Anna Mulrine and Nancy Bentrup | "The Power of Secrets," *U.S. News & World Report*, January 27, 2003. |
| John Podesta | "USA Patriot Act: The Good, the Bad, and the Sunset," *Human Rights*, Winter 2002. |
| Romesh Ratnesar | "The State of Our Defense," *Time*, February 24, 2003. |
| Karina Rollins | "No Compromises: Why We're Going to Lose the War on Terrorism . . . and How We Could Win," *American Enterprise*, January/February 2003. |
| Michael Scardaville | "Public Health and National Security Planning: The Case for Voluntary Smallpox Vaccination," *Backgrounder*, December 6, 2002. |
| Abraham D. Sofaer and Paul R. Williams | "Doing Justice During Wartime: Why Military Tribunals Make Sense," *Policy Review*, February 2002. |
| Gene Stephens | "Can We Be Both Safe and Free? The Dilemma Terrorism Creates," *USA Today*, January 2003. |
| Jessica Stern | "The Protean Enemy," *Foreign Affairs*, July/August 2003. |
| Joseph Summerill | "Homeland Security: The Challenge of Finding Jail Space," *American Jails*, January/February 2003. |
| Eric R. Taylor | "The New Homeland Security Apparatus: Impeding the Fight Against Agile Terrorists," *Foreign Policy Briefing*, June 26, 2002. |
| Stuart Taylor Jr. | "How Civil-Libertarian Hysteria May Endanger Us All," *National Journal*, February 22, 2003. |
| Jonathan Turley | "WMD in Our Own Backyard," *Los Angeles Times*, January 18, 2004. |
| Douglas Valentine | "Homeland Security: Where the Phoenix Came Home to Roost," *CovertAction Quarterly*, Fall 2003. |
| Patricia J. Williams | "Loose Lips and Other Slips," *Nation*, March 17, 2003. |
| Philip Zelikow | "The Transformation of National Security," *National Interest*, Spring 2003. |

# Index

Abraham, Spencer, 55
Air Line Pilots Association (ALPA), 109,
    110
air travel
  arming pilots for
    arguments against, 109–10
    arguments for, 106–108
    cultural constraints and, 119
    is not experimental, 106
    lack of support by pilots for, 110
    need for, 104–105, 108
    resistance to, 105–106
  costs associated with security of, 105
  failure of security in, 59
  increased security in, 20
  not addressing proper problems with, 62
  U.S. Department of Homeland Security
    and, 83
  vulnerabilities in, 18
Anaya, Lillian, 55
Anti-Terrorism Intelligence Tools
    Improvement Act (2003), 134
Antiterrorism Tools Enhancement Act
    (2003), 134
Ashcroft, John, 14, 156
Atef, Mohamed, 38
Aviation and Transportation Security Act,
    122–23

Beers, Rand, 18
bin Laden, Osama, 38–39
biometrics, 34–36, 63–64, 97, 137
biotechnology companies, 44
bioterrorism
  gas masks for, 32
  inadequacy of current system for dealing
    with, 45–46
  infectious diseases and, 45
  is unlikely, 28
  preparation for, 32–33
    lack of, 43
  reasons for fearing, 43–45
  smallpox and, 30–32
  steps for improving federal response to,

    46–49
  U.S. Department of Homeland Security's
    success with, 84
  water safety and, 33
Blix, Hans, 57
Boxer, Barbara, 18
Brown, Michael, 21–22
Bureau of Immigration and Customs
    Enforcement, 134
Bursky, David, 111
Bush, George W., 30, 81
  criticism of war in Iraq and, 17–18
  on homeland security, 19–20
  on preemptive strikes, 102
  vigilantism against immigrants and, 143

California's Campaign Against Marijuana
    Planting (CAMP), 152
Carafano, James Jay, 43
Card, Andrew, 123
Carter, Jimmy, 130
Centers for Disease Control and Prevention
    (CDC), 22, 30
Central Intelligence Agency (CIA). See
    intelligence agencies
chemical attacks, 28
  see also bioterrorism
chemical-plant security, 20
Cheney, Richard, 12–13
Chertoff, Michael, 169
ChoicePoint, Inc., 116
Cilluffo, Frank, 20
civil liberties
  balance between homeland security and,
    14
  information technology and, 123
  law enhances, 156–57
  mistreatment of immigrants and, 140–43
  national ID cards and, 111–12, 114
  new surveillance technologies and,
    137–39
  racial/ethnic profiling threatens, 129
  treatment of detainees does not violate,
    173–75

USA PATRIOT Act protects, 157–58
USA PATRIOT Act violates, 130–31,
134–36
con, 160
U.S. Department of Homeland Security
protects, 71
Clarke, Richard A., 22
Cockburn, Alexander, 55
Cole, David, 13, 14
Collins, Susan, 19, 21
color-coded terrorist-alert system. *See*
Homeland Security Advisory System
computers
federal databases and, 65–66
improving security on, 67–68
networked, not secure, 65
Congressional Research Service (CRS), 19
costs
for air travel security, 20
for arming airline pilots, 105
for rescue personnel training, 16
for U.S. Department of Homeland
Security, 92–93
*see also* federal funding
Cottrol, Robert, 117
credit-card numbers, 66
Crews, Clyde Wayne, Jr., 137

data-mining technologies, 137, 162–65
Davis, Tom, 64
death penalty, 134
DeFazio, Peter, 105
Defense Advanced Projects Administration
(DARPA), 123, 162–68
Democrats
on chemical-plant security, 20
critique of war on terror by, 17
on federal homeland security spending, 24
on funding for homeland security grants,
22
Department of Defense (DOD)
bioterrorist threat and, 45, 47, 48
bureaucracy and, 91, 92
National Guard and, 118
war on drugs and, 153
Department of Health and Human Services
(HHS), 45, 47, 48, 49
Department of Homeland Security. *See*
U.S. Department of Homeland Security
Department of Veterans Affairs (VA), 45, 47
Dershowitz, Alan, 114
Dodson, Dan, 133
Dority, Barbara, 130

Eberhart, Ralph E., 145, 148

Eggers, Andrew, 121
Eland, Ivan, 90
Ellison, Larry, 61, 65, 114
Ellison, Willie, 105
El Shukrijumah, Adnan G., 41
emergency personnel. *See* rescue personnel
Engler, Mark, 140
Environmental Protection Agency (EPA),
20
Epling, Jimmy, 81–82
European Union (EU), 92

FaceIt software, 63
face-recognition technology, 62–63, 138
Falk, Richard, 102
Faris, Iyman, 40–41, 158
Federal Bureau of Investigation (FBI)
commitment to homeland security of, 37
disruption of terrorist activities by, 39–41
pre–September 11 failures of, 29
prevention of terrorist funding by, 41–42
USA PATRIOT Act and, 130–31
*see also* intelligence agencies
Federal Emergency Management
Administration (FEMA), 23–24, 45,
75–76
federal funding
debate on, 24–25
increase in, for homeland security, 82
for police and firefighters, 84
Federal Law Enforcement Training Center,
74
fingerprinting, 66, 97
Finnegan, Patrick, 145
fire departments. *See* rescue personnel
First Amendment, 156
food contamination, 45
food poisoning, 28
Foreign Intelligence Surveillance Act
(FISA), 132–33
Fourth Amendment, 138, 139
Franti, Michael, 132
Freedom of Information Act (FOIA)
(2001), 123

Goode, Stephen, 50
Graham, Mary, 121
Guantánamo Bay, 12, 131

Hamas, 42
Hauptli, Todd, 20
al-Hawsawi, Mustafa Ahmed, 38
Healy, Gene, 144
Hernandez, Esequiel, 149–50
Hinderberger, Ron, 107–108

# Index

Hizballah, 42
homeland security
  balance between civil liberties and, 14
  Bush administration on, 17
  FBI's commitment to, 37
  gaps in, 18–19
  need for improvements in, 16–17
  September 11 created concern for, 117–18
  *see also* security measures; U.S.
    Department of Homeland Security
Homeland Security Act (2002), 78
  *see also* U.S. Department of Homeland
    Security
Homeland Security Advisory System
  criticism of, 19
  function of, 86
  importance of information and, 88–89
  is not practical, 100
  levels of threat established by, 86–88
  partnership encouraged under, 88
hospitals, 33, 48
human rights, military courts violate, 13–14
  *see also* civil liberties
Hutchinson, Asa, 34

immigrants/immigration
  American laws and, 53
  America's assimilation ethic and, 50–51
  amnesty for illegal, 51–52
  arriving at a consistent policy on, 51
  detainees and, 140–41
    fair treatment of, 173–75
  discrimination against, 141–42
  homeland security and, 53–54
  improved monitoring of, 34–36
  need for aggressive approach to, 172–73
  relationship between national security
    and, 52
  southern border and, 53
  USA PATRIOT Act's unfair treatment of,
    131
  wave of vigilantism against, 142–43
Inhofe, James M., 20
intelligence agencies
  change in structure for, 124
  guidelines for protecting openness and
    privacy by, 125–27
  increasing communication among, 16–17
  need for new counterterrorism and,
    121–22
  new information strategies and, 122–24
  should assess information needs, 124
  U.S. Department of Homeland Security
    and, 93–94
Internal Revenue Service, 116

Iraq war
  preemptive strikes and, 102–103
  relation between war on terror and, 17–18

Kady, Martin, II, 16
Kean, Thomas, 19
Kerry, John F., 18
Khemais, Essid Sami Ben, 28
Kinsley, Michael, 129

Laboratory Response Network (LRN), 33
law, liberty enhanced by, 156–57
library records, 158
Lichtblau, Eric, 133–34
link analysis, 165
Los Alamos (nuclear laboratory), 55
Lott, John R., Jr., 104
Loy, Jim, 81
Lynch, Timothy, 113

Malkin, Michelle, 50
Mann, Charles C., 58
Maritime Transportation Security Act
  (2002), 21
Al-Marri, Ali Saleh Kahlah, 41
Mefford, Larry A., 37
Metzl, Jamie F., 23
military. *See* U.S. military
military courts, 13
Minner, Ruth Ann, 25
Mohammed, Khalid Shaikh, 17, 38
Moran, Jim, 64
Moussaoui, Zacarias, 40
Murad, Abdul Hakim, 27

National Commission on Terrorist Attacks,
  19
National Governors' Association, 24
National Guard, 118, 147
national ID cards
  are a threat to privacy, 115–16
  civil liberties and, 111–12, 114
  increase government surveillance, 113–14
  paranoia about, 111–12
  possible abuse of, 116
  uses for, 112
  will not make people safer, 113–14
National Security Advisor, 94
National Security Council (NSC), 94
Nokes, Dave, 55
nuclear attacks, as unlikely, 28
nuclear plants, security lapses at, 55–57

Odeh, Mohamed Sadeek, 171
Office of Domestic Preparedness, 74–75

Office of the Secretary of Defense (OSD), 91–92
Operation Liberty Shield, 24, 52

Patriot Act. *See* USA PATRIOT Act
Peña, Charles V., 99
police departments. *See* rescue personnel
port security, 21
*posse comitatus,* 144–45, 148
Posse Comitatus Act (1878), 144, 146, 148, 152, 155
privacy issues
 information gathering and, 123–24
 protection of secrets and, 126–27
 surveillance technology protecting, 167–68
Public Health Security and Bioterrorism Preparedness and Response Act, 48–49

al Qaeda
 disruption of terrorist activities by, 40–41
 "sleepers" in, 171
 threat from
  is exaggerated, 27
  is serious, 42
  lack of future, 26

racial/ethnic profiling, 129
Reid, Richard C., 40
rescue personnel
 funding for, 22–23, 84
 improving preparedness of, 16, 21–24
Reserve Officers Training Corps (ROTC), 119–20
Ridge, Tom, 86
 Bush's appreciation of, 81
 difficulties faced by, 96–97, 98
 on success of homeland security, 17
 *see also* U.S. Department of Homeland Security
Roberts, Craig, 103
Rogers, Harold, 19
Romero, Anthony D., 13
Rothkopf, David J., 61
Rove, Karl, 51
Rumsfeld, Donald, 13

San Francisco, California, 23
Scherer, John L., 26
Schneier, Bruce, 58–59, 68
security measures
 home guard force and, 118–20
 mistreatment of immigrants and, 140–43
 need for aggressive approach to, 172–73
 need for new, 111

preemptive strikes in Iraq and, 102–103
 success with, 82–83
 suggestions for, 94–95
 technological
  breakdown of, 59–60
  failures in, 62–66
  improving computer security and, 67–68
  overlooking other security measures and, 61–62
  people vs., 68
  post–September 11 increase in, 60–61
  will not solve security problems, 58–59
  *see also* air travel; national ID cards; surveillance technology; U.S. Department of Homeland Security
September 11 terrorist attacks
 federal commission to investigate, 19
 illusions shattered by, 117
 terrorists of, relations among, 26
Shelby, Richard, 94–95
smallpox virus, 30–32
Social Security numbers, 116
Spencer, Jack, 102
state health departments, 32–33
Steinberg, James B., 121
Stephen, Andrew, 96
Stuber, Doug, 132
surveillance technologies
 attack scenarios and, 164–65
 built-in privacy protection of, 167–68
 compulsory databases and, 138
 detecting patterns in stages and, 165–67
 monitoring of immigrants and, 34–36
 new tools and approaches to, 162–64
 safeguarding civil liberties with, 138–39
 violate civil liberties, 137–39

Tatel, David S., 141
technology. *See* security measures, technological; surveillance technologies
Terrorism Information Awareness (TIA), 137
terrorist attacks
 difficulty of launching, 28–29
 disruption in, 39–41
 likelihood of future, 26–27
 at nuclear plants, 55–57
 preparing for future, 16–17
 preventing funding for, 41–42
 threat of
  exaggeration of, 27–28
  investigative response to, 169–71
  al Qaeda and, 38–39
  wide range of, 42
 *see also* bioterrorism

terrorists
death penalty for, 134
detainment of suspected
criticism of, 13
U.S. officials defending, 12–13
violates civil liberties, 140
disruption of activities of, 40–41
military courts for suspected, 13–14
relations among September 11, 26
"sleeper," 171–72
Terrorist Threat Integration Center, 17, 83
Tether, Tony, 162
Thompson, Tommy, 32
Thornberry, William M., 23
Tiahrt, Todd, 78
transportation safety, 79
*see also* air travel
Transportation Security Administration
(TSA), 19, 20, 74, 79, 104–106
Treece, Tom, 131–32
Turner, Jim, 16
Twight, Charlotte, 113

Udeen, Jamal, 12
USA PATRIOT Act (2001), 122
accomplishments of, 159
application of, 158
enhances investigations, 169–70
expansion of federal powers and, 132–33
judicial scrutiny and, 160–61
lack of abuse of, 158–59
law enforcement looking for "un-
American" material under, 131–32
legislative oversight of the executive
branch and, 159
preserves civil liberties, 161
protects rights of citizens, 157–58
technology and, 60
unfair treatment of immigrants and, 131
violates civil liberties, 130–31, 134–36
U.S. Citizenship and Immigration Services,
75
U.S. Customs and Border Protection, 73–74
U.S. Department of Homeland Security, 70
bioterrorism and, 47
Bush's appreciation of employees of,
81–82
continual improvement in, 77
criticism of, 29
does not make sense, 99–100
does not solve intelligence problem, 93

effectiveness of consolidation in, 79
government bureaucracy in, 91–93
growing pains in, 18–19
guiding principles of, 71–72
intelligence gathering by, 123
is not necessary, 94
is riddled with holes, 97–98
mission of, 80
need for, 78–79
progress in, 84–85
purpose of, 70–71
reduces security, 90–91
strategy of, 72–73
success of, 83–84
tasks and functions of, 73–77
*see also* Homeland Security Advisory
System
U.S. Environmental Protection Agency
(EPA), 33
U.S. Immigration and Customs
Enforcement, 74
U.S. military
for domestic security
dangerous implications of, 148–52
historical background to, 145–48
opposition to, 154–55
proposal for, 144–45, 148
war on drugs and, 152–53
weapons of mass destruction and, 154
foreign nationals in, 53
smallpox vaccine and, 31
treatment of prisoners by, 12
*see also* Department of Defense
U.S. Visitor and Immigrant Status Indicator
Technology (US-VISIT), 34–36

vaccinations, smallpox, 31–32

Warner, John, 144–45
war on drugs, 152–53
war on terror
critical tools in, 157–58
Democrats' critique of, 17
relation to war in Iraq, 17–18
water contamination, 45
water safety, 33
weapons of mass destruction, 154
Will, George F., 109

Yousef, Ramzi, 27